Lives Between Cultures

A Study of Human Nature, Identity and Culture

D1243827

Lives Between Cultures

A Study of Human Nature, Identity and Culture

Richard M. Swiderski

The Denali Press
Juneau   Alaska

Denali, derived from the Koyukon name *Deenaalee*, is the native name for Mount McKinley. Mount McKinley, the highest mountain on the North American continent, is located in Denali National Park and Preserve. The lowlands surrounding this majestic mountain provide a diverse wildlife habitat for a variety of animals including grizzly bears, wolves, caribou and moose.

Copyright © 1991 by The Denali Press

Published by The Denali Press
Post Office Box 021535
Juneau, Alaska USA 99802-1535
(907) 586-6014
FAX: (907) 463-6780

Library of Congress Cataloging-in-Publication Data

Swiderski, Richard M.
    Lives between cultures : a study of human nature, identity, and culture / Richard M. Swiderski.
        p.   cm.
    Includes bibliographical references.
    ISBN 0-938737-24-4 (alk. paper) : $25.00
    1. Culture.   2. Acculturation.   3. Socialization.   4. Ethnicity.
I. Title.
GN357.S85   1991
306--dc20

90-49515
CIP

∞ The paper used in this publication meets the minimum requirements of the American National Standard for Information Sciences—Permanence of Paper for Printed Library Materials, ANSI Z39.48-1984. This book is printed on recycled paper.

For Sandi

Contents

Photographs appear on pages 6, 28, 48, 100, 122, and 144.

Introduction

"Her odyssey from the middle-class gentility of Plymouth to the rural poverty of a remote Egyptian village sounds bizarre," wrote Christopher S. Wren (*New York Times* April 17, 1979: A8) of an Englishwoman originally named Dorothy Eady who had been living for years under the name Om Seti amid the ruins at Abydos, an eccentric who could recall in intimate detail a previous life among the pharaoes yet whose knowledge Egyptologists valued. Her name "Om Seti" she had taken in keeping with the practice of Egyptian peasant women, and actually of women throughout the world, of designating themselves solely after the name of a son. Wren listened to Om Seti's story sympathetically, recorded her explanation that a childhood fall downstairs "knocked a screw loose" and took her photograph to accompany the article. The story of another soul carried off by the charms of a distant, drier, more barren, more ancient place was chronicled and placed securely on the margin: a service newspapers have long been performing.

A survey of writings of all sorts from the beginning of time turns up many stories like that of Om Seti, though not always so gentle and not so faintly melancholy. In the Anastasi Papyrus of the Ancient Egyptian New Empire is a series of letters sent by one scribe to another flaunting his wit and compositional skill in giving an account of his correspondent's trip across the Syrian desert on a mission for the pharaoh.

> Thy groom awakened in the night, and took away with him what was left. He then went off to some bad fellows, joined the tribes of the Beduins, and transformed himself into an Asiatic. . . .

The Egyptians of that time had little regard for the "Asiatics," who undoubtedly would welcome a thief into their ranks. The translator expresses his understanding of the character of these people by naming them "Beduin," nomads who wander far from the civilized centers living an existence unregulated by regard for property. Each age had these faraway beings and those inclined to join them. The Roman poet Horace in his fifth Ode berated the soldiers in the army of the triumvir Crassus who upon defeat by "Syrians" decked themselves out in the manner of the victors, took native wives and joined their ranks. Going over to the other side was the way of thieves and turncoats, abandoning the proper way of life for an escape into savagery.

Om Seti obviously was not described as a robber or a traitor. Her double retreat to modern and ancient Egypt was remarkable for the degree of rejection, "from middle-class gentility to rural poverty," "from England to Egypt," but she was not morally debased. Like the Egyptian valet and the Roman soldiers, however, she was a renegade. Whatever the cause, a fall down the stairs or moral depravity, the transition from one way of life to another was noticed in its time as a rejection of one way in favor of another, less highly valued way of life. The Egyptian scribes who formed the audience for the letters and the literate Romans of Horace's time may have been as curious about Asiatics as the readers of the *New York Times*; they all were susceptible to the tensions between their own group and outsiders brought to a point by someone crossing over to the others.

People of every civilization notice and comment upon reported crossings. Whether deliberate or not, a crossing is a single person's direction with respect to the body of observers. The direction is invariably judged as having moral qualities: away from the center (civilization, the good, the true) it is the movement of a renegade; toward the center (and away from the foreign, the barbarous, criminal and false) it is the movement of one becoming civilized. In history and in fiction the lives of people who have taken these directions are the common stock of cultures. By their recounting they help define what is "ours," defined as the right and civilized way, and what is "theirs," usually the antithesis.

A crossing (or a refusal to cross when offered the chance) is an event worth rehearsing, examining and pondering. Studying such an experience may yield to the interested observer conclusions about the unerring consistency of (our) noble civilized spirit (General Gordon trampling the pilgrim's robe and accepting death rather than conversion to Islam) or about the malleability of the human spirit (the defeated Roman soldiers turning Syrian). Travelers, captives, missionaries, spies, anthropologists and many other interesting types of people are formed of these qualities. The interest which governs the attention we pay to these lives and experiences is born of the sense that they are (or seem to be) crossings. The motion first draws the attention. It establishes "us" and "them" by setting a direction from one to the other. A crossing is the inertia of motion to a culture's inertia of rest.

In a tale of the Tang Dynasty collected by Xu Tang in his *Wu chao xiao shuo*, entitled "Zhi-nan-zi-quan," or "A Tale of the Far South," a young scholar-official named Guo is captured on the train of a defeated expeditionary force and held by the "southern barbarians" for an enormous ransom. He writes to his friend Wu that he is not enduring his captivity with the patience and firmness of the four exemplars of antiquity, and pleads with Wu to procure the ransom from Wu's uncle, a high imperial official. The uncle is dead, however, and Wu, beholden to Guo for past favors, undertakes to amass the amount of the ransom through trading endeavors. He passes years neglecting his wife and family until a military commander, Yang, moved by Wu's devotion to his captive friend, completes the amount from his own stores and sees that Guo is returned (Bauer and Franke 1964: 162).

> During the time he had to spend with the southern barbarians Guo had adopted some of their uncouth habits. So he sent people into the cave cities of the barbarians and had ten girls brought thence, all of them of ravishing beauty. They had just arrived when he had to make a farewell visit to Commandant Yang, who was about to return to his northern homeland. As token of thanks for his benificence he expressed the wish to be allowed to make him a present of the girls. But the Commandant refuse.

Better, says the Commandant, that the ransomed Guo use his money to care for his aged parents, though he finally is persuaded to accept the youngest of the girls for the sake of civility. Guo has obviously forgotten the fundamental relationship that binds him to his parents and to the friend who has slaved for years to ransom him; he neglects the Five Relationships that form Chinese society and in being strictly observed elevate the Chinese above barbarians.

Commandant Yang's good example—civilized enough to reject all the girls and polite enough to accept one—restores Guo to a sense of priorities. He visits his parents and when he obtains his imperial post takes them to live with him. After his parents die and the prescribed period of mourning is over Guo seeks out his friend Wu and finding he and his wife have died carries their bones back to their native village. Guo mourns his friend for three years then resumes his post. He cares for Wu's orphaned son and upon the son's reaching maturity resigns his position in favor of the younger man.

During his fifteen years of captivity Guo's frequent attempts to escape were severely punished: he may have become habituated to barbarian ways but he was always a captive who never gave in. He required only a good man's reminder to quit himself of barbarian influence and complete an exemplary Chinese life of his own. His passage away from civilization was involuntary and incomplete; it was recounted, or fabricated, to underline the determination and permanence of his adherence to the values of his own people. While in motion from one culture to the other, Guo remained in the same place.

In Paul Bowles' story "A Distant Episode," a band of nomads seize a French professor studying the dialects of Moroccan Arabic, cut his tongue out and train him to be a capering fool. At the end a French soldier who fires at him as he runs madly through the streets of town takes him to be a holy man (Bowles 1989: 1-12). The professor's career diverges radically from Guo's where it becomes clear that he is thoroughly, if ironically, assimilated to the other culture, and has become unrecognizable to his own countrymen. He has completed a crossing in one direction only. It is only through the imagination of the writer that we may know this. Bowles does suggest that some of the characters whom we take as part of a different, foreign life may be familiar people transformed perhaps unwillingly, having accidentally fit into that life. The professor also moves to reach cultural stasis as one completely and impenetrably other.

A crossing is observed, recorded or invented to say something about human nature, about identity and culture. How firm is our culture; how frail is our culture. How revolting is their culture; how tempting is their culture. The motives for a crossing are as endlessly debatable as the qualities of the culture itself because the culture (identity, human nature or some such principle) acquires concreteness in a crossing.

A crossing tells what a culture is. It is language, dress, social customs especially those regarding marriage, expressions, food preferences, and a myriad of other ways if the list is to be extended—but mostly it is language and dress. In crossing publicly from one life to another a person first and most ostensibly shows a change in appearance and behavior. Conversely, a person wishing to suggest a crossing dresses and acts, especially speaks, differently. A crossing is managed in this way: the commentator responds first to these differences; the captive or the voluntary crosser (why isn't there an adequately neutral word for this person in English?) has them engineered.

This book is an array of lives of people who made crossings. It is devoid of a specific theoretical program beyond the cumulative effect of presenting these lives together. In each life the chief emphasis is upon the trend of the recounting which makes this life known and knowable: how and to whom is this "news" worth hearing. Here well-known figures mingle with the marginal; one-source biographies are alongside those with extensive bibliographies. While there is some pretense to breadth and variety there inevitably appear trends: British Arabesque or the quest for "Greater

Hungary" or the struggles of Native Americans for a viable identity among whites.

The single common quality is the cultural location of the observer and the motion of the crossing with respect to that observer: toward or away as the observer accounts it. While Tahitians, Seneca, Japanese or for that matter Italians, English, French, Germans and other distinctive cultural identities figure among these lives, none is recounted strictly from that standpoint.

Culture is a fixed location specified by motions in its regard. Watching a crossing successful or not, away from or toward, exposes the stance we must occupy to see any motion at all. Frauds occur in these pages as well, showing how much a culture is a place we occupy, how much what is different can be a place apart from ours, until the familiarity of that apparent difference is recognized. The exotic castaway may indeed turn out to be an English farm girl; but the man brought to England from Tahiti himself can be a practiced impostor. Crossings are judged from a place; they pass an apparent distance from that place and over a seeming boundary.

Today the mixing of people long separated by geography and temper is proceeding at an accelerated pace. Culture is brought into questions of rights; identity is asserted by military action. Human nature is held to be specified by genes, of a natural variety which should be preserved, or changed to make life better. Crossings are judged political. But here it is shown that they never have been innocent of politics. They are a prime reflex of politics.

References

Bauer, Wolfgang and Herbert Franke, eds. and trans.
 1964 *The Golden Casket: Chinese Tales of Three Millenia*. London: George Allen and Unwin.

Bowles, Paul.
 1988 *A Distant Episode: Selected Stories of Paul Bowles*. New York.

Wren, Christopher.
 1979 "Briton with a Sense of Deja Vu Calls Ruins 'Home'." *New York Times*, April 17: A8.

Roberto de Nobili
Anonymous seventeenth century portrait, courtesy of the
Nobili Research Institute, Madurai.

I

Jesuit Adaption:
Roberto De Nobili in India

Francis Xavier never expected to die on a sweltering island off the coast of China. The missionary drive that carried him from Rome to India then to Japan he hoped would sustain him as far as Peking, where his conversion of the emperor would bring the entire Far East over to Christianity. Thus Xavier lay ill on the island of Chang Chuan Shan awaiting the boat that would never bring him to the Chinese mainland.

Xavier was one of Ignatius Loyola's first converts to the Society of Jesus. He met his Basque countryman at the University of Paris and, fascinated by his teachings, followed him to Italy. There, along with others, he performed good works while awaiting official confirmation of the order. Not long after the Papal bull instituting the Society of Jesus Loyola selected Xavier to catechise the Asians. With the momentum of tremendous zeal Xavier took ship to Goa and labored there to clear away superstition and convince the people that the only true faith was in the stone temples built by the Portuguese. Working among the mass-converted Paravas on the Coromandel Coast, he learned a little Tamil and taught prayers to whoever would learn them. He incited the children to wreck the images. Here and there about the Portuguese dominions he established Jesuit priests in permanent stations, "four on the Moluccas, two in Malacca, six at Cape Cormorin, two in Bassein, and four on the island of Sokotra" (Fulop-Miller 1963:208). Xavier did not devote much attention to the native Christians in India who traced their conversion back to the Apostle St. Thomas. These "Syrian Christians" at first had friendly relations with the foreign Christians, but soon their ignorance of the Pope and the Roman rite caused trouble (Neill 1964: 143-48).

In 1548, while stopping at the Malacca mission, Xavier was visited by a Japanese whose name Xavier wrote in his letters as Anjiro. This man convinced the Jesuit that Japan was the ripest field for Christianity, that the Japanese were, before all other Asian peoples, the most tolerant. If the missionaries could demonstrate to the Japanese that their religion was superior to all others then this reasonable people would embrace the faith wholeheartedly. The prospect appealed to Xavier, not only because he preferred men whose belief was tied to reason but because he was exasperated with the Indians and their brahmans — "de gente non sancta, ab homine iniquo et doloso, eripe me," ("deliver me from the profane people, from the false and cunning man"), he wrote, turning a passage from the Psalms against these pagans (Brodrick 1952: 147). With Anjiro as a guide Xavier departed for Japan.

The country was hardly the complaisant land of Anjiro's stories, and the informant himself turned out to be an uneducated rogue who seriously misled the missionaries. Once Xavier overcame the difficulties caused by his ignorance of the language and customs, however, he found the Japanese an ingratiating people, "the delight of my heart." He made nearly a thousand conversions in short order, though many of them may not have grasped enough of the new faith to distinguish it from Buddhism and quite a few adopted it because it was stylish. Apostolic poverty, a winning device in Europe, aroused nothing but contempt among the Japanese, hence Xavier presented himself as a person of consequence, attired in Japanese style and surrounded by retainers. His disputes with Japanese Buddhists assured him that China was the fountainhead of all heathenism in the East, and that the spiritual conquest of that nation would have universal repurcussions. He left Japan to his successors.

In 1579, twenty-seven years after Xavier's death, Alessandro Valignano, specially appointed Jesuit Visitor to the Far East, arrived in Japan. The Visitor's task was to examine existing missions and report to the General recommendations for improving their work. In August 1580, he set down his conclusions in a *Sumario* (Boxer 1951: 72-90). He is full of admiration for the "cultivated and intelligent" Japanese who contrast markedly with the "base and bestial" people of India. Native Japanese, he advises, should be permitted to enter the Society of Jesus since they are the only Asian people qualified to uphold the ministry with true devotion. Conversely Valignano suggests full-scale adaptation of European missionaries to Japanese customs, for he had learned that the Japanese allow a foreigner two years to assimilate himself. Anyone unchanged after that period is shunned as an "ignorant lout."

Valignano admits that the Japanese language is unlearnable, the customs bewildering and the food undigestible, but for all that he can see no other way to impress the Japanese and forward the mission. Francisco Cabral, the Superior of the Mission, disputed Valignano's contentions: Jesuits should not forsake their cotton for luxurious silks, nor should the proud Japanese be allowed into the Society of Jesus. But Valignano had the General's ear. His reforms were instituted.

On this tour the Visitor also undertook to reorganize the China mission. Jesuits attempting to enter China had been deported or murdered, and those attempting to learn the language were mightily discouraged by the multiplicity of dialects and the preposterous writing system. However, in Matteo Ricci, a young Italian Jesuit recently posted to Asia, Valignano found a man able to crack the rock of China.

Ricci and a companion gained a foothold in Canton and established missions in a succession of South China cities. At first they presented themselves as Buddhist monks, but on learning that this earned them no respect took on the character of scholar-teachers. The method of adaptation practiced by Francis Xavier and advocated by Valignano became Ricci's chief missionary tool (Bettray 1955). He mastered the language and the elaborate rituals of social intercourse to the extent of gaining admittance to the socity of mandarins, whom he entertained with philosophical discourses and feats of memory. Ricci's aim, like Xavier's, was to reach the Emperor with his message. Slowly, tortuously he made his way to Peking. Though the ruler never gave Ricci a personal audience he did accept the missionary's services in various technical problems. The Jesuit was consigned to repairing clocks and predicting eclipses, but he also wheedled favors from the Emperor. By the time of his death in 1610 he was simultaneously a Chinese court official and the minister of a Christian church numbering over 2,000 converts (Pfister 1932-34).

Ricci inaugurated a Jesuit presence at the Chinese court which was filled by a succession of Jesuit-mandarins making themselves useful, enduring persecutions and forever proffering Christianity to the elite. Despite a change of dynasties, the church grew in size and spread in the provinces with little serious interruption. Other missionary orders, the Franciscans and Dominicans, severely criticised the Jesuits for taking on Chinese customs and allowing their converts to preserve ancestor worship in the bosom of the church. This "rites controversy" nettled the Jesuits throughout the period of their success, but did not curtail the spread of doctrine (Bontinck 1962).

Elsewhere, success varied. The promising Japan mission was suppressed by the newly centralized government just as the Chinese mission was getting underway, and succumbed completely to the persecutions and martyrdoms of the mid-seventeenth century. In India there was neither dramatic prosperity nor wholesale failure, just indifferent stagnation as missionaries in the country forsaken by Xavier and degraded by Valignano pushed their task.

The Portuguese authorities in Goa and other settlements decided that the natives could not be persuaded and must be forced into European beliefs. Brahmanic practices were banned in 1546, and the next year this policy was intensified to allow the outright demolition of temples and mosques. During Francis Xavier's visit the maneuver known as *compelle intrare*, forced conversion, came into play (Boxer 1973:73-9), and Thomas Aquinas' dictum in the *Summa Theologica*, "The infidel is to be brought to the faith not by coercion but by persuasion," was forgotten. Persuasion was for China or Japan, where coercion was impossible. The slovenly civilization of India demanded the exercise of brute force.

In the areas outside of Portuguese rule the invaders took advantage of the parlous state of Indian politics to back one petty ruler against another. They approached the Mughal emperors in the north with the usual gifts and treaties while working to undermine the Muslim Empire wherever possible. The Jesuits situated themselves at court even more tenuously than in China, winning again through their application of the arts and sciences a measure of attention from the monarchs (Maclagan 1932). In the provinces and especially in the south they were perpetually stymied by those same brahmins and their "monumental pagan lies". On November 20, 1609, Alberto Laerzio, Jesuit Provincial of Malaber, wrote a letter to the General of the Society of Jesus, Claudio Acquaviva. Laerzio recalled the desparate condition of the Jesuit mission in the South Indian city of Madurai. "At the time of my arrival in Madurai in December 1606 with Father Roberto de Nobili, Father Goncalvez Fernandez had been applying himself for 14 years in a fruitless effort." Laerzio's companion de Nobili was inspired to revive the mission using a new method (Bertrand 1848: vol. 2: 3).

> Touched by the deplorable blindness of these people imprisoned in the shadow of death; filled with the great notion that Jesus Christ came for the salvation of all men and that he should triumph over the Devil everywhere, destroy the Devil's empire and free his slaves; and at the same time recognizing the true causes of the mission's delinquency, Father de Nobili resolved to apply an effective remedy. Like St. Paul, who made himself all things to all people; like the Word of God, who became Man to save men, Father Roberto said to himself 'I shall become an Indian to save the Indians.'

De Nobili's quiet resolve seems a small voice at the end of Laerzio's long winded homily, but that mass of verbiage places it in context.

For Laerzio, de Nobili's interest meant a new vitality in the problematic Madurai mission, and a chance to substitute a fellow Italian for the bothersome old Portuguese Fernandez. When Laerzio says that Nobili "recognized the true causes of the mission's delinquency" he means something very specific. Fernandez, a Portuguese Jesuit working in territory under Portuguese military influence in an era when all Asian missionary work had to be overseen by the Portuguese, had converted only a few Hindus by offering treatment in his European-style hospital or by catching them at death's door. Like many missionaries working in the overseas field, Fernandez packaged cultural conversion with religious conversion. The new Indian Christians were required to adopt Portuguese dress, food and manners along with their new faith.

From the first arrival of the Portuguese the South Indians, who perceive all humans as caste members, needed to find a caste category for the novel beings, who seemed but scarcely human. The Portuguese and their native imitators soon came to be known as "*Parangis*". Ever since the Crusades, when the Frankish nobles made their presence known in the Near East, Europeans of any description were called Franks; "*Parangi*" was a Tamil version of the Persian word for Franks (Yule and Burnell 1968: 352-54).

One of the major principles differentiating castes in India was the degree of ritual cleanness or pollution. The *brahmans* were acounted the purest, the *ksatriyas* and the *sudras* next. Outside of the caste system entirely were the pariahs, or outcastes, who were so unclean that others solemnly avoided them. Even a wrong glance from a pariah could defile a *brahman* and require elaborate purification rituals. Actually there were many castes, of course, and their relations depended upon the individual's standpoint, but the *brahmans* saw the *Parangis* eat unclean foods, perform unclean acts and behave in a manner so uncouth that they could be nothing but pariahs. Fernandez, unaware of the meaning of caste and the outcaste quality of *Parangi* status, accepted the label for himself and his converts and was forever trying to persuade the higher castes to join them in this degraded state. Naturally the mission did not prosper (Hollis 1968: 5).

Roberto de Nobili arrived in Madurai with an exemplary Jesuit education and a fair speaking knowledge of the Tamil language gained during a year's mission work among the pearl divers of the Fishery Coast. His first impressions of the natives were not favorable. He wrote to one relative that he considered himself a sheep among wolves, ready to be devoured, and to another that the natives were so depraved they actually gave worship to an unmentionable object (probably a lingam) (Wicki 1968: 131, 133). De Nobili's opinion of the Hindus matched the Hindu's opinion of the *Parangis*.

Overcoming his distaste, the young Jesuit began to investigate the causes of the mission's failure. Conversations with a sudra school teacher, one of Fernandez' articulate converts, taught him the reasons for the odium attached to the *Parangis*. With Laerzio's firm support de Nobili made plans to renew the mission. First he dissociated himself from the *Parangi* caste and let it be known that he was a *ksatriya* or *raja*, a member of the warrior caste. De Nobili himself felt that there was justification for this claim since his family was of old Roman stock (Bertrand 1848: vol. 2: 66). But the assertion alone was worthless: De Nobili asked of his superiors permission to "adapt."

The example of Ricci in China was known to the Jesuits of India and actuated similar moves among some of the more liberated missionaries. Another Jesuit on the Malabar Coast, Rubino, had already petitioned Laerzio, his Superior, asking that he be allowed to "dress, eat and act like them in political matters" (Dahman 1925: 31). But it is an indication of how tentative a practice adaptation always was that Rubino later proved one of Nobili's most implacable foes.

Further inquiries convinced Nobili that the optimum caste identity would be that of *brahman sannyasi*. A *sannyasi* character would best comport with his missionary ideals, de Nobili felt, because he serves as a teacher to a wide range of upper-caste types while practicing stern asceticism. By his nature a *sannyasi* criticises normal beliefs and offers some personal system as well. Any mistakes in language or behavior can be set down to *sannyasi* eccentricity, and any desciples he wins are of course his personal followers and not *Parangis* (Bachman 1972: 55).

Laerzio seconded this idea. Unfortunately he was not empowered to give approval since he was but de Nobili's immediate Superior in the Society of Jesus. The entire issue had to be referred to the highest ecclesiastical authory, the Archbishop of Cranganore. The Archbishop convened a council of theologians to pass on the doctrinal correctness of this approach. The testimony of Laerzio and others convinced the doctors that adaptation was allowable, yet they could not bear the thought of a missionary preaching the Gospel in the saffron loincloth the *sannyasi* must wear. The Archbishop put his seal to an intricate statement which permitted de Nobili to adapt, but as a *ksatriya* not as a *sannyasi*.

De Nobili immediately moved out of Fernandez' mission house, where he had been awaiting the decision, rented a suitable residence, employed *brahman* cooks, restricted himself to a vegetarian diet, ate all his meals from leaves with his fingers and spoke only courtly Tamil, all deemed proper behavior for an upper-caste person. Though he began to attract followers the *Parangi* associations still lingered about him while he wore the black Jesuit soutane. Local *brahmans* instigated unpleasant incidents, and whispered that he was nothing but a pretentious *Parangi*. De Nobili pressed Laerzio, who in turn pressed the Archbishop for leave to make the full switch to *sannyasi*. Finally, in 1607, approval was handed down; de Nobili might wear the deplorable costume for the sake of the Church. De Nobili abandoned the *raja* insignia, the ear pendants and palenquin preceded by shouting desciples (Dahmen 1931: 132-33). He confined himself to his dwelling and there commenced the discourses that would earn him the title *Tattuva Podagar*, the "Teacher of Reality".

The *sannyasi* dress and habits which de Nobili was eager to assume were not just an episode in Jesuit mission history. They were an epoch in de Nobili's personal experience, a culmination of themes already prominent in his life. From early in his life de Nobili was preparing himself for an existence like that which he attained in the *sannyas* role.

The pattern of the wealthy young man who forsakes paternal bounty for religious privations was frequently repeated in the thirteenth through sixteenth centuries. St. Thomas Aquinas, St. Francis of Assisi and many other holy men left along their march to sanctity an entire history of frenzied mothers and raging fathers. God's good work demanded loyalty to a higher, more abstract family than one based on blood. The spurning of riches by these young saints symbolized the sundering of earthly ties and submission to the sacred patriarchy of the religious orders.

De Nobili saw his own relative, Fabius de Fabiis, sole heir to one of Rome's oldest names and fortunes, successfully defy all opposition to enter the Society of Jesus and become a respected Superior. Even more imposingly, he had before him the example of his namesake and uncle, Roberto de Nobili, a youth of great piety and learning who gained a Cardinal's hat before his death at age 13. De Nobili resisted his parent's plans for his future as the perpetuator of an ancient line and practiced severe austerities in preparation for holy orders (Tornese 1973; Cronin 1959). When they became insistent de Nobili decamped to the house of a wealthy noblewoman who protected him as he progressed through the steps of his religious education. Agents of his family discovered his whereabouts, and there were further quarrels, but finally the young ascetic succeeded in cowing his relatives. In 1599 he was allowed to abdicate succession to his father's titles and estates—not without wrangling with the family over the disposal of his inheritance. De Nobili wanted to distribute his money among the poor; others, including his cousin, the formidable Cardinal Sforza, preferred that the fortune remain in the de Nobili coffers. Only after General Acquaviva pointed out that willfulness ill becomes a Jesuit did de Nobili agree to a compromise: the family kept most of the estate and a token sum was reserved for charity. These events suggested that de Nobili's response to authority was closer to a Roman noble than a Jesuit priest. His enemies later took frequent occasion to remark on the commanding quality of his supposedly humble petitions. Submission was a positive act of will for de Nobili; his right to poverty and asceticism was the result of assertion, not accession.

Taking Jesuit orders isolated de Nobili from his family and his hereditary role in society; it also allowed him a life more amenable to his asceticism. The departure to India severed his connections with his beginnings even further: throughout his life he rejected pleas from family, friends and superiors to return even for a brief while (Wicki 1969: 323). The adaption of *sannyasi* lifestyle was the final abdication. As a *sannyasi*, de Nobili left everything behind for the life of a penitent and missionary. He was allowed greater austerities than a Jesuit could normally undertake, and yet he had an odd new freedom too. The strictures of the Hindus added to those of the Jesuits framed a space for invention. Under the sharp scrutiny of his ecclesiastical superiors and of his potential converts, each watching from a radically different viewpoint, de Nobili performed the life of a *sannyasi*.

He had to move precisely and deftly, like a skilled actor knowing all the restrictions of the stage yet able to fashion original performances. Unlike an actor though, he did not see the results of a single performance for months or years. Step by step de Nobili had gone as far away from his past as he could go on earth. In leaving off the things of this world he sustained a tremendous preoccupation with with things of a new, Indian world.

Each aspect of the *sannyasi* identity acquired for de Nobili a significance related to his own Christian asceticism. Clothing, the first and most urgent sign of the change, he altered thoroughly. Laerzio described the ambiguously transformed de Nobili after the Archbishop's permission arrived (Bertrand 1848: vol. 2: 4):

From this moment Father Roberto de Nobili admitted only *brahmans* to his service. Rice, milk, vegetables and water, taken once a day, comprised his diet. A long yellowish silk robe, covered with a kind of rochet of the same color; a red or white veil for his shoulders; a toque in the shape of a turban for his head; sandals of wood set on supports two inches high and attached to each foot by a loop over the toes-these things comprised his dress. He added to them a string, the distinguished sign of the *brahmans* and *rajas*, but instead of the three threads usually twined to form it he used five, three in gold and two in silver, with a cross suspended from the center. The three gold threads represent, he said, the Holy Trinity; the two silver threads represent the body and soul of the human state; and the cross recalls the passion and death of our Savior.

De Nobili included the elevated sandals to punish the flesh in the place of the heavy Jesuit robes, which he had relinquished in favor of the more comfortable loincloth.

De Nobili knew that any example he set for the locals would be comprehensible to them only if his asceticism was presented as the asceticism of a native holy man. The costume, while communicating this message to the people, must actually bite into his own flesh. An improvement in his pain was the costume's truest efficacy. Invisible alterations in its meaning kept him close to his purpose, lest he forget.

De Nobili's new diet was also a heavy imposition. Meat and fish-eating were, in the eyes of the Madurai *brahmans*, one of the *Parangi's* most vile habits. They even called the *Parangis* by an epithet meaning "fish-breath." De Nobili realized that he could never claim *sannyasi* status without revising his diet to include only those foods deemed acceptable to the *brahmans*. And the *brahmans* knew of his diet through the cooks whom he employed. Any sight of meat or fish would have excited general revulsion.

Unfortunately de Nobili had always found dietary restrictions onerous. Troubled by a perennial condition of the stomach he was excused from Lenten fasts while a Jesuit novice, so grave was his affliction from the lack of substantial food. The tropical climate of South India aggravated his suffering, and nearly brought about his demise soon after he reached Goa. In December, 1607, one month after he assumed the *sannyasi* role, he wrote to Cardinal Bellarmine that hardly a day went by without severe headaches and stomach-aches (Bachman 1972: 70-71). Many Jesuits arriving in India had similar troubles and not a few died. De Nobili's adherence to the single daily vegetable meal of the *sannyasis* intensified his susceptibility and thus his self-flagellation.

Peter Lombard, an eminent theologian called upon to determine the propriety of de Nobili's practices, found the fasting especially Christ-like in the light of de Nobili's earlier inability to sustain a fast. And Father Pero Francisco, one of de Nobili's most determined adversaries, declared (Dahman 1935: 185):

> The life of these two Fathers (de Nobili and his companion Vico) will not fail to give devotion to all those who see them and to excite their admiration as it has done with me. It is one thing to see them with your own eyes, to treat with them as I do, to console them, and quite another to write about them. Your Reverence must know that no Carthusian monastery is more strictly secluded from the world, no Capuchin convent is poorer, no anchorite or hermit of Thebais more abstemious. In rigor and austerity of life they rival the greatest penitents of the world

No matter how much they might carp about de Nobili's adaptation and his concessions to converts no one ever accused him of softness. Having bound himself into this structure of pain, de Nobili vowed he would live this way until death (Bertrand 1848, vol. 2: 6).

The criticism came quick and loud. De Nobili and his converts avoided Fernandez and the other *Parangis*, explaining that the Portuguese had only offered him hospitality for a brief time while he located a residence. Privately de Nobili continued to visit Fernandez for the confession of sins, but for his part Fernandez stayed away from de Nobili's dwelling and muttered disapproval to all who would hear him. A visiting sea captain complained to de Nobili's superiors that the *sannyasi* refused him admittance to church services and denied him the sacraments (Wicki 1968: 142-43). Laerzio visited Madurai in answer to the repeated accusations and stayed in de Nobili's house under the character of de Nobili's own guru. He wore *sannyasi* garb and followed the correct diet. What he saw satisfied him though he regretted the necessity of dissociation from the smaller *Parangi* congregation. For the time being nothing was done to curb the new mission, but forces were at work in India and in Rome.

The adaptation which excited so much praise and resentment was only initially a matter of clothes and of diet. The real labor of the mission was the recasting of Chruch dogma into a Hindu form which would not compromise its domestic integrity (Dahmen 1925: 43-45). This was a philosphically delicate labor requiring a firm grasp of what the Hindus expected in a valid teaching. De Nobili, like Ricci, first had to distinguish Hindu religious practices from purely "social" customs in order to determine what could and what could not be legitimately retained by his converts. He became an ethnographer of sorts and roughed out a concept of culture, but most important he mastered the Tamil and Sanskrit scriptures and used them to explain himself both to the *brahmans* and to the Church.

In 1613 he composed his treatise *Informatio de quibusdam moribus* for the edification of the Father General of the Jesuits, and to reassure him about the mission's proceedings (Rajamanickan 1970, 1972a). This clear summary of the caste system and of the *brahmans'* role is intended to prove that the *brahmans* are a hereditary social group upon whom priestly duties devolve and not necessarily pagan priests. The sacred thread, tuft of hair and sandal paste annointment always found among the *brahmans* are not in themselves associated with the Hindu gods; they are merely signs of the *brahman* estate. To forbid them is to destroy the quality of a *brahman* and isolate him from his own caste and from society in general. For determining whether a usage is religious (hence un-Christian) or customary de Nobili offers a rule of logic typically Jesuitical; the purpose of an object's use determines its nature. The sacred thread and other instances have only social significance and are therefore not religious.

From this thesis one obtains insight into de Nobili's Christianisation of Hinduism. Only those things which in use offend dogma require extirpation, and they can be detected only through concentrated inquiry. The eagerness which de Nobili saw in his compatriots to ban traditional customs was insensitive and impractical. Hindus who had all their lives remained under the rule of custom were not about to transform themselves at the behest of a few foreigners. In effect de Nobili did not subscribe to the common notion that any "pagan" intelligent enough to understand Christianity's basic tenets must instantly become a convert. As his many writings in his own defense make clear, he was honoring the theories of Augustine and Aquinas and the practice of early missionaries to the pagan tribes of Europe when he separated out the heathen elements and put Christianity in their place, urging the people on to a better religion risen up from within their old faith (Bertrand 1848: vol. 2: 264-65).

De Nobili's translation of the sacred thread was the primary symbol of his policy. Outwardly the same as the thread which a boy of the "twice-born" castes recieved upon coming of age, it was also to de Nobili a Christian symbol. The *sannyasi* did not hesitate to explain the meaning of his idiosyncratic thread to his converts and probably allowed them to wear the same. When the number of converts grew large enough to require a new church, the structure built resembled a Hindu temple on the outside. Inside the plan of a simple basilica was followed but with the proviso of a side chapel, connected with the main chamber by a narrow passage, for accommodating the pariahs separately from the high castes during services (Dahmen 1931: 28n). De Nobili circumvented the *brahmans'* dread of pariahs and the Church's insistence on uniformity in one contrivance. The church provoked constant protests from among de Nobili's detractors. (Dahmen 1925: 26).

In language de Nobili fared as in building. Previous missionaries demanded that converts learn Portuguese or they selected terms for Christian personages and concepts on the basis of very limited acquaintance with the languages. De Nobili learned Tamil, the vernacular, and Sanskrit, the sacred language, well enough to compose texts in either, and he soon invented a Christian vocabulary for both languages.

De Nobili's predecessor in Jesuit mission work among Tamil-speaking people, Henrique Henriques, in 1578 printed in European type a Tamil Catechism which set usage for the few Christian Tamils. Upon attaining proficiency in the language de Nobili was shocked by the mistakes and confusions. The use of the Tamil word "*chorcam*" for "heavenly bliss" engendered a heresy because the word actually connoted a garden of carnal delights on the banks of the Ganges. When the Christians commissioned a Tamil poet to write verse on the joys of Heaven they received (what they considered) obscenities. An even more absurd blunder was in the rendition of the Latin word for "Mass" (missa), as de Nobili shows in his *Apologia* (Rajamanickam 1967: 3-4).

> In the Catechism the word for Mass is translated [into Tamil] by *Misei*. Now, this word means here *beard* or *moustache*. I have therefor substituted '*pujei*' a Tamilized word meaning and expressing sacrifice. I called Mass thus because during Mass, Christ is truly sacrificed to God, his Father. Never mind if pagans use the word. For the gentiles, when they as gentiles offered false sacrifices, called them sacrifices; after their conversion they gave that name to the Mass. Besides to remove all ambiguity I added '*Christu Pujei*' which means sacrifice instituted by Christ.

Consistent with his stated procedures de Nobili identified the function of the term "*pujei*" (Tamil version of the Sanskrit "*puja*"), and, analogous to the Latin word "*sacrificatio*," pressed it into service for the Holy Sacrifice of the Mass. This was a daring innovation, and ultimately unacceptable to the Church, but it did convey to the converts precisely what was happening in the Mass. Less infuriating to his superiors, but still discounted, was de

Nobili's devising Tamil names for the saints and for his converts: St. Peter became *Malaiaggan*, St Elizabeth *Devannamal*, Joachim *Devarambar*, Lazarus *Devashayam*, and so on (Rajamanickam 1967: 4).

Many of the Tamil words de Nobili derived from the Sanskrit terms, the better to make a case before the brahmans. Here the task was even more complicated because of the plethora of highly technical terms which had arisen over the long history of Sanskrit text transmission. A would-be teacher had to know all the implications of his phraseology before speaking. De Nobili felt it was safe to designate Christ by a Sanskritized version of the Latin name "*Khristu.*" He referred to Him also as "*putra,*" "the Son," and as "*satguru,*" "the true teacher." The latter was appropriate because it had a special meaning for members of the Siddhanta sect of Shivaism from which de Nobili drew many converts (Dahmen 1925: 25). There it meant a divine intermediary between the supernatural and the human-de Nobili again assimilated a parallel native idea to convey a Christian doctrine. The difficult concept of grace de Nobili translated as "*parapadam,*" a gift of food made to celebrants after a temple service. Though misleading it at least gave de Nobili an opening through metaphor to induce in his followers appreciation for the divine bounty of grace freely bestowed by God.

Images, so important in Christian teaching, also required careful revamping to meet the biases of converts. De Nobili found that he could use the crucifixion to exposit Christ's passion because the Hindus understood perfectly well the spiritual meaning of sacrifice. Here at least the India missionaries did not come to the same impasse Ricci and his successors reached in China, where death by torture irretrievably marked Christ as an insurrectionary and criminal. However, it was much more difficult to convey to the people of Madurai the reason why this particular sacrifice was more important than any other. They were accustomed to sacrifices often repeated, in honor of many different gods.

Whenever de Nobili spoke of that devisive tenet, the Incarnation, he ran into confusion. According to this belief Christ was the Son of God made Man, or the Word of God made Flesh. Determining the proportion of man to God in Christ was the fountainhead of great and bloody heresies from the early Church onward, though the Council of Chalcedon decreed that Christ incorporated two "substances," and anything beyond that is a mystery. The Hindus were ready for their own deviation; they immdiately confused the Incarnation with their traditional concept of reincarnation, which teaches that all creatures are endlessly reborn in different bodies and states until they escape rebirth entirely. De Nobili had to monitor himself constantly to

Chapter One: Roberto de Nobili | 19

prevent the retreat from dogma accompanying a too easy marriage of Christianity with Hinduism. In one of his Tamil religious dialogues the *Punar Jenma Aksepam*, he nimbly executed the contortions required to avoid referring to transmigration which preserving other doctrines associated with it (Rajamanickam 1972b: 206-07).

> Disciple: It is a well known fact that those outside the revealed religion not knowing the reasons for the inequality that exists in the world by the ordinance of the just God, have invented the theory of transmigration. If you explain the reason why God has established such a order, even children will understand that transmigration, which they have invented in vain, is false.
>
> Guru: To prove the reason why God has ordered a certain hierarchy among men, we shall bring forward as the first argument the dictum which the people of this country admit. They also admit that 'what is in the microcosm is also in the macrocosm and vice versa.' This dictum is quite in consonance with the providence of God.
>
> Disciple: I am ignorant of the meaning of this dictum. So please design to explain the meaning and import of that dictum.
>
> Guru: The Human body is called the microcosm, while the world is called the macrocosm. So whatever is found in the small world, i.e. the human body, is also found in the big body which is the world. That is the meaning of the dictum; what is in the microcosm is also in the macrocosm. Now the import of this saying is this: Just as various organs are necessary for the welfare of the human body, so also various kinds of people are necessary for the world. Otherwise no man can live on earth and there will be anarchy. When we explain all this in detail, we shall have proved that a certain hierarchy is necessary for the welfare of the world.

De Nobili infiltrates the stepwise proof of scholastic logic into a written (and, unusual for Tamil of this period, prose) version of the oral guru-disciple dialogue which he conducted with the catechists. He opposes transmigration but, hardly a social bandit, he is not about to negate the social hierarchy which transmigration always explained.

De Nobili turns from a supernatural argument to a functional one; the castes, the privileges and functions exist because of a cosmic order that assigns each working unit to its place. The body, with its organs in line from stomach to brain, is a gross simulacrum of the prevailing condition of society. This was a popular rationalization of slavery and dominance in Europe at the time: Shakespeare had put a merrier form of the same into the mouth of the old Roman Senator Menenius Agrippa, who was trying to assuage the wrath of the people against the haughty Coriolanus. De Nobili took advantage of a Hindu belief in macrocosm-microcosm correspondence to introduce this acceptable alternative to transmigration, and in so doing again turned Hindu prejudice into Christian faith.

Outwardly, then, from the church building to the sacraments it housed de Nobili adapted and adapted well. Any survey of his compositions must occasion wonder at the deftness of his articulating Hindu parts into a Christian whole. He even introduced concepts of Western science, especially of the new astronomy, to the *brahmans*, and urged them on to a less superstitious view of nature (d'Elia 1960: 15-17).

Amid all the wealth of material that is available to the serious (and Tamil-speaking) student of de Nobili there really exists almost none of the information about his personal life a twentieth century biographer would require. His controversial and didactic writings are intended to obscure him, for it was unseemly in a *sannyasi* or a Jesuit to indulge in autobiography (Sommervogel 1894: vol. 5: 1779-90). A Jesuit especially relied on the institution of personal confession to unburden himself of the inner dissonances that at later dates ended in narrative. De Nobili's letters to kin and acquaintances are likewise unrevealing; they concentrate on the progress of the mission, its frustrations, his own spiritual state. He never weathers a crisis, thrashes with a doubt. The perfectly rounded self-containment that franked him through nearly sixty years of turbulent, exhausting mission work was not broken anywhere. De Nobili kept his doubts to himself and spread his assuarances to the world. Only an occasional murmur about his health escaped his lips.

This impassivity was, of course, in the spirit of the time and of the Society of Jesus. But it would be hard to believe that silence about one's life and feelings was culturally incumbent upon a man who was born in the year Benvenuto Cellini died, Jesuits notwithstanding. De Nobili was a man of unbreakable reserve. In a Tamil manifesto he posted not long after beginning the mission, designed to quell suspicion about his origins and intent, he apologized even for setting down a few sentences about his home country and travels, behavior disgraceful in a *sannyasi*, who knew neither home nor relatives. De Nobili's silence on the subject of his own transformation is itself autobiographical; his alien hermitage was proof against any need to describe himself. He became a character subject to his own determination yet also with a purpose in the scheme of things. All that we know of him, and can know, is austerity, escape and volition. Everything else is history or fable.

De Nobili was not wholly solitary in his *sannyasi* life. He asked for companions and recieved a steady stream. Few, however, had his stamina, or, more vulgarly, his intestinal endurance. Emmanuel Leitao, the first sent, lasted only a few months on the diet that the supposedly frail de Nobili maintained until the age of 80. De Nobili's reception of Leitao, detailed in one of Laerzio's annual reports to the General, shows how de Nobili handled the daily ambiguities of his situation, if not how he felt about them (Rajamanickam 1972b: 24).

> As soon as Father de Nobili was informed of my arrival he sent Visuvasam and his brother Alexis to meet me. They welcomed me with great tokens of affection and led me to the Church. On entering it I prostrated myself according to the custom of the country, and gave thanks to God who had granted my desire. The church is very poor but to me it is rich in devotion. I was next taken to the place where Father Robert was waiting to welcome me as his disciple according to the custom of the gurus. On entering I prostrated myself before him and saluted him with a deep bow, for all this was required by the circumstances. He received me with great joy. He then ordered evryone to withdraw, had the doors closed, and having thus recovered his freedom, put aside all the ceremonial prescribed by etiquette, and embraced me with great affection. He was delighted to see my *sannyasi* costume and also my complexion which is not very different from that of the local *brahmans* . . .

The Jesuit end of De Nobili's condition was transacted separately from the *sannyasi* end, but they both were joined as far along as de Nobili could manage. Leitao and his more persistent successors were willing to accede to the subterfuge of discipleship which was the most natural way of introducing them outside the odor of *Parangi* suspicion (Rajamanickam 1967: 6). Some few accommodated themselves adequately to the pattern de Nobili had established; those who became disgruntled with the unreasonable demands de Nobili imposed turned evidence against him in the hearings his opponents finally instigated.

The history of de Nobili's struggle with the local Church authorities occupies a disproportionate amount of his life history simply because the documentation from de Nobili's side and from that of his opponents far exceeds all other material. Jealousy and national hostility (Portuguese against Italian) played more of a part than most Jesuit writers are willing to admit, but a fundamental ideological cleavage was the cause or at least the symbolism of the differences. To a line of critics from Fernandez to Pero Francisco, Laerzio's replacement as Jesuit Provincial (1611-15), de Nobili's adaptation looked like surrender. And surrender to these heathens was an affront to European, that is Portuguese, civilization.

In this period the Portuguese seaborne empire was under fire from the rising Protestant powers and it would be only a matter of years before it was quit of many prize possessions, as well as control of the Asian trade routes. The Portuguese Jesuits tended to favor the intrusive conversion methods since there was a real possibility of infiltrating political control once there were enough Christians; the Portuguese considered themselves on a religio-political mission which became more mystical as the century progressed. The Italians, on the other hand, with no hope of conquest, had the time to ease the natives into Christianity. De Nobili and a few others, including the remarkable English Jesuit Thomas Stephens, were under fire for their concessions, for their failure to broadcast an externally European Christianity. Political, economic and ethnic motives directed the assault.

De Nobili, aware of the crude energies that were shaking his delicate structure, made adjustments. Around 1610, for instance, he left off wearing the sacred thread entirely, having discovered that *brahman sannyasi* of the Shivaite sect do usually give up the thread (Bertrand 1848: vol. 2: 110). He could not concede enough to give the right appearances, however. When the new Provincial, Pero Francisco, visited Madurai in 1612 he inspected de Nobili's mission and reported his findings in a letter to the General of the Society. Pero was pleased with Fernandez' accomplishments and even devoted a paragraph of fulsome praise for de Nobili's saintly life, as was seen before. But he sharply condemned de Nobili's method which he though nothing less that a slavish imitation of the most superstitious brahman customs.

This missive devastated de Nobili's good name among his family and the Church hierarchy. It was noised about that he had gone over completely to the Hindus and officiated at loathsome rites; his cousin, the learned Cardinal Bellarmine, refused to answer his letters for over three years (Bertrand 1848: vol. 2: 160-70). General Acquaviva's reply to Pero is not preserved but it was sufficient to permit the Provincial to lay stifling restrictions on de Nobili's mission including, eventually, a ban on new baptisms. Pero's death in 1615 lessened de Nobili's travail momentarily, but soon afterward he had to withstand the attack of the new Archbishop of Goa, Cristovão de Sâ e de Lisbôa.

Archbishop de Sâ was able to mount his assault on higher levels. He wrote to Rome requesting permission to curtail the mission radically.

However, de Nobili's stock had recovered somewhat and theologians examining his writings found justification for the adaptation method. In 1617 the Archbishop received a papal brief ordering a conference at which the opinions of de Nobili's procedure were aired. This went poorly for de Nobili, who had to endure the jibes of opponents while scarcely restraining himself from sharp rejoinders. When a richly clad monk alluded sarcastically to de Nobili's *sannyasi* dress the beleaguered missionary replied by asking if Christ ever accoutered himself like the monk (Bertrand 1848: vol. 2: 160-70).

The opinion of the conference, not favorable to de Nobili despite the support of Archbishop Ros of Cranganore, was passed over to Rome whence the final decision should be issued. As with any motion in the Church, it took years. The bull *Romanae Sedis Antistites* (1622) settled the controversy with the finality of papal authority: de Nobili was allowed his adaptation but with a few minor changes. His family influence, and his argumentative skill, had bested his detractors, and though they might sneer that Rome always vindicated her own, the mission was under the Papal aegis and subject thereafter to no designs.

Significantly enough 1622 was also the year in which the Sacred Congregation for the Propogation of the Faith was created in Rome. This body, composed of three cardinals, two prelates and a secretary, was charged with overseeing all activity touching on the spread of the Roman Church. Francesco Ingoli, the first Secretary of the Propoganda and the man most responsible for its later influence, was especially committed to halting the Spanish-Portuguese preponderance in overseas missions. Probably de Nobili's case contributed to the creation of such an organization, or the attitude which permitted its creation may have aided de Nobili (Neill 1979: 179-80). After 1622 de Nobili had mainly the agitation of the *brahmans* to combat (Bertrand 1848: vol. 2: 26-33).

Though triumphant against those who would obliterate it entirely, de Nobili's missionary alternative was never the dominant one. His personal adaptation formed the template for individual transitions from Christianity to Hinduism to the medial state he had so doggedly fashioned. The conversion of natives to Christianity was one obvious direction; de Nobili's example also provided for the conversion of Europeans to native Christians that they might teach and minister. The change of clothing, diet and customs accompanied this as did an introduction to a very different order of the world.

De Nobili himself was removed from the Madurai mission in 1645 and died in Mylapore in 1656. Later there developed among the transformed missionaries a caste ranking which mirrored the Hindu system (Dahmen 1925: 86). Missionaries were especially designated for the upper castes or for the pariahs, even for separate divisions within those levels. Presumably the members of the different Jesuit castes had to observe the same relations toward each other as were normally observed among real castes in Indian society. De Nobili escaped the worst consequences of this inverted conversion by his own ingenuity but he left a heritage of caste-separated ministry.

In the early eighteenth century, when the progress of the Muslim conquests had driven the Jesuits from many parts of South India, the dominant figure in the Tamil mission was Constantine Giuseppe Beschi. Beschi, a Tamil stylist of renown, assumed the status of a *brahman*, and it is said that Jesuits of lower "caste" had to prostrate themselves in the street as he passed (Besse 1918). The tradition which de Nobili originated, insofar as it remained in force after his demise, apparently lost the direction which he himself provided. The missionaries started truly to resemble what they had come to alter.

De Nobili was the unintentional catalyst of these excesses. He had wished to give in his life, teaching and writings the principles of a Christianity which did not violate the innocent commonplaces of native life. He filtered out only the "superstition," and with the finest sieve. De Nobili asked only that his hermitage be left in peace so that he could spend all of his days locked in the substance of another culture, for the exaltation of his faith, which he served beyond any culture.

References

Bachman, Peter R.
    1972 *Roberto Nobili*. Rome: Institutum Historicum S.I.

Bertrand, J.
    1848 *La mission de Madurai*. 3 vols. Paris: Poussielque- Rusand.

Bontinck, Francois
    1962 *La lutte autour de la liturgie chinoise*. Louvain: Editions Nauwelaerts.

Bettray, Johannes
    1955 *Die Akommadationsmethode des P. Matteo Ricci, S.J. in China*. Rome: Gregorian University.

Besse, L.
    1918 *Father Beschi of the Society of Jesus*.

Broderick, James
    1952 *St. Francis Xavier*. New York: Wicklow Press.

Cronin, Vincent
    1959 *A Pearl to India*. New York: Dutton.

Dahmen, Pierre
    1925 *Un Jesuite brahme: Roberto de Nobili, S.I., 1577-1656*. Bruges: Charles Beyaert.

    1931 *Roberto de Nobili: l'apôtre des brahmes*. Premiere Apologie, 1610. Paris: Editions Spes.

    1935 "Trois lettres sprituelles inedites de Roberto de Nobili." *Revue d'ascetique et de mystique* 16:179-194.

d'Elia, Pasquale
    1960 *Galileo in China*. Rufus Soter and Mathew Sciascea, translators. Cambridge: Harvard University Press.

Fulop-Miller, Renee
    1963 *The Jesuits*. F.S. Flint and D.F. Tait, translators. New York: Capricorn.

Hollis, Christopher
    1968 *The Jesuits: A History*. New York: Macmillan

Maclagan, E.
    1932 *The Jesuits and the Grand Moghul*. London.

Neill, Stephen
  1964 *A History of Christian Missions.* Harmondsworth, Middlesex: Penguin.

Pfister, Louis
  1932-4 *Notices biographiques et bibliographiques sur les Jesuits de l'ancienne mission de China.* Shanghai.

Rajamanickan, S.
  1967 "Roberto de Nobili and Adaptation. The Indian Church" *History Review* 1, 2:1-10.

  1970 "The Newly Discovered 'Informatio' of Roberto de Nobili." *Archivum Historicum Societas Iesu* 30:221-267.

  1972a *Roberto de Nobili on Indian Customs.* Palamkottai: de Nobili Research Institute.

  1972b *Roberto de Nobili: The First Oriental Scholar.* Salamkottai: de Nobili Research Institute.

Sommervogel, Carlos
  1894 *Bibliographie de la Compagnie de Jesus.* 7 vols. Paris: Alphonse Picard.

Tornese, P. Nicola
  1973 *Roberto de' Nobili.* Cagliari: Facolta Teologica del S. Cuore.

Wicki, Joseph
  1968 "Sei lettere inedite del Roberto Nobili, S.I." *Archivum Historicum Societas Iesu* 37:129-44.

  1969 "Lettere familiare del P. Roberto Nobili, S.I., 1609-49." *Archivum Historcum Societas Iesu* 38:313-325.

Yule, Henry and A.C. Burnell
  1968 *Hobson-Jobson.* Originally published in 1886. New York: Humanities Press.

Omai

II

Captives and Visitors: Omai

As with all tides the European advance into the outer world traveled both ways, though the main draw was outward. On the backflow there arrived an odd collection of flotsam, some pieces cast ashore and left there, others staying only for that moment of inertia between the rise and fall of the waters, dragging back with them a bit of the European shore when the flow was outward again.

In 1287 a Turkish Nestorian Christian from China named Rabban Sauma made his way to Rome where he quarreled over theology with the Cardinals, and to Bordeaux, where he administered the Eucharist to King Edward I of England (Budge 1928). Rabban Sauma was already a Christian, although a heretical one by the standards of the Roman Church. He needed nothing but a correction in his views and he would be a proper European. He did not stay long enough, however. His visit prompted the dispatch of missionaries in the direction of the Mongol Empires, in the hope that the fierce Mongol warriors might be inspired with a Christian fervor and consent to attack the ruling Islamic empire of the Turks, who were slowly strangling all Western commerce with the East.

The next outreach brought back more outsiders. Cabral, the Portuguese navigator, stopping on the Southwest coast of India, at Cranganore, took aboard a St. Thomas Christian named Joseph and carried him to Europe. Little is known of the real Joseph's fate. A book, *Novis Orbis*, was fathered upon him, giving a spurious account of his travels and of the Indian Christian community (Brown 1956: 12-13). The English, in their tour of India, brought back a Bengali boy, who, having been instructed in the Anglican faith, was baptised in London in 1616 with King James as godfather (Neill 1964: 232). The Roman Church tried to better their northern rivals by consecrating a Brahman convert, Matthew de Castro, a bishop and giving him a see in Japan. Matthew antagonized the Portuguese authorities, most of whom were hardly prepared to accept native clergy, not to mention native bishops. Matthew was shunted from see to see and finally ended being deprived of his titles and being removed from all active involvement in the missions (Ghiesquière 1937). Later waves brought to

Europe Chinese Jesuit seminarians and Japanese samurai making a visit to Rome. Brahmans were seen walking through Covent Garden and an Arab prince presented King George with an oddly calligraphed document.

The seas reached west also. In about 1010 Thorfinn Karlsefni an Icelandic merchant exploring Markland (most likely Labrador) came upon some Skraelings, a name given by Icelanders undiscriminatingly to Eskimos and American Indians. Karlsefni's men captured two Skraeling boys (Magnusson and Palsson 1965: 102).

> They took the boys with them and taught them the language and
> baptised them.

We are not told of the fate of these converted Indians, but perhaps it was more kindly than that of the Eskimos Martin Frobisher captured on his second voyage to the north Canada coast, in 1577. The captives were a man and a woman with her child. On the return voyage Frobisher's sailors amused themselves by packing the man and woman together into the same tight bed only to be disappointed by the savage modesty exhibited. When the ship put into port at Bristol the Eskimo man was called upon to exhibit feats of kayak maneuvering and duck spearing in the harbor. In less than a month all three captives were dead in spite of being fed according to the British conception of native diet and permitted Eskimo clothes (Morison 1971: 521-30).

In 1629 ambassadors from an American Indian tribe stood before Louis XIV in courtly costume, but the next year feathered Tompinambus brought from Maragnon Island by the Baron de Razilly excited polite awe at the barbarity of their dress. The savages had every reason to prefer their wild accoutrements, as Baron de Le Houtan discovered when he tried to make a coxcomb out of an articulate Indian (Boucher 1967: 288). "How could I," exclaimed the redman,

> ever get used to spending two hours dressing and preening myself,
> wearing a blue coat, red stockings, a black hat, a white feather and
> a green ribbon . . . .

If the people could not resist being brought to Europe they could at least decline the imposition of European manners, thus reflecting the absurdity of their civilized hosts. This criticism would become quite potent in the hands of satirists and commentators of a later period, all writing as

Chinese, Persians, Turks and Indians who found little to admire in European civilization.

From the late seventeenth century onward there was a procession of Indians bearing tribute out of the New World and to the great courts of Europe, to Whitehall, Versailles and the Vatican. It was a mark of imperial success to make a show of these elaborate outsiders: other European monarchs might know the measure of a kingdom's power in the New World and the tribesmen, brought into scenes of regal splendor, might return to their country with breathless reports of the King's godlike state. At times, however, these ambassadors (the English and French wanted to think of the Indians as weak nations within the scope of European diplomacy) were not treated very warmly by their hosts. In October 1766 some Indian chiefs waiting for a return ship at Gravesend after delivering a petition to King George were conducted into a church. One of the chiefs was suddenly set upon by a woman who raved, "You scalped my husband." She wounded the man and scratched his "consort" in the face before she could be restrained. The crowd in the church, thinking there was a fire, stampeded, causing other injuries. Only the minister retained his composure and waited in his pulpit for the scattered parishioners to return (*Gentleman's Magazine* 1766: 490). There is little wonder that the Indians did not choose to settle in Britain, and usually were eager to be repatriated as soon as possible.

Nor were the savages considered genial guests able to impress polite courtiers with their good breeding. There seemed no chance of reconciliation between the high manners of Europe and the low custom of savages. Even the noble savage theorists who held that men were best in their natural state and were corrupted by laws and balls, could find no excuses for the savages who actually visited European nations. The people who had been tossed up on European shores could not last in the rarified milieu of social niceties. Europeans might find homes in other lands; some might even fall into savage ways. But falling was always easier than climbing. When Captain Wallis' ship the *H.M.S. Dolphin* touched Tahiti in 1767 the ship's master George Robinson noted in his journal that the Tahitian natives would have gladly voyaged to Europe and (Robertson 1948: 229)

> there were some of our men who said they would stay in this place
> if they were sure of a ship to come home in a few years.

Precocious, canny men, and well civilized knowing that a few years would suffice to suck Paradise dry. But no men stayed and no natives came. If one had come to England could he ever have raised himself to the level of teas and royal levees? Hundreds of years had intervened between the primitive origins of Europe, at which point most savages were stalled, and the present, higher state which savages might attain only with hundreds of years of their own. Many said that no individual could ever move in advance of his backward people to join the greater ranks of civilized Europe. Then Omai appeared.

In September, 1773 Captain James Cook's expedition to the Pacific was at anchor near Huahine, one of the Society Islands. Two ships formed Cook's small force, the *Resolution*, commanded by Cook himself, and the *Adventure*, under the orders of Cook's subordinate Captain Furneaux. Cook had won the amity of a local chief on an earlier voyage and was renewing the friendship. The layover was relaxed, marred only by small hostilities. A native armed with clubs had to be quelled by Cook and the ship's botanist was stripped bare by a pair of robbers. As the ships unmoored one of the natives who had come on board the *Adventure* expressed a wish to travel to Britain.

Furneaux was quite willing to gratify the whim but Cook himself was not generally well disposed toward transporting natives. On his previous trip he had carried two Tahitians as far as Batavia, where they died, and he already had another Tahitian named Porio on board the *Resolution* bound for Britain (Cook 1961: II; 400).

Experience in America and in the Pacific had given Cook a dark vision of civilization's effects upon the "happy tranquility" of the natives (Cook 1961: II; 174-75). Earlier in the same expedition Cook had observed the damage done by his men to the morals of the Maori on Queen Charlotte's Island. The women previously had seemed to him

> more chaste than the generality of Indian women . . . but now we find that the men are the chief promoters of this Vice, and for a spike, nail or any other thing they value will oblige their Wives and Daughters to prostitute themselves whether they will or no. . .

Reflecting broadly on the melancholy effects of the intrusion of "civilized Christians" into these isolated societies Cook concludes

> If any one denies the truth of this assertion let him tell me what the natives of the whole extent of America have gained by the commerce they have had with Europeans.

Cook himself was no noble savage visionary, but he was well aware of what could make any savage ignoble.

Cook's attitude was reinforced by the protest from a chief that he was taking young men away from the island, and it looked for a moment that Omai, as the islander on board Furneaux's vessel was called, would be obliged to return to shore. But something, perhaps the charm that Omai never failed to exercise when needed, caused Cook to relent. Omai was on the *Adventure* soon afterward, and for the rest of the trip (Cook 1961: II; 873: Omai is on the *Adventure*'s muster books in December 1773).

Omai outlasted the Tahitian Porio: while the ships rode at anchor by the island of Uliatea some of the officers decked Porio out in European clothes giving him such an edge with the women that he could not be coaxed back. Porio's spot on the *Resolution* was filled by Odiddy (Hitihide), a native of Pora Pora, taken on board the *Resolution* in August 1773 after being warned ominously of the trip's rigors. Odiddy did not last beyond June 1774 when, appreciating fully the gravity of Cook's forebodings, he asked to be let ashore at Raiatea.

Only Omai persisted. Cook did not like him. Cook compared Omai unfavorably with Odiddy, who (Cook 1961: II; 428 fn. 2)

> would have been a better specimen of the Nation in every respect which the man on board the *Adventure* is not, he is dark, ugly and a downright blackguard.

Cook might grumble as he liked. By default Omai quickly became a shipboard oracle in matters Polynesian, being asked to comment upon the customs and languages of the various people encountered and providing a degree of amusement to the jaded men. He served Cook a solemn and fabricated recital of ritual killings on his native island (Cook 1961: II; 238). Faced with the decapitated head of a cannibalism victim Omai exhibited such an excess of anguished feeling that the display prompted William Wales, the ship's astronomer, to write in his journal how Omai (Cook 1961: Appendix V; 819)

> . . . seemed as if Metamorphosed into the Statue of Horror: it is, I believe, utterly impossible for Art to depict that passion with half the force that it appeared in his Countenance. He continued in this situation untill some of us roused him out of it by talking to him, and then burst into Tears nor could restrain himself the whole evening afterwards.

Although Omai was a savage and in Cook's view not a noble one he was at least a sentimental savage who clearly enjoyed his own ascendant position as the only native on board. He could placidly delineate the bloodthirsty rites of the priests on his own island while recoiling in horror that was more than a little theatrical at the sight of a severed head. By this time Omai had already begun a performance gauged to impress his hosts, whom he knew to be far from all-wise or infallible. Omai, like Francis Xavier's Japanese cicerone Anjiro, gave himself off to be more knowledgeable about his own people than he actually was. To make up for what he lacked he used his keen insight to ascertain what the Europeans expected of Polynesian natives and what they expected of gentle, humane persons. Soon he began to act a part, the part of a civilized gentleman rather than that of a barbarous Polynesian.

Cook's men were not the first Europeans Omai had met. Years before, Captain Wallis, whose men had wanted to stay on the newly discovered island of Tahiti for a few years, had fired upon the Tahitians and wounded several of them including Omai, who recieved a musket bullet in the side. Omai remembered Dr. Solander and other members of Wallis' crew when introduced to them upon the *Adventure* reaching Hertford. Solander, captivated by the native, announced to a friend in a letter that Omai had been living "as a Gentleman of private fortune" on Huahine when Furneaux took him on board the *Adventure* (August 19, 1774; Cook 1961: II; 949). This is already an improvement in Omai's status over his actual rank on Huahine where he was a refugee and a dependent, and certainly a sharp contradiction of Cook's low opinion.

Undoubtedly this exalted state was the result of Omai's machinations while on the *Adventure*, as he bestirred himself to behave in the way most advantageous to his own interests. A Polynesian gentleman was not so ridiculous or unlikely. A gentleman at the time of King George III was not just a person who held a high social place through a fixed revenue for which he performed no visible labor. A gentleman was a person possessed of a natural, hereditary gentility which could never be diminished by downfalls or vicissitudes of material fortune. Though struggling against poverty or indisposition a born gentleman would always manifest his nature. Omai was known to be a gentleman and hence gentlemanliness was expected of him and induced in him. The circular logic of the label was not noticed. No one presumed to pass judgement on a gentleman's breeding but other gentlemen and Omai had yet to meet such persons in any number. The evidence of his quality was great. Dr. Solander noted with satisfaction Omai's behavior toward the Duchess of Gloucester (Cook 1961: II; 951).

We dined with him at the Duchess of Gloucester's. At going away the Duchess gave him her pocket handkerchief, which he properly recieved with thanks, and observing her name marked upon it [Omai could read!], he took an opportunity when she looked at him to Kiss it. Many more instances of his own Gallantry could I mention if I had not already dwelled to[o] long upon the subject.

It reminds one of scenes from Sterne's *Sentimental Journey* or, on a lower level of quality, of any of the swarm of sentimental novels that began to fill bookshelves in that era. "Sensibility" was coming into vogue. Gentlemen everywhere were studying sentiment, if only in the devious, superficial manner of the characters in Sheridan's *School for Scandal*. A gentleman would be expected to respond effusively to a severed head and to flirt engagingly with a Duchess. Omai was much with fashion. Omai's nature showed itself to be of the most elevated sort. He was a gentleman, as Dr. Solander described him, and fit to mingle with peers and ladies.

All that followed during Omai's sojourn confirmed the best estimates of his deeper being: he was a natural aristocrat. Thomas Blake Clark in his small but substantial volume on Omai's visit, has adduced much evidence to show that the Polynesian instinctively responded to the current picture of refinement and conducted himself as the living image of what was most wanted in a polite savage (Clark 1941: 90-93). Clark attributes this result to Omai's Polynesian preoccupation with manners and mimicry, his practice in observation when an apprentice priest back on Huahine, and a quantity of natural shrewdness as an observer of mores.

The evidence in favor of this view is ample. London intellectuals, dissatisfied with the Eskimos, Indians, Arabs and Brahmans that had been paraded before them found Omai's actions a comforting return to orderly and composed self-presentation. On numerous occasions Omai betrayed a natural grace and sentiment which pleased such luminaries as Lord Sandwich, the First Lord of the Admiralty, Joseph Banks, the naturalist, and the sentimental novelist Fanny Burney whose brother Jem, the future admiral, had given Omai English lessons on board the *Adventure*. Magazines and journals announced Omai's prestige in admiring terms. Even Captain Cook, seeing Omai petted by the well-born, relinquished his earlier opinion possibly to the extent of editing some hard passages out of his journals. Dr. Johnson was more cautious in his estimate (Boswell 1866: 497).

He had been in company with Omai, a native of one of the South Sea Islands, after he had been some time in this country. He was struck with the elegance of his behavior and accounted for it thus:

Sir, he had passed his time, while in England, only in the best company; so that all he had acquired of our manners was genteel. As proof of this, Sir, Lord Mulgrave and he dined one day at Steatham; they sat with their backs to the light fronting me so that I could not see distinctly, and there was so little of the savage in Omai, that I was afraid to speak to either lest I should mistake one for the other.

Dr. Croker, the editor of Boswell's *Life*, sourly adds that the confusion of appearances between savage and Lord must have been due to Dr. Johnson's defective sight. But there could be no clearer indication of its sharpness than this statement. Dr. Johnson recognized the learned nature of Omai's attitude and slyly, maybe even a little archly, suggests the superficiality of all noble estate while almost giving voice to the disturbing realization that all cultivated behavior is learned, not genetic.

It is not difficult to agree with Dr. Johnson and Professor Clark that Omai was in a situation where any virtue was bound to be appreciated and rewarded. His reception in Georgian London is at once an easy metaphor for the frailty of intellectual pretentions in that age. A simple islander could, by deploying his charm and using his insight, deceive the best minds and most powerful personages of fashionable society. This delights the removed onlooker who may then fashion through Omai a smug vision of that other time. Even in those days Omai was an excuse for everything from mild commentary on modish happenings to more severe political indictment (e.g. Anonymous 1775; Preston 1777; Bell 1780). It is quite pleasing to watch today as Omai dances, bows, gives up his seat to ladies and recoils from fishing with live worms because it is such a murderous sport, knowing that Omai himself may have kept a smile inside as he watched others practice seriously the habits he was feigning.

Omai's experience did not exist as an awareness of how he was fooling London high society—which is just as well since he did not fool them for very long. Despite our desire to see him as a quick-eyed commentator on the world of his "betters," Omai never narrated his life in the way satirists and philosophers would have him. He left no account of his adventures: his only writings have been written for him. A taste of his experience can only be had by guessing, by reaching toward him through the words of others. Even though he lived for almost two years in the heart of eighteenth century London, Omai himself is silent. He is as remote as he would have been had he stayed in Huahine, for there is too much consistency in his reported actions, and no assurance that the narratives are accurate, that Omai was not already being manipulated for various literary purposes. Within all his own efforts to seem like an Englishman and beyond all those efforts to *make* him seem like an Englishman (or a Polynesian acting according to English motives) Omai was learning, while in London, not to be an Englishman but to be a grander Polynesian.

De Nobili at a distance is somewhat comprehensible because his intentions and the movement in which they were formed can be seen. He declared his intentions, at least on the surface, while Omai made no such declarations, and has no visible intellectual origins. Both were holding themselves in the mold of another people to gain acceptance among those people. But de Nobili brought himself to "become" an Indian for his own reasons. Omai might seem to be the same only moving in the opposite direction, trying to be an Englishman while living among them. This idea of Omai does not take him seriously enough. Mimicry of English habits was not his aim. He did not have de Nobili's deep message which to deliver he must take on the characteristics of a native. He cavorted amid the applause of his friends, but that applause made him into someone greater than it could make most people.

It would be extremely inaccurate and unfair to say that applause was all Omai wanted, that he was naught but a childish savage having his fling. Omai was not playing. He was gaining the appreciation of people whom he could see were well-situated, chiefly personages in their own nation. The regard of the important increased the load of importance which Omai himself bore. This England was very like his native Huahine, where the attentions and gifts of an exalted person elevated the receiver for as long as the gifts and attention were bestowed (Sahlins 1970: 210-13).

Much of what Omai did to win esteem must have been in fact incomprehensible to him beyond its gratifying effects. He tread a numb matrix drawing its strings in accord with observable responses. His work consisted of gaining the status he desired by associating with certain kinds of action with definite results. His inquiry was a social one where de Nobili's was cultural. His problem was to elicit behaviors attached to status-enhancing responses, just as de Nobili's was to discover which practices and ideas were religious and which secular. Both problems were equally artificial but equally characteristic of the individual Omai had no goal, no preformed conception of what he should become. There was just soliciting responses and discovery. What worked best was most often repeated. If Omai gained the reputation of a natural gentleman it was because when his efforts finally proved successful in awaking esteem all his mistakes were forgotten and he was seen as a person of inborn gentility. Omai's uniqueness was an advantage.

While de Nobili strove to hide or excuse his foreigness Omai converted it into prestige. He employed his position and skills to elicit from the English the marks of esteem most valued in his own society. What he *became* mattered little since he did not see himself becoming anything except renowned, as far as he could tell. He used his "natural" quality to make himself important, a man of regard, a Polynesian chiefling in English drawing rooms.

As with most pets and playthings Omai's appeal soon began to wear thin. By the second year of his residence he was making a nuisance of himself to Lord Sandwich, who felt motivated to order another Pacific expedition under Cook. Although his hosts had wearied of the suave savage, Omai had not tired of England. His departure meant he would have to strut on another terrain, one that he knew well enough. Although he preferred to remain in England, where there were still conquests to be made, he prepared to return to Huahine gracefully. All that he had accomplished qualified him to return a better man than he had been before. Cook and his sponsors thought this too, only they were rather idealistic: they assumed that Omai had been civilized by his stay in England and that he would spread the benefits of civilization to his people. If people were beginning to realize that Omai "was not (poor soul) the ideal man," that he was not the neoclassical native that Sir Joshua Reynolds made of him in his portrait (Tinker 1922: 89), at least he was capable of carrying the goods of England back to the South Seas.

The English King was not so eager to extend his authority over Polynesia as he was to secure the soon-to-be-lost American colonies, but Omai's success was a beginning and his return would foster a cadre of British supporting natives in the South Pacific, a useful counterpoise against French ambitions in that area. But the native Tahitian the explorer Bougainville brought to Paris in the year Omai entered London had nothing of Omai's success. Civilization would spread with ease there once solidly introduced. Omai was to be regally equipped so that he might impress his people with the generosity of the English nation. This was much to Omai's own purpose. What the English considered evidence of civilization Omai's fellow islanders would consider evidence of power. Omai would return a better man, not on the scale of British imperial cosmology but on the social scale of his little island. Tinker (1922: 80) cites sources contending that Banks deliberately kept Omai ignorant, a simple savage.

Cook's description of Omai's departure from London shows that the Captain had penetrated Omai's mystique even while retaining his perplexed regard for the man (Cook 1961: III; 1: 5).

> His behavior on this occasion seemed truly Natural; he was fully sensible of the good treatment he had met with in England and entertained the highest ideas of the Country and the people but the prospect he now had of returning home to his native isle loaded with what they esteem riches got the better of every other consideration and he seemed quite happy when on board the ship. He was furnished by the King with everything that was thought usefull or ornamental in his Country besides many presents of the same Nature which he received from My Lord Sandwich, Mr. Banks and several other gentlemen and ladies of his acquaintance. In short every method had been taken during his abroad in England and at his departure to make him convey to his Countrymen the highest opinion of the greatness and generosity of the British nation.

Behind him Omai left material for years worth of mock epistles and bombastic verse. In 1785, almost a decade after his visit, Omai was still large enough in the public imagination to be the main figure in the Theatre Royal's stage extravaganza *Omai: or a Trip Round the World*. Here, amid Philip de Loutherbourg's lavish sets, Omai, the heir to the kingdom of Tahiti, wooed an outlandishly dressed maiden (Smith 1900: 80-82 & plates 63-68). On the somewhat less accommodating sets of the real South Pacific Omai, hardly a noble himself, did not fare so romantically.

The journals of Cook and his officers show that the Omai whom they were bringing back to his home island was not the same low-class creature they had carried to England two years earlier. Contact with lords and ladies had magnified him to a visible size, though he never grew so large as on the Covent Garden stage, he was at least assured of some stature as long as Cook was present. Omai served as interpreter for the expedition, frequently going ashore first and establishing contact with the local strongmen. He insinuated himself into the company of the mighty, using his knowledge of English and his privileged place on the English ship to impose upon the islanders.

He was always eager to bring Cook into conference with dignitaries on shore since his role as an intermediary between Cook and the natives could only generate prestige. Omai was especially pleased when he could be the instrument of bringing about some high conference at which he could occupy the seat of honor (Cook: III; 1: 128-29). When one Tongan chief appeared to be greater than another to whom Omai had equated himself by exchanging names Omai became quite annoyed and, in a fit of pique, refused to accompany the greater chief ashore after he had visited the *Resolution*. Lieutenant King, in his *Journal*, adds that Omai spent so much effort downgrading the chief and shoring up the reputation of his friend: "it was therefore impossible Omai cou'd consent to be so degraded" (Cook III, 1: 116 fn. 2).

Indeed by this time Omai had become so big with his own grandeur that he struck a marine sentinel on duty, having imagined some insult. The Corporal replied by shoving Omai away (Cook III, 2: Appendix III, 1341-42).

> Omaih, who amongst these islanders had always been looked upon as a Great Man, was so much incensed at this rebuff that he immediately left the Tent and repaired to one of the Indian Chiefs, taking the two young New Zealanders with him [two Maoris Omai had persuaded to join him] declaring his resolution to return no more to the Ships. The Affair, however, was accommodated the next day.

Lieutenant Burney, who records this incident, adds that the chief whose eminence Omai had so petulantly protected promised to make Omai Agee, or viceroy, were he to remain. The passage concludes with a sparse sentence that speaks volumes concerning Omai's real position on the islands: "his continuance in that station after the Ships were gone, would have been very precarious."

We learn further from the journal kept by the Surgeon's second mate David Samwell that Cook refused to placate Omai, but that he sent a messenger calling him back, and "matters were made up to his satisfaction" though Cook would not punish the Corporal (Cook III, 2: Appendix II: 1032). Cook's own *Journal* remains decorously silent about the whole affair.

The Captain does remark on the invitation of chiefdom extended to Omai, and stresses his disapproval of the step (Cook III, 2: 158)

> but altho I disapprove of it, it was not because I thought he would do better in his own Native Isle.

Like most truly effective sea captains Cook shared the deeper sentiments of his officers and men. His orders required him to return Omai to Huahine, and this he would do, but not without a sense of tart resignation over Omai's probable end.

Landfall in Tahiti confirmed Cook's apprehensions. Omai's brother-in-law and a local chief came out to meet the ship. They were not very open-armed in their welcome until Omai brought them below and gave them both red feathers, thus exciting a display of amity as exaggerated as the original indifference. Cook and King were disgusted by the fickleness of Polynesian affections while Samwell thought to see much affability in the episode-but he had not seen the distribution of the feathers (Cook 1967:III, 1: 1386; III, 2: 1369; 1052). Cook's disgust turned to distress when he saw Omai being duped at every turn and making no effort to use his property for a real advantage or to make himself "courted by the first persons in the island." Instead Omai squandered his goods in buying himself importance with his brother-in-law and other "rascals" (Cook III, 2: 186, fn. 2).

> He always went drest in the most tawdry manner he could contrive and was constantly attended by a large train of followers whose only motive was to profit by his profusion and carelessness.

The officers of the expedition joined their captain in a chorus over Omai's fatuity. They deplored his poor strategy in not making the most of his possessions. Omai ignored all of this. Even though Cook "preached" to him of how little he could count on his return to Huahine, Omai threw himself into Tahitian politics with verve. He tried to attract a significant following by distribution of gifts, the best method, and by making as great a noise in the land as possible. His efforts were bound to be ineffectual since his means were his sole recommendation in a society where power could only exist in terms of complex social constellations formed from hereditary webs. Omai did not have the backing of a strong family or a tradition of rulership, nor did he have a body of supporters who had been bred to his service since youth. Omai could hardly lay claim to any familial prestige in the islands. Indeed Omai was far less noble than even Cook had supposed, as became clear when they both visited one of the Tahitian chiefs. Lieutenant Williamson reports (Cook 1967: III, 2; 1343)

> . . . poor Omai was of so little consequence here as not to be known, we found that Omai was an assum'd name, his real name being Parridero; Captn Cook ask'd why he had taken the former name in preference to his own, he replied that ye names of all the great Chiefs began with O. & that he thought to pass for a great Man, by assuming ye name of a chief who was dead . . .

Omai was an impostor, and though he might dress in his finest clothes and give the grandest presents, both superficial qualities of a chief, he was ignored, partially, as Cook thought, out of envy (Cook 1967: III, 1; 192).

Lacking nobility of birth or favor of the powerful, Omai gathered a rabble dependent only on his largesse, and thus became the caricature of a Polynesian chief, with bonds of anticipated gain replacing the profounder loyalties expected of a chief's following. These people plundered Omai and by their ruffian conduct fostered scornful disregard for Omai among the Tahitian chiefs. When Cook tried to settle Omai on Tahiti advantageously by marrying him to a chief's sister Omai's ragamuffin followers persuaded him to forego the match, and instead introduced him to a young woman who offered him distractions while her accomplices robbed him of everything portable, giving Omai venereal disease into the bargain (Cook 1967: III, 1: 193, fn. 2). Omai had a vision of how to gain ascendence among his own people but he mis-calculated profoundly in implementing it, for he chose the wrong medium for expressing his power. He only ended by alienating the chiefs and amusing the officers of Cook's ships. He achieved only a slipshod replica of what he desired since he had not perceived anything but the most obvious concomitants of chiefdom: the subservience of multitudinous followers and the ever-present bounty. He lacked the consciousness and concern to work himself methodically into a chiefly role, and rejected all efforts of the determined, if culture-bound Cook to secure him in some stand of British solidity by marriage into a "good" Tahitian family.

Omai was not born to command; this Cook could see. Omai held the typical underling's view of the powerful. He saw the great man as the cynosure of crowds and a distributor of benefits. And, as in such fantasies, he assumed that having all the requirements of a chief he would become a chief. He did, but only in musical comedey fashion, and ended significantly poorer for the effort.

The accident of his prominence in London was not perpetuated in Polynesia. He had failed to consider and was unable to impress his own people as he had the English. Cook had a little more insight into the politics of the islands than did Omai, and his insight lead him to a conclusion that was shaped by his own English biases: Omai must be secured against his own foolishness.

Cook preferred locating Omai on Tahiti since Huahine was to his mind politically unstable. Omai resisted and Cook finally acceded: Omai was brought to his native island. On arrival there Cook noted that Omai was showing far greater prudence, now that he had got clear of his "gang." Cook even aspired to regain for Omai a piece of land from which Omai's father had been dispossessed, but this required reconciliation with old enemies and Omai was "too great a patriot to listen to any such thing" (Cook 1967: III; 1, 233). Cook saw that Omai was provided with a plot of land and had a house constructed for him, planted a garden and gave him horses, goats, dogs and pigs to fill his new estate. Cook also tried to ensure Omai's safety against marauders by promising to return and make inquiries after his protege. He advised Omai to give away most of his belongings to a few prominent chiefs, and thus diminish the jealousy of his equals and promote the goodwill of his superiors.

Having divested himself of the expectation that "from his first appearance all woud bow to him," Omai and his small following were settled on the plantation (Cook 1967: III; 2, 1387). Where he had not agreed to a peaceful repossession of his father's properties he tried to prevail upon Cook to take them by force, but Cook refused and readied his ships for departure, leaving Omai to the care of the local chiefs. The leave-taking was quite touching. Omai was especially affected as he bade farewell to Cook.

The Captain continued to have apprehensions about his passenger. No longer would Omai be able to call upon Cook to put men in irons if they threated life or property. Soon after Omai was left behind, in November 1777 Cook set down a series of remarks on Omai's character, describing him as a typical specimen of his race, without application or observational skill, frivolous but not, for all that, an ingrate, blackguard or a complete fool. Cook was chagrined at Omai's disinclination to learn anything important from the British. The only hope he had for Omai's settlement was agrarian, that the animals might multiply and supply the islands with their kind. He sputtered at the thought of Joseph Banks having given Omai a useless electrical machine. Thus Cook parted company with Omai and went off toward Hawaii and his strange death.

Captain Bligh, who had been on Cook's last expedition, inquired after Omai in 1788 when he brought the *Bounty* to Tahiti. Omai, said Bligh's informants, has assisted the Huahine chief in a quarrel against men from another island, and had wreaked havoc on the enemy with his muskets, but had expended all his ammunition gaining the victory. Bligh inquired if Omai had advanced himself in any way by the martial prowess, and the natives replied no, he stayed the same as before (Bligh 1938: 65-66). Omai was also said to have entertained a local chief by killing a man with his gun. Bligh was told that Omai had died of natural causes, along with his Maori companions and most of his plants and animals. His house was burned or somehow destroyed and fragments of his riches fell into the hand of chiefs who showed them to exalted guests for some time afterward. The land on which Omai's house had been bore the name Bretania (Ellis 1969: 365). People in the locale showed leg tattoos of a man on horseback and Bligh heard that Omai often did ride out while the horses survived, wearing his boots and cutting a figure, so that Bligh was convinced that Omai did not immediately "lay aside the Englishman."

Back when Cook was preparing to leave Omai had been very insistent that he take no one back to Britain with him. But at parting Omai himself desired to go back (Cook 1967: III, 2; 240 fn. 4),

> saying, his time should be spent in learning what would be useful to him instead of throwing his time away at cards, however sincere Omai might be at this time, I believe had he gone to England again (which was greatly his wish and desire) he would have acted the same part over again being extremely fond of a gay life & of being thought a great man.

Omai must have known by then that his entire being was made of loose illusions, that he lived with all the means of greatness but greatness would never be his. In London he had obtained prestige on a scale beyond all imagining. He was a Polynesian for a brief while in Britain, having all his native wishes gratified materially. On returing to his own habitat all the charm that had been cast upon him by the adulation of the elite melted away, and he was left to fumble. He carried out his vengeful war against his father's foes, but it won him nothing. He had been a chief in London but he could not be a man who had been a chief in London, living in Huahine.

Omai had taken on the appearance of an Englishman only because it brought him attention. He was a better Polynesian for seeming to be English while in London, but being English in Huahine would not make him any better, just a useful curiosity. To return to his old self was impossible, not in keeping with the honor given him. But to move anywhere else was equally impossible. He could adapt himself temporarily to English society, but could find no way of reassimilating himself to the society of his own people at a higher level, of parleying his experiences and gains into a new native identity that would continue his preferred place in Huahine as it had been in England. His Tahitian adventure as a mock chief had chastened him a little.

In the long run, however, Omai and his English patrons were deceived about the role of goods in Polynesia. Like good Englishmen the patrons, from Lord Sandwich and Joseph Banks to the considerably more astute Captain Cook, had assumed that a hoard of possessions and a plot of land would assure Omai respectable (gentlemanly) if not chiefly status, as it would have in Britain. Omai himself never having been a chief and never having analysed chiefly behavior as effectively as he had the posings of the English upper class, may have assumed that his goods would assure him permanent and unequivocal status. But Polynesian chiefdoms are hereditary, and it is a chief's responsibility to assuage his followers by doling out useful objects or food. It does not follow that anyone endowed with and giving out a supply of frivolous objects is a chief. It is true that Omai may have been wealthy beyond the dreams of chiefs and commoners, but his wealth was ill-bestowed in the absence of any personal quality or of any traditional loyalties it might have reinforced.

As Omai's stock dwindled he himself dwindled into a mere oddity of no particular importance. To gain importance Omai should have declared himself a reformer or a messiah and overthrown the old order to build a new one around himself. But he lacked the force and the acumen to do this. He died on Huahine, once again a commoner, always an outcast and unable to adapt himself to his own culture from a new angle. Omai was still Parridero, and although Britain had allowed him to be Omai in the play world of the aristocracy the islanders knew better and Omai ended as a symbol of his own strangeness, a tattoo.

de Nobili had tried to be authentic in his adaptation and so, in his way, had Omai—it would have benefited him most to be an Englishman. But in Europe itself no one seriously thought of actually becoming another, not when the traits of another could be so easily donned for a moment in masquerade. Yet masquerade could become too serious . . .

References

Alexander, Michael.
    1977 *Omai: 'Noble Savage'*. London: Collins and Harvill.

Anonymous
    1775 *An Historic Epistle from Omaih to the Queen of Otaheite*. London.

Bell, J.
    1780 Letter from Omai to the Rt. Hon. Earl of (xxxxxxxx). London.

Bligh, William.
    1938 "A Voyage to the South Sea." *In A Book of the Bounty*. London: Dent.

Boswell, James.
    1866 *The Life of Johnson*. ed. by John Wilson Croker.London: John Murray.

Boucher, Francois.
    1967 *A History of Costume*. London: Thames and Hudson.

Brown, Lesley W.
    1956 *The Indian Christians of St. Thomas*. Cambridge: Cambridge University Press.

Budge, E.A. Wallis.
    1928 *The Monks of Kublai Khan, Emperor of China*. London: Religious Tract Society.

Clark, Thomas Blake.
    1941 *Omai: First Polynesian Ambassador to England*. London: Colt Press.

Cook, James.
    1961 *The Journals of Captain Cook, II: The Voyage of the Resolution and Adventure, 1772-1775*. ed. by J. C. Beaglehole. Hakluyt Society, Extra Series, Vol. 35.Cambridge: Cambridge University Press.

    1967 *The Journals of Captain Cook, III: The Voyage of the Resolution and Discovery*. ed. by J.C. Beaglehole. Hakluyt Society, Extra Series, Vol. 36. Cambridge:Cambridge University Press.

Ellis, William.
    1969 *Polynesian Researches: Society Islands*. Rutland, Vermont: Tuttle.

Ghesquiere, T.
    1937 *Mathieu de Castro*. Bruges.

Magnusson, Magnus and Herman Palsson, trans.
   1965 "Eirik's Saga." In *The Vinland Sagas*. Harmondsworth, Middlesex: Penguin.

Morison, Samuel Eliot.
   1971 *The European Discovery of America: The Northern Voyages*. New York: Oxford University Press.

Neill, Stephen.
   1964 *A History of Christian Missions*. Harmondsworth, Middlesex: Penguin.

Robertson, George.
   1948 *The Discovery of Tahiti: A Journal of the Second Voyage of H.M.S. Dolphin Around the World*. Hakluyt Society, 2nd Series, Vol. 98. London:Hakluyt Society.

Sahlins, Marshall.
   1970 "Poor Man, Rich Man, Big Man, Chief: Political Types in Melanesia and Polynesia." In *Cultures of the Pacific*, ed. by Thomas J. Harding and Ben G. Wallace. New York: Free Press.

Smith, Bernard W.
   1960 *European Vision and the South Pacific*. Oxford: Clarendon Press.

Tinker, Chauncy Brewster.
   1922 *Nature's Simple Plan*. Princeton: Princeton University Press.

Chevalier d ' Eon
English popular print, late eighteenth century, courtesy of
the British Museum Print Collection.

III

Masquerade: The Chevalier d'Eon

Masquerade is an amusement, a design for idle toying with identity. The masquerade balls that occupied European elites of the seventeenth and eighteenth centuries were territories for playful masking where wearing a costume was less important than the costume being worn. The balls grew out of the masked court processions of the Renaissance and even more remotely out of the traditions surrounding Carnival, the rude gaiety that signaled the beginning of stern Lent. The Carnivals of Venice were the model for these masquerades; an increasingly distracted, court-bound nobility filled their time with variations and imitations.

The masked balls were the herding places of power. The ability to digress from a life of grandeur into the form of a lion or a clown was emblematic of the indefinite identity which was the prerogative of the noble. Monarchs such as Louis XIV of France and the Empress Elizabeth of Russia delighted in the many shapes of splendor their rank allowed them and the change in shape their courtiers would exhibit on command. In the French Court Carrousel of 1662 the King's brother appeared as a Turk, the Duc d 'Enghien as a rajah and the Duc de Guise as a "savage chief." At a carnival ball in 1685 Monsieur, the King's brother, outdid them all, bringing all nations and estates together in his person (Honour 1961: 62).

> First he appeared masked as a bat, then fluttered away to return dressed as a Flemish woman; having cast away his wide brimmed hat and voluminous skirt he made his last entry somewhat surprisingly clad as a workman—but the costume was the most ingenious of all for by pulling a string he shed his rustic clothes to emerge ' vetu en Grand Seigneur chinois'; and in this guise he danced and postured for the rest of the night.

As in the reception of embassies at Versailles, as in the panegyrics of poets and the portraits of painters all nations were convened before King Louis, only here entertainingly. The thick decorum of court life was broken up and inverted; but the privilege remained.

In the latter decades of the eighteenth century the masked ball descended to common usage. Mozart, royalty among composers but no nobleman in his time, attended a ball in 1785 dressed as an Indian philosopher complete with laconic riddles which he insistently posed to passersby. Boswell, much to Johnson's distemper, attended a ball in the costume of a Corsican. From there the balls degenerated into far less respectable events, the excuse for random mixing and the cause of brawls, though occasionally there was a stiff, staid promenade at court. Later ages, regarding the masked balls of the past, saw their glamour but beneath that detected grimness, death-like torpor and scheming wickedness. Poe's *Masque of the Red Death*; Le Fanu's *The Room in the Dragon Volant*; Verdi's *Un Ballo in Maschera* (based on the story of a Swedish King's assassination at a masked ball) and a drove of Gothic romances each with its obligatory masked ball scene, were the nineteenth century's judgement on masquerade. There was rich evil in scenes where no one's identity was known for sure—Death might be present in some costume, perhaps even disguised as himself. The righteous people of the nineteenth century looked back and shuddered. Disguise was for the public good, for Richard Burton reconnoitering the dangerous Arabs or for Sherlock Holmes set upon undoing some skulking Moriarity.

The era of masked balls spawned a few prodigies whose masking went beyond masquerade. With just a switch of clothes and the sincere wearing of a novel face any person was as if foreign, knowing an experience like that of de Nobili or Omai but in his own land, among his own acquaintances. This extenuated masquerade could happen in one of two ways: either as a public change into costume, open for all to see, or as an impostor, an effort of the masker to convince those who had not seen the change that he really is the person he resembles. The public change is simpler, but not any the less artful the full imposture. This open masquerader must make a pact with society to permit the assumption and perpetual retention of a new identity. But often such a legislated masquerade is not so easily abandoned once the pact is made. The masker can never be as he was before; something inside him clings to his exterior. This first type of masquerade was practiced then suffered by the Chevalier d'Eon. The natives which he joined were neither Indians nor Polynesians but much closer to home.

No doubt the Chevalier d'Eon would have protested his name being used by Havelock Ellis to designate the aberrant act of wearing the clothes of the opposite sex (Ellis 1936: II; 2, 1-110). The Chevalier was always sensitive to issues involving the honor of his good name, and only the intervening centuries have protected the English sexologist from a challenge to arms. But Ellis could have defended himself with words rather than swords by asserting that even when quite young the Chevalier (not yet the owner of that title) did much to warrent the neologistic slur. Ellis, like anyone else explaining the Chevalier's career in strictly psychological terms, would have been wrong.

The Chevalier's mother consecrated him to the Virgin Mary at the age of four and for three years thereafter he wore the habit of the sisterhood of the Virgin, until his father ordered that he assume male dress (Telfer 1885: 3). The mother attributed her son's safety in many risky enterprises to the prevailing protection of the Virgin Mary. But a deeper reason, not the idiosyncrasy of the parents, lies behind this precocious transvestism.

It was the custom in Europe during the Chevalier's time to clothe male infants in female dress. This was not spontaneous in that era—some of the most formidable Greek heroes (Achilles, for example) were raised as girls, and the pattern can be traced through cultural history in most European societies (Aries 1962: 51, 58). Even the Chevalier's royal master, Louis XV, appears dressed as a girl in one of his infant portraits (Pitou n.d.: 252-Chantilly Gallery, Paris). Malign forces, the evil eye and the beings who wield it, always tended to strike a family through its male heir. If they found nothing but a worthless female child they would be frustrated-better to let her live and cost her parents a dowry. The Chevalier's transformation into an infant nun was not unusual; it added the Virgin Mary's potent shield to the ploy of female disguise. It may have prediposed the Chevalier to later flights into female costume-but neither was *that* very unusual in the upper reaches of society. And many male children dressed as girls in infancy grew up to evince only those occupations generally considered male (Kiener 1965: 110).

The reports of the Chevalier's wearing of female dress on his own account are extremely controversial. Whether or not, in 1755 Eon traveled to Russia and served as confidante to the Empress in female disguise will never be fully decided. The main source for this story is Gaillardet, whose *Memoirs of the Chevalier d'Eon* (1970 [1836]) are mainly a historical romance though originally passed as truth. The *Memoirs* show the young Eon cajoled into female costume by Madame de Barry and other court ladies in order to trick the King during a masked ball. The "royal boa constrictor" is deceived and arranges to have the young "woman" led to a private apartment to await his pleasure. Madame de Pompadour enters and furious at the usurpation is about to claw the new favorite when she discovers "her" true sex. Captivated, she yields herself instead. Then the King arrives and he fortunately is good enough to be amused when he discovers the deception. He forgives everyone and enrolls the talented young man in his secret service. The trip to Russia and sundry other adventures follow suit.

But they may not be as much of an invention as the King's attempted seduction. There exists a portrait of the Chevalier in female dress painted when he was 25 years old, by the fashionable court painter La Tour (preserved today in a copy by Angelica Kauffman; Nixon 1905: 125). The exact meaning of the portrait is undetermined; it only implies that the Chevalier took to female dress seriously enough to want a record. Somewhat later it was a persistent rumor in aristocratic circles that the Chevalier had infiltrated the household of the Empress Elizabeth as a femme de chambre. Whatever dress he did wear the Chevalier certainly was in those years an important contact in Louis XV's spy network, the Secret du Roi which, like many similar organizations in history, was operated as if it were a monstrous cruel child's game, hidden from public scrutiny, destroying friends and enemies alike.

The years following Eon's obscure Russian adventure (1755-63) thrust him into the tangles of espionage and the glories of war. The enormously complex story of these is best left to Eon's many biographers, each with his or her own rendition of the many plots and counterplots that buoyed their hero along (Coryn 1932: 246-47). At the end of this surge Eon, now Chevalier d'Eon, is in London guarding a bundle of papers that make the King and his Councillors very uneasy, and is fighting a battle of nerves with the Comte de Guerchy, French Minister to London, who is under explicit orders to do anything to wrest the papers from the tenacious Chevalier. Guerchy negotiates: Eon refuses: Guerchy tries to poison Eon and kidnap him back to France: Eon turns his house into a garrison and mines the stairs up to his chamber. And so it goes through law courts and on duelling fields until 1774 when Louis XV dies leaving Louis XVI and the deluge for France.

There had always been some speculation concerning the Chevalier's sex. He was of short stature and rather delicately featured. He had a curious lack of interest in sexual matters, bound to provoke notice in Hogarth's London. During the heat of the battle Guerchy commissioned some hack writers to contrive epithets for Eon. The keenest abuse of his sexuality they could devise was to call him a "hermaphrodite" (oddly prognostic, as will be seen). On one occasion Eon had disguised himself as a woman to evade pursuers— this much he admitted. All of the rumors came to a head in 1769 when many bets ("insurance" as they were then called) were being laid upon the Chevalier's true sex. Eon was bitterly displeased by this notoriety and offered to face on the field of honor any policy-maker who persisted taking insurance on his sex. He was beset with offers of money for submitting to an examination which would decide the issue once and for all. The contradictory reports of the newspapers and the conflicting testimony by the Chevalier's associates added to the fascination surrounding the "little Frenchman."

Amazingly enough the Chevalier had the composure to continue his lifelong researches into economic history. The scandal of his life has overshadowed these extensive writings, but it did not detract from his concentration when he was at work. His long historical essay on taxation, *Considerations historiques et politique sur les impots*, which followed the subject from the Egyptian to the Persian Empire, was in its third edition in 1764, when he arrived in London. During the years of his running battle he accumulated 13 volumes of essays on miscellaneous topics in trade, finance and economic history. They were published in Amsterdam under the title of *Loisirs* in 1774, the year when matters came to a head.

The death of Louis XV actually improved Eon's prospects. He wanted badly to return to France and petitioned the new King, reputedly more benevolent than his royal grandfather, for the requisite passport. The King was advised concerning the *Secret de Roi* and Eon's role in its activities. He knew that among the papers in Eon's possession were detailed plans for the French invasion of England. A stream of negotiators issued from Versailles, but none could work the mechanism of Eon's consent until Caron de Beaumarchais arrived in London.

The author of *The Barber of Seville* (not yet *The Marriage of Figaro*) had already served Louis XV in London by bribing a blackmailer named Morande into withdrawing from print a scandalous biography of Madame du Barry. Now Beaumarchais was sent forth by Louis XV to treat with the impossible Chevalier. And he was successful not only in retrieving the incriminating documents but in managing one of the most curious stage effects of his career.

The canonical version of the parley between Eon and Beaumarchais, and the one reported by Beaumarchais in his letter to the King, is that the Chevalier broke down before Beaumarchais, disclosed her true identity and pleaded with the playwrite-emisary to intercede (Loménie 1880: I; 416-17). This is difficult to believe either of Eon or Beaumarchais considering the proud soldiership of the former and the perceptivity of the latter. And Eon was, as the curious learned after his autopsy years later, a "fully formed male" (Nixon 1965: 240-41 reproduces the death certificates). But Louis XVI

Chapter Three: Chevalier d'Eon | 53

did believe the story, and made the assumption of female dress a condition of Eon's return to France.

The disclosure was quite opportune for Eon. As a man returning to France he would be harassed by enemies eager to avenge the memory of the Comte de Guerchy, for Eon had insulted the man savagely and was thought to have driven him to his grave. As a woman she would pass freely. The retrospective interpretation of the Chevalier's behavior as that of a woman explained everything; only a woman would be so mercurial and petulant. Now that she was ready to drop the foolish masquerade as a man and recover her skirts she would be "forgiven all." Also the Chevalière, placid and tractable, would, Beaumarchais intimated, surrender the secret documents. An agreement was drawn up and signed by Eon and by Beaumarchais on the King's behalf. Eon received a pension and sundry emoluments along with permission to return to France—*but as a woman only.* She was to refrain from taking any action, legal or other, against Guerchy's heirs and was protected against prosecution by the same (But who would prosecute a woman?). The King gained custody of the papers and peace of mind about relations with England. And Beaumarchais, the author of the pact, rose in the King's favor— but that was unwritten.

Loménie, the main biographer of Beaumarchais, and a number of other biographers of Eon and Beaumarchais are convinced that the Chevalier duped the playwright into thinking he was really a woman. Judging from Beaumarchais' later activities and from his mentality in general this is unlikely. The ambitious son of a watchmaker, he longed to move in court circles and win the notice of the powerful, because arbitrary authority intrigued him. It is the crux of all his plays: the wily manipulator tricks the authority figure into surrender. Like his immortal Figaro, Beaumarchais delighted most in assembling motley groups of people under strange circumstances to observe the results of the interactions.

Here, as in the Carnival itself, the masquerade of everyday life is undone. The Count or the wealthy doctor becomes the clown; the barber or the strolling musician takes command. Only the playwright standing behind the scenes can watch with impunity and make these happenings known to his audience. Beaumarchais' plays were like children to him, he says in his *Lettre* answering critics of *The Barber of Seville:* he sent them out into the world to grow and encounter the severity reserved for foundlings.

Beaumarchais proclaimed that he wished to create a truly French theater. The Chevalier's situation provided him with all the materials he needed for an excellent mise-en-scène. A few adjustments of costume from man to woman and of setting from England to France and the poised tendencies would converge into an amusing spectacle. The King, his Ministers, all of France, even Beaumarchais himself were in the cast of characters with Beaumarchais in his Figaro role. The Queen of France, Marie Antoinette, was already asking to see this man-woman marvel. Beaumarchais stepped back and the curtain rose.

Eon started treating the matter archly and basking in the transformation. From London he wrote a letter to Beaumarchais in Paris, using the female forms of the adjectives (Pinsseau 1945: 152-53).

> All my life I have been as solicitious of military honor as a young
> girl should be of virtue and chastity.

The equation between woman and soldier had a particular force in Eon's mind, as if one were part of the other. Being known as a woman did not, to the Chevalier at least, preclude being known as a soldier. While he was still in London, and persisted in male dress while Beaumarchais obtained funds to purchase female clothing, his suppositions about his new life were not challenged.

The news of the agreement, though vague on particulars, aroused interest in Eon's sex and instilled new life into the flagging policy market. Eon pilloried the policy-makers in print and, when he learned that Beaumarchais was involved in their insulting demands, quarreled with him furiously. The playwright had just returned from Versailles with less money for Eon than the Chevalier considered his due. Together with his new crony, the blackmailer Morande, Beaumarchais had staked great sums on the outcome of a scientific investigation into Eon's true sex and tried to persuade the Chevalier to submit to the doctors' probing while clandestinely taking an interest in the results. Could it be that Beaumarchais, knowing Eon was a man, had done everything to convince the public he was a woman so that he might earn a profitable triumph in a witnessed examination? Art was one thing; profit did not have to be another.

Eon attacked Beaumarchais in a letter to Vergennes, the minister of Louis XVI charged with overseeing the delicate affair. He complained that he was not being given enough money to discharge all his debts which he, like a gentleman, had amassed during his years in London. The Chevalier had a taste for rare books, first editions of Horace and other classical authors in fine printings and exquisitely tooled bindings, but he did not have the means to accumulate such holdings as were listed in the auction catalogue of his collection (which went under the hammer at Christie's in 1791) and live

Chapter Three: Chevalier d'Eon | 55

the life of a gentleman. Eon was eager to pay off his creditors because they could prevent him from leaving London, and he expected he would be free of this burden once the King accepted the agreement. But he was deceived in this as in many things. Beaumarchais may have alienated some of the cash for his speculations in policies and perhaps he did miscalculate assuming that Eon's insolvency would cause him to violate his conception of honor. The policy exchanges thickened; Eon held himself aloof and took part only to malign Beaumarchais and anyone else who offended him.

In the midst of the scurrilous pamphlet exchanges it was rumored that Eon was in love with Beaumarchais and wished to marry him, that their harsh words were the result of a lover's quarrel. Even before the main act was underway the play had reached out to absorb its author. Eon's landlord paternally advised her not to marry Beaumarchais because he was not handsome enough, and in the midst of many-leveled charges and counter charges came the innocent query of Miss Wilkes, the daughter of Eon's friend John Wilkes. The convent-bred young lady was "very anxious" to learn whether Eon was a man or a woman. In a court case growing out of a disputed policy payment, Eon was more or less legally accepted as a woman. Then the cloud-cuckoo land of the policies was obliterated in a stroke when the unsuccessful defendant in that case cited an Act of Parliament under which he could not be made to pay. If Beaumarchais had actually expected material profit, he was disappointed.

So far Eon had only endured verbal controversy over his sexual image. The image was public property, even to the extent that it could be defined in a court of law. Suddenly, however, he was faced with the serious condition that governed his return to France: as far as Louis XVI was concerned he was a woman. It was always an autocrat's singular advantage that the world around him must be made to conform to his knowledge of it. The King knew Eon for a woman and, as Vergennes reminded him, women are not allowed to wear men's clothing in France. He might have added that the precedent was set as early as Joan of Arc. On August 6, 1774 Eon appeared "in her real character as a woman." She dined with friends, among them C.J. Bach and the society riding-master Angelo, who left an account of the supper in his *Memoirs*. Then, having staved off her creditors, she parted for France.

Eon materialized in France in his old military uniform and was immediately ordered back into female clothing. Marie Antoinette, thinking that this contrariness was due to an incomplete wardrobe, promised to have a trousseau made. The Chevalier used this excuse to hold off the return to "proper" dress begging, in a letter to Vergennes a little while to compose himself into a correct woman and signing it pathetically "The Chevalier d'Eon for a little while longer" (Telfer 1885: 291).

A day was officially slated for her first public appearance as a woman and she came forth arrayed in all the splendor of court dress, taking Communion in the Chapel of the Virgin to confirm her submission. In a passage written around this time she reflected that she had not only lost a "man's estate," but that she had to become a woman "in spite of myself to adopt the vocations and virtues incumbent thereon" (Telfer 1885: 293). The society of woman was her sole resort and her sole frame of reference. Everyone from the King down knew this must be what she desired, and expected she would be happy in her life if she would be calm and arrange herself accordingly.

Much of the Chevalier's misfortune derived from the common confusion of sex with gender. Sex is a biological fact usually stated unambiguously in the body at birth; gender is the social and cultural quality of being "male" or "female" (the dress worn, language used, occupations followed, behavior expected) developed in the child as it is brought into the realm of human action by parents, teachers and others. Gender is planned on the basis of sex but goes far beyond it. Though the male or female sex has been the same throughout history and is the same in all cultures the modes of inculcating and expressing gender vary widely. One culture's "female" might well be uncomfortably close to another culture's "male." The association of sex with gender in infants leads most people to assume that the two are identical thus believing that children who are female in sex are drawn to "female" crafts while those who are male in sex naturally aspire to "male" exploits. It follows then that a woman no matter how long or well her sex is concealed will always evince "womanly" behavior after the standards prevailing in her time and place. A woman must always be a "woman," and a man is nothing but a "man."

It was therefore logical for everyone in the Eon farce that the Chevalier, although a soldier who had worn the King's uniform for many of his 40 years and shown conspicuous bravery on the field of battle (not "womanly" traits, despite Joan of Arc) would, on being revealed as a woman, instantly revert to female dress and occupations. No one will ever know why the Chevalier, from his side, accepted Beaumarchais' solution but most likely he did not foresee what it would be like to be thrust into conformity with women and have no chance of escape. As he discovered, there is a great difference between masquerading as a woman with the hope of changing back and being accepted as a woman in fact. He may have thought this was another secret service game and that the King would relent. But the King was persuaded.

The Chevalier found adherence to female usages unendurable. The dress worn in earnest brought with it immobility and sequestration, and the perpetual company of women only, which was a culture apart from males and from the world at large. The rigidity of gender identities fostered what amounted to a cultural division between the two genders, assumed to be sexes. Women lived with a sanctum fortified by an ideology which upheld chastity and the dominance of men while keeping distance from men through a round of activities both domestic and pious from which men were implicitly excluded. Some upper-class women made their way into the ruling councils—Madame de Maintenon and Madame de Pompadour had virtual control over the French state at times—but their power was contingent upon a skilled management of their obscurity and personal attractiveness to the men in control.

There developed a whole class of institutions which permitted women the relations which men in their condition traditionally denied them but their importance indicated they might have. The salon, foremost among these, was an arena where relations among men and women could be more fluid that in the traditional world (Picard 1943). Beneath a light surface of gallantry men discussed literature with women or arranged for the transgression of those customs which normally governed lives. Women presided over these brilliant gatherings, wrote diaries, letters and memoirs but still guarded a deliberate community among themselves, their own relations with men and with each other becoming the substance of communication within this community and the main subject of the literature produced. From Madame de Lafayette in the time of Louis XIV to Madame de Rambouillet on the eve of the French Revolution the salons offered space and protection for men and women who wished to stand together just a bit apart from their time and everyday obligations.

The Chevalier-Chevalière, seen in the perspective of social history, was a symbol of this paradoxical mingling of two very distinct genders. The main vehicle for his symbolism, dress, was well chosen because nothing seperated the genders more completely than the clothes they wore. The women in their expensive *grands habits* or, less formally, in their *robes volantes*, had grown vast and billowy yet unimaginably delicate, everything from shoes to hairdos announcing the grace, susceptibility and grandeur of womanhood; while the men were encased in tight-fitting breeches and hose, exacting wigs, heavy, blocky shoes with perhaps some concession to the spirit of casual looseness in the swing of their coats (vid. Monet's engravings for Rousseau's *La Nouvelle Heloise*, 1776). Exchanging one for the other was a monumental change, but the act in itself suggested the bridging of the gap.

But it is painful to be a symbol. Eon made efforts at resigning herself to simple participation in the collective life of court ladies. She visited convents and went on retreats, wrote long prayers and learned dressmaking. Her companions noticed that everything she did had an unladylike crudity; the deftness born of lifelong training at being a woman was absent. Despite her innumerable pleas to be allowed to reemerge as a soldier, not as a man, just as a soldier, the King applied pressure for her to adapt to female routines. Louis and his ministers maintained that Eon, having known the liberty of male life for many years, could only be tamed when confined in the female world. Her pleas were refused or ignored.

The petticoats were physically a prison, as Eon asserted repeatedly in letters. She suffered from acute depression and was told there could be no cure. With every inducement to conform totally to women's ways and become a woman to all appearances, Eon resisted. He would not cross the wavering line between protracted masquerade and permanent masquerade; he would not change genders entirely. Although she wrote coy notes to other women she did not let even the most superficial camaraderie absorb her. The King had to order her confined to a prison and threatened to inter her in a convent (the usual punishment for wayward females) before she would, after one foray in soldier's uniform, return to the ponderous petticoats. Even her struggle to regain manly estate was treated as a form of female deviance.

After reaching a certain point, the adoption of female dress and a few mannerisms, the Chevalière moved only infinitesimally closer to full womanhood. Not that this was impossible for a man: the superficiality of gender markings made it possible for men and women to become each other with little difficulty. The eighteenth century has a long roster of women who spent their lives as males, sometimes even marrying and raising an adopted family. More relevant for the Chevalier men were able to live completely within female gender. His contemporary the Abbé de Choisy had done this, made a woman of (and for) himself by wearing woman's clothes and joining wholeheartedly in women's occupations in a circle of women friends. He was persecuted for this unauthorised transformation and sought refuge in sanctity and travel. Had Eon been willing to do the same he would have been left in peace. But he struggled and was crammed against the glass of his masquerade never able to fuse himself into the costume, draw the costume into himself or escape entirely.

Chapter Three: Chevalier d' Eon | 59

Where the Chevalière failed to give herself a stable gender the public provided her with one, with an inventiveness that reached mythic proportions. Eon masqueraders began to appear at Parisian masked balls and "even at ordinary evening parties." These masked imitators brought the affair back to the manageable dimensions of masquerade. Before smiling audiences they recounted at length the affecting story of Beaumarchais' courtship of Eon, and alluded to the playwright's mismanagement of the King's money.

Time began to flow backward for the Chevalière. Stories of youthful appearances in female dress circulated thickly; they were the beginning of the fabrications which culminated in Gaillardet's biographical romance long after Eon's death. These stories required that Eon's military career be a fable (no woman could have actually fought in war) and opened her entire life to reinterpretation. In 1779 one Monsieur de la Fortelle authored the first full-length biography of Eon, *La vie militaire, politique et privée de Mademoiselle Charles-Geneviève-Louis-Auguste-Andrée-Timothée d'Eon de Beaumont* in which everything from Eon's names to his exploits were transferred to the female gender.

Beaumarchais, caught in the accelerating whirl of myth-making, was concerned enough to procure a statement from the King, that final arbiter of reality, and publish it around Paris with the hope that it would free him from heckling. The Chevalière herself was alternately pleased and distraught at the proliferating forms she took. The Masons, a fraternity always at variance with the King, voted the Chevalière a member. Since only males could be admitted into the Masons she was overjoyed. A print showing her as a warlike Pallas standing before the tents of an army appealed to her so much that she sent a copy to some women friends at a convent. The idea of a divine woman warrior consoled her even though she was denied actual soldierhood.

Another widely disseminated print gave her little joy, though it enrolled her in a class of mythological beings even more arcane than Pallas: she was shown as a man-woman, an androgyne, one half a soldier with a sword, the other a court lady with a feather fan, thus evoking the hard/soft dichotomy which was one of the main gender distinctions. The late eighteenth century evinced a growing taste for androgyny; a number of prints and drawn images attest to the popularity of the concept outside its application to Eon. The masked balls themselves took notice. Along with the frequent cross-dressing one sometimes found costumes like that of a "female mask" who arrived at a 1776 London ball "dressed partly as a man with a woman's head-dress surmounted by a huge clerical cap. . . ."

The man-woman was, of course, no innovation. The Hebrew (Kaballah) Adam, the Hindu Krishna and the Greek Hermaphrodite were but a few instances of its appearance, each having its own significance in a religion. Its eighteenth century occurrences were most likely conditioned by social change, by the need to find a concise picture of relations between the two genders. The appropriation of Eon as a living androgyne was one turn in the pattern's history, which continued after him into the occultism of the early nineteenth century and beyond. Eon fulfilled the mythic promise of his childhood by being apothesized while yet alive, a rare honor, but it was more as a god in the theatrical Olympus of the Comédie Francaise than in the Pantheon of the Ancient Greeks.

The rest of Eon's personal history shows that she actually fell into the androgyne image that had been cast for her. Permitted to leave France in 1785, she repaired to London, where her household effects were stored, and tried to prevent their auction for debts. She remained there, obscure but still in female dress until 1787 when in a spectacular try at raising funds she arranged a public fencing match with the formidable young swordsman Saint-George. Although Eon was 60 years old and in full petticoats she touched her adversary repeatedly. The oft-reproduced print of the match (Coryn 1932: opp. 65) shows the Chevalière in full female costume stretching the limits of her petticoats to cross Saint-George in a masterful *coup de temps*. From the sidelines the Prince of Wales and other notables stare at the androgynous image in wonder. On another occasion the Chevalière actually appeared before the Prince Regent dressed as Pallas, fulfilling her favorite picture. Her relations with the dissipated Prince were the stuff of satire too, as in the comic print which has the dress-wearing Eon drubbing the cowed Heir Apparent at fisticuffs (Vizetelly 1859: opp. 316).

None of this capitalizing on her androgyny helped pay her nagging debts. Chess matches between her and the master Philidor came to naught; the French Revolution exacerbated her penury by wiping out the pension. Yet the Revolutionary army received an offer of help from the still strong sword arm of Citoyenne Genevieve d ' Eon, and accepted with thanks. Something, most likely her creditors, detained her in London. Her treasured book collection was liquidated. Still in woman's clothes she declined into deep poverty and finally, in 1796, into an obscure death. After her decease a committee of physicians, under the eyes of officials, drily dissected her body and found her to be a male. No one has ever dissected the conceptions which led them to expect anything else.

The Chevalier's life proceeded from masquerade to continual masquerade to enforced (but incomplete) change of gender, then back to masquerade as a being of inter-gender qualities with special meaning for his/her contemporaries. The artistry of Beaumarchais and the authority of the King only brought Eon so far into the masquerade; she never dissolved into her costume, into either gender costume, but floated between, where he was finally caught.

The other type of masquerade, where the change is private and the disguise foisted upon the world as a reality, was also common in the masked ball period. But first a brief pastoral.

References

Aries, Philippe.
    1962 *Centuries of Childhood.* trans. by Robert Baldick. New York: Vintage Books.

Beaumarchais, Caron de.
    1966 *La trilogie de Figaro.* Paris: Livre de Poche.

Coryn, C.S.
    1932 *The Chevalier d ' Eon.* London.

Cox, Cynthia.
    1966 *The Enigma of the Age.* London: Longman's.

Eliade, Mircea.
    1965 "Mephistopheles and the Androgyne." In *The Two and the One.* New York: Harper and Row.

Ellis, Havelock.
    1936 *Studies in the Psychology of Sex.* 2 v. New York: Random House.

Gaillardet, F.
    1970 *Memoirs of the Chevalier d ' Eon.* trans. by Antonia White. London: Anthony Blond.

Graham, Harvey.
    1950 *Eternal Eve.* London.

Honour, Hugh.
    1961 *Chinoiserie: The Vision of Cathay.* London: John Murray.

Hughes, Talbot.
    1933 "Costume. "In *Johnson's England.* ed by A.S. Tuberville. Oxford: Clarendon Press.

Kiener, Franz.
    1956 *Kleidung, Mode und Mensch.* Munich: Ernst Reinhardt.

Lomenie, Louis.
    1880 *Beaumarchais et son temps.* 2 v. Paris.

Nixon, Edna.
    1965 *Royal Spy.* New York: Reynal and Co.

Picard, R.
    1943 *Les salons litteraires et la société française.* New York: Brentano's.

Pinsseau, Pierre.
    1945 *L'etrange destinée de Chevalier d ' Eon*. Paris: Raymond Clavreuil.

Pitou, Camille.
    n.d. *Le costume civil en France du XIIIe au XIXe siecle*. Paris: Flammarion.

Telfer, James Buchan.
    1885 *The Strange Career of the Chevalier d ' Eon*. London: Longman's.

Thompson, C.J.S.
    1974 *The Mysteries of Sex*. New York: Causeway.

Vizetelly, E.A.
    1859 *The True Story of the Chevalier d ' Eon*. London.

IV

Interlude:
Marie Antoinette Never Dressed As A Milkmaid

One of the entrancing images gleaned in a liberal education is Marie Antoinette, Queen of France, dressed in the simple rustic costume of a milkmaid. That the splendor of the Versailles court should be balanced by a pastoral in the Queen's private life is charming, gentle, a little wan and self-conscious, like a Watteau painting. It is also the starting point for many potential discourses on the nature of society and culture in the period, the search for simplicity in a complex world, the dialectic, or dialogue of art with nature. Even outside scholarship the image is a human tableau that gives palpable emotion to an otherwise unliving time in history. It attracted me, for while considering the intricacies of grand masquerade I might step aside for a moment to quieter pastures. But alas! Marie Antoinette never did dress as a milkmaid, not even in jest.

The revelation was long in coming. I hunted through the *Memoirs* of Madame de Campan, one of the Queen's ladies in waiting and a chatty source of small observations. No luck. Lots of intrigue, entrances and exits of enough characters to fill many Louis XVI reveries, the Chevalier d'Eon, cardinals and the like but no milkmaid masquerade. I pushed forward into a hoard of books, on Marie Antoinette, on Louis XVI, on eighteenth century France, on eighteenth century Europe. Often the milkmaid episode was mentioned along with the model dairy and herd of cows the Queen kept but without any reference to a contemporary source. More often the whole matter was ignored for the Affair of the Pearl Necklace or some other tasty crumb of court gossip. No one denied that the Queen dressed as a milkmaid...

Finally, in a regal French biography of the Queen (Nuignan & Jalliet 1970: 139) I located a firm statement:

> Contrary to a persistent belief Marie Antoinette did not dress up as a peasant woman and never took part in field chores, but she did maintain easy and familiar relations with the peasants of her domains, filled herself with country life and felt the promptings of an ideal.

Marie Antoinette maintained an *hameau* near the Petit Trianon, a little palace on the Versailles ground intended itself as an escape from court routines. The *hameau* comprised a farmhouse, a water mill with a man-made brook to drive the wheel, a gardener's house, a dovecote, a still smaller more isolated house for the Queen and of course a dairy and a herd of cows. The buildings were painted to suggest the worn, vine covered exteriors of rural architecture, and the whole gave a prospect of country calm and simplicity. Inside, however, were elegantly furnished rooms serviced by uniformed lackeys.

According to Madame de Campan in this place the Queen "adopted all the ways of country life." This means that she allowed people to continue their cardgames in a room she entered, dressed her daughters informally, fished in the lake and, on occasion, watched the cows being milked. Her love for the bucolic brought with it an increasing aversion to the magnificence of the Versailles court and to the King's sumptuous outings at Marly. The King himself was not completely enmeshed in these galas. At times he retired to a workshop where he tinkered with small watches and other mechanical pieces. In the company of the Princes and a few Courtiers he sometimes visited Marie Antoinette to watch her perform in pastoral romances on the stage of a small theater. Possibly there she played the part of a milkmaid, but for royal eyes only.

Queens became peasants only in theater, romance and folklore. A French folktale makes a swineherd out of an unkind princess (and a princess out of a swineherd) as punishment for supercilious cruelty. Saintly Queens disguised themselves as commonfolk to go among their subjects and learn of their woes, that they might rule more fairly. During the pastoral vogue of the early seventeenth century the Flemish engraver Crispijn de la Passe (1640: I), member of an illustrious family of engravers, released an album of poems and pictures in which he made shepherdesses out of the "grandest ladies of Christiandom," placing them in the unchanging rustic habit because "fashion and clothing style are ever changing and even with the times seem almost ridiculous." Crispijn began his gallery with the Empress of the Holy Roman Empire then moved on to the Queen of France, showing them as the most sumptuous shepherdesses who ever graced an Arcadian bower. The Queen of France is wearing her crown and holding a staff with a bouquet of lilies. The accompanying epigram reads:

By virtue and by prudence
she manages her sheep,
and keeps within her power
the Invincible Fleur-de-Lis.

Gallant sentiments befitting the pastoral, but there are no sheep and the only countryside is that visible through the window of the palace in which the Queen stands. Our materialistic outlook is disappointed: the Queen as shepherdess is still a Queen.

Marie Antoinette, over a century later, was much the same as the royal object of Crispijn's flattery. The only concession she made to milkmaids (who had evidently taken the place of shepherdesses) was to wear dresses in the "dairy maid" style that became *de rigeur* in the 1760's. This was a bouffant effect originating in the dairy maid's habit of fastening their long overskirts up on the sides to clear the country ground. Marie Antoinette did not simply fasten her overskirts; she had her dressmakers loop, buckle, festoon and embroider them. Any direct resemblance to the milkmaid's practice dissolved in the thickness of draped cloth artificially held in its place by wire frames and cork pieces. Though the Queen made this nod to the countryside and might even indulge herslef in a *robe du matin à la mode Creole* or *à la Turque*, the Creole ladies, Turkish beauties or milkmaids were but reflected in the Queen.

The Queen, in fact, could reflect any state of being while still remaining herself—that was part of being Queen. She was a Queen-milkmaid in a world where she was already, and uninterruptedly, Queen. She could live on a farm *without* being a milkmaid and still have the freedom, as she imagined it, of a milkmaid, the best of all her possible worlds. Had she gone out among the people dressed as a milkmaid she would be in disguise, for an intrigue or for some lofty reason. She never imagined until the very end that the perpetual masquerade and the open choice of costumes would come to an end. The image of Marie Antoinette being brought to the guillotine, a plain, middle-aged woman in a cotton dress and clutching a rosary is a disguise she never assumed until there was no other choice. That disguise had to be the reality.

References

Campan, Marie de.
    n.d. Mémoirs. Paris.

Huisman, Philippe and Marguerite Jallut.
    1970 Marie Antoinette: l'impossible bonheur. Paril: Vilo.

Passe, Crispijn de la.
    1640 *Les vrais pourtraits de quelques unes des plus grandes dames de la christiené, disguisées en bergères.* Amsterdam: Joost Broersz.

V

Princess Caraboo of Javasu

Every masked ball had its unmasking. At that moment it was seen how effective the costumes were in shielding their wearers from discovery. The Turk might in truth be a Christian, the sailor a physician and the young dandy an elderly lady. The commonplaces of social relations were thus suspended during a masked ball; all could flirt or converse indiscriminately as if born anew or in another place. As long as the masking continued these new relations became broader and deeper and tensions rose to a point that the unmasking was welcome relief.

People at a masked ball had the advantage of knowing they were at a masked ball and that those around them were in costume. On occasion however a masker in plausible costume ventured out into the street hoping to impose his identity upon the world at large. He demands the honor or the charity owing to one of his standing and he strives to postpone his personal unmasking as long as it pays him to stay hidden.

People who lead these lives are often called impostors—but the name is misleading. An impostor must have been discovered. To the impostor the act of deceit is usually a consequence of a long personal history completed by fictionalization of his life. If enough people respond to the fiction the disguise then becomes his proper clothing for as long as they continue to respond. Those caught in the act of deceiving are scorned because they are maladroit, not because they are dishonest.

George Psalmanazar, one of the most celebrated eighteenth century impostors, counterfeited himself into a Formosan of high birth, baffled a few churchmen, was unmasked and spent the rest of his life penitent among the ruins of his fraud. He undertook the deceit, he says in his *Memoirs* (1764), because he was indolent and hankered for the easy life of an honored guest. As a bedraggled student he never begged alms so successfully as he did when he became a Formosan.

Psalmanazar was only one member of a class of impostors who sought to elevate themselves from obscure want to eminent having (by means of credit). For example, late in the year 1764 *Gentleman's Magazine* (34: 394) abstracted an article in a foreign newspaper:

> A person who appeared at Paris with some splendor under the chracter of Prince of Angola, has lately been apprehended and committed to prison as an impostor. On examination he appears to have been valet to an Irish merchant, and to have contracted debts to the amount of 100,000 livres to support his dignity.

Likewise, a few months later (34: 543),

> Was committed to Newgate a famous mulatto man, who called himself King Kadgo, and who for some time past hath preyed upon the public, pretending to be a king, or foreign prince, and hiring livery servants, taking genteel lodgings, obtaining rich clothes from taylors, and such like impositions; when apprehended he had two footmen to attend him, had a crown upon his head composed of rich gold lace, stolen from a taylor whilst he was chusing a pattern for a rich suit of clothes.

Both these men saw in the ignorance of Africa and in the uncommoness of dark-skinned men in Europe a chance for fortune. Unfortunately they overstepped the reasonable and were caught in their excesses. Still, one wonders how many foreign kings, queens, princes and princesses won their way to modest profits before tactfully absconding. There was room for them in the credibility of merchants and userers who mistook the appearances of "quality" for the fiscal concomitants and let both real and pretended nobles run up debts.

One "Princess" who was unmasked before she fled with her very limited gains was Princess Caraboo of Javasu. Her brief but vivid masquerade is known in greater detail than most of the self-elevating impostures because she is the subject of a biographical tract compiled by a magistrate named Walter Bates (1817) from depositions and interviews. Bates' smug officer-of-the-law prose holds no compassion for the pathetic young criminal, but it yields information which justifies a very different reading of the events. Bates starts with the deceit itself and then traces his subject's life backwards to her origins; instead I will start at her beginning and enter the imposture at her trajectory, as an event in her life.

Mary Baker was born to an impoverished family in Witheredge, Devonshire. Energetic and ambitious as a child she had a drive for excelling in all she did, even the games of childhood. Her lack of formal schooling left her undisciplined and thus, Bates implies, free to proceed with her fantasies and lies. Her father and other relatives testified that Mary was a learned young girl, that she even knew French though they were at a loss to explain how she might have acquired it. The father ventured that a bout with rheumatic fever at age 15 (1806) had addled the child's brains and made her the prey of whimsies and odd notions. That, at least, was his only explanation for what followed.

At age 16 Mary was sent off to work on a farm some distance away. This was a common practice among poor families of the towns; on a farm the girl would learn useful skills and perhaps find a husband. It also made one fewer claimant to the family's limited resources. Mary threw herself into the farm work in her old spirit of competition, undertaking even to do men's work in order to draw notice to herself. The meanness of the wages by which her zeal was compensated offended her and she left the farm.

She wandered a bit, invested her wages in a fine white dress and returned home thus improved intending to impress her parents with her rise to gentility. This ingenuous conceit was smashed when her father accused her of stealing the dress. He could not believe that his daughter gained a piece of ladylike finery honestly even though its purchase was within her means. Stung by this rejection of her fantasy character she fled her own home and commenced a series of picaresque wanderings which were much in the spirit of Tom Jones and other celebrated vagrants over the English Landscape. In the open air she was freed from her humble life and the drudgery which surrounded her as long as she stayed with her parents.

First she tried begging in Exeter but was rebuffed and unable to earn even her sustenance: begging was a profession too. When she tried to end her despondency by hanging herself a heavenly voice intervened with a warning about the results of suicide. Her life was blessed enough to go on, with no change of luck. Her feeble attempts at seeking charity from house to house never went further than the donors' question about her background and parentage, at which she hastily took flight. Brain fever sapped her strength and it was only the kindness of a friendly carter who picked her up along the roadside that she was conveyed to a hospital, St. Giles in London. She lay in a delerium for a long time and was bedridden for months afterward.

When she was able to talk she told the physician an embellished version of her life story. Mary Baker could not speak of herself anymore without embellishment; she was a fictional character who had lived whatever life accompanied the character she was trying to play. She only aimed at pathos and a better ancestry for the moment, but on her release one of the physicians recommended her to service with a lady, who unwittingly supplied her with the absent materials. Mary's new employer taught her to read and gave her books; the lady's daughter gave Mary writing lessons. Bates juxtaposes two letters, one sent to her parents in 1812, around this time, and the other to the same recipients four years later. The difference is astounding: over that span of time Mary Baker learned the grammar, diction and style of a well-bred lady. Her fantasy was beginning to work itself out in her life.

This quiet moment in Mary Baker's life did not last long. She was befriended by the Jewish cook of a family next door, sharing much talk with this informative acquaintance. Mary's mistress forbade her to attend a Jewish wedding to which she was invited, through her friend's offices. Mary went anyway and when questioned about her disappearance fabricated an excuse. This independence cost her the secure position. By pure naivete she allowed herself to be taken to the Magdalen, a residence for reformed prostitutes only to be expelled when it was learned she was "unsullied." Thus began her next period of wanderings, this time with the added experience of her reading and observation.

First she chose an obvious change—to a man. Her adventure in men's clothing ended in embarrassment but luckily no worse: the band of rogues she had unwittingly joined released her unharmed when they learned of her true sex on the promise that she not disclose the location of their hideout to the authorities. She resumed female dress and tried another domestic position. Her eccentricity, her rash likes and dislikes and her posings made her disagreeable to one mistress after another. Years later, after Mary had been connected with Caraboo, a Mrs. Starling, one of her former employers, wrote offering details about Mary's tenure in her house (Bates 1817: 51-52).

> She was very fond of her children, but told them such strange stories about Gypsies and herself that she frightened them out of their wits. She once came into the parlour, and had dressed herself up so like a Gypsy, that the children did not know her.

Mary was dismissed from this position because she set two beds afire in order to incriminate another servant against whom she had conceived an animus. Mrs. Starling told Bates that she hesitated before writing her letter lest Mary hear of it and seek vengeance by "waylaying" Mr. Starling some dark night. Mary must have cut a wild figure among the Starlings to cause this awe. But servants were in general to be feared, and Mary was just more likely to act upon her low class impulses.

Mary's Gypsy outfit, and the complete alteration of appearance it induced, was a monument in her development. This is the first recorded sign of her putting on a completely different aspect. The choice is significant. To the nineteenth century English the Gypsies were a mysterious, nomadic people who spurned the settled life of property and comfort for the rootless voyaging and wanton thievery. Romanticism had intensified the image, making the Gypsies seem darker still, and more passionate. Caraboo when she was at the Starlings' knew the Gypsies only by repute and distant observation; she summoned herself into playing one well enough to terrify children. Mary obviously felt that the traits attributed to Gypsies were her traits too.

Yet when she fell in with a band of real Gypsies after being evicted from another house and was invited to join them she toyed with the idea only briefly then went her way, adding a few Gypsy words to her double-talk vocabulary and a few Gypsy elements to her costume. The Gypsies as people were left to George Borrow, who was starting his adventures among the travelers in the period; Mary was only interested in having people respond to her as if she were a Gypsy. The run-down caravans and hand-to-mouth livelihood held no attraction for the imaginative wanderer.

Another disillusionment followed: Mary's initiation into sex. She claimed that she was seduced by a persuasive gentleman who plied her with promises but in the manner of a villain out of sentimental literature left her alone, and pregnant, never to return. She bore the child clandestinely and left it at the Foundlings' Hospital to die, like most of the other children left there. Bates ascertained, however, that the fathering of the child was far more prosaic than Mary made it sound. She had been the (not unwilling) victim of the master of a family she stayed with in the country. Every interlude in her life was inflated to literary proportions in the retelling; the fictional character she was becoming moved closer to the present all the time.

Once the death of the child had released her from responsibility she determined to have another go at begging. The perceptive girl noticed that foreigners displaced by the Napoleonic wars found a ready welcome in English homes. They were usually aristocrats or wealthy bourgeois and thus fit for Mary's emulation. She started by approaching house-owners babbling in an invented jargon but with indifferent success. Seeing some Norman lacemakers with their high peaked bonnets she concluded that the more absurd the costume the more credible the wearer. Mary therefore "outlandized" her dress, donned a turban and resumed her visits. Her application of her insight was incomplete; when she assented to being French or Spanish there was invariably a French cook or a Spanish governess to test her. She slipped away before being discovered and finally decided that without a knowledge of French or Spanish she stood no chance of masquerading as a Continental.

Something more exotic and less easily assessed, something oriental, would mask her better from the disbelief and scientific prying of her potential hosts.

Mary Baker judged wisely in postulating that an oriental mask might be mistaken for an oriental face. Although there was a steady flow of information into Europe concerning the Far East, first from the missionaries and later from the traders and political missions, and although reliable compendia of facts on China, Japan and the Southeast Asian kingdoms had been in existence since the early eighteenth century, the Orient was still a decorative surface. The European exoticism called chinoiserie was the design of this surface: breezy mandarins fishing beside pagodas or flowery screens where monkeys played were the only China, the only Orient, that most people knew. Europe had synthesized its own Orient in these settings, to the point of building entire Chinese villages, as did Catherine the Great, or at least erecting a pagoda or a tea house among the well-tended shrubbery of a garden. As Oliver Goldsmith's canny Chinese visitor to England, Lien Chi Altange, declared, even those English who were wealthy enough to own authentic Chinese artifacts placed them around the house in utter ignorance of their real uses, which seemed ludicrous (Goldsmith n.d. : 43-46). But to most English the Chinese had no daily life outside of the endless dreamy calm resembling an opium sleep.

This casual vision of the Orient was already moribund in most of Europe in the early nineteenth century; it had long been replaced in favor by other styles, the Gothic or the Classical. The démodé taste of King George IV for chinoiserie kept it artificially alive for a time, and the sheer conservatism of the countryside assured it a presence on wallpapers, lacquer ornamentation and wistful framed drawings collecting dust on the walls of great houses. Mary Baker made herself into a living example of this late Georgian chinoiserie, subsiding, idiosyncratic and out of place. She considered herself safe in weaving her fantasies in Chinese silks, but she misjudged the quality of her wares and the eye of the buyer. If, like a scene painted on a porcelain teapot, she lingered just a moment in the mind, she would have passed. But Mary Baker wanted applause all out of keeping with the costume she had selected.

When she was admitted to the house of the Overseer of the Poor, Gloucester, studiously speaking her own "language" and not responding at all to English, she was believable. She had put together a distinctive costume (Bates 1817: 30)

> a black stuff gown with muslin frill around the neck and a red
> and black shawl around her shoulders; both loosely and tastefully
> put on, in imitation of Asiatic costume; leather shoes and black
> worsted stockings.

The costume was not "in imitation" of anything, yet it seemed Asiatic to those who saw her. Bates, in the sections on the imposture, writes as if no one ever fell for the inept posturing of the deluded young girl. For the magistrate Mary never stood a chance of misleading better and wiser people; as a result his attitude toward her never tallies with the scenes he describes. The only justification he can provide is by making everyone suspect her while behaving as if they are under her spell. It would be well to take Mary Baker more seriously than Bates wishes because there can be no other explanation for the events that followed. Bates' narrative is a retrospective vindication of those people who were actually taken in, but feared having this gullibility known. The truth is much more indefinite, and far less elevating.

The girl whom the Overseer brought to Mr. Worrall, the magistrate, was not yet identified as "Asiatic", unless her costume, which bore no similarity to either real or imaginary Asian wear, was labeled that way. Pending discovery of the stranger's origin Worrall committed her to the care of his wife, who lodged the girl at a local inn. There she exhibited some odd predilections. A picture of Annana (pineapple) excited her; she rejected a second cup of tea until the cup was scrupulously cleaned; she tremulously refrained from lying in bed until one of Mrs. Worrall's daughters reassured her by lying there first. After muttering a few words of prayer the visitor fell fast asleep.

The next day a session with the local clergyman (the person always summoned to deal with extraordinary events) who had brought books on oriental subjects, demonstrated the girl's enthusiasm for Chinese landscape scenes. Whimsical chinoiserie vignettes on Mrs. Worrall's parlor furniture also stirred her. After a period of hand-waving and shouting her name was elicited: Caraboo. Several people tried to browbeat her into confessing she was a charlatan but even in the face of the most solemn exhortations she kept her silence or spoke in the incomprehensible tongue in which she introduced herself. During the succeeding days a congress of authorities and scholars examined Caraboo. The Mayor of Bristol blustered through a cross-examination; scores of self-proclaimed Orientalists labored to pinpoint her native land.

Caraboo was undeviating in her response. She paid no attention to words spoken in English, whatever their import, and she arbitrarily voiced a few syllables in her own language when a reply was demanded. She seeded the imaginations of her interlocutors with a few offhand clues derived from the very chinoiserie in which she conceived her disguise. With a rare grasp of human fatuity she avoided any strenuous assertion; instead she touched the acceptable identity's nascent shape and molded her actions accordingly. Mary Baker-becoming-Caraboo simply followed the line of least resistance which was in this case the line of greatest ignorance. She fit herself into the gaps in her hosts' knowledge and materialized what was needed to fill out the shape she was acquiring.

The advent of a Portuguese named Manual Eyenesso, who had lived (he bragged) many years in Malaya gave Caraboo her final boost. He conversed with the mysterious stranger (which must have been, from Caraboo's viewpoint, a strange discussion: the Portuguese babbled in his lingo, she in hers), and announced that she was a person of consequence who had been abducted from her home in the East Indies and abandoned in England. Her language, he added with an expert air, was a hybrid spoken on the coast of Sumatra. Thus he startled the Worralls out of their skepticism and insulated Caraboo from any immediate threat by removing her to a place so obscure and so remote from the British sphere of influence in Asia that she could not readily be tested. To Caraboo herself he gave the gift of a more detailed fiction which could still subsist on the diet of chinoiserie while evading accountability.

All further questioning of Caraboo departed from these impressive findings. A sign language was perfected between the Worralls and their guest since it was unlikely that many people knew her tongue and it would be a while before she knew English. She was soon given quarters at the Worrall residence, the Knole, that she might be observed more closely. There a gentleman from the East India Company "interviewed" Caraboo and assembled an even more generously circumstantial life history. Bates himself remarks that the interviewer in his eagerness to gain data unconsciously abetted an imposture with his own knowledge of China and Malaya.

In the resulting tale Caraboo, the offspring of a noble Chinese man and a Malayan (Mandin) princess, is kidnapped by the pirate Chee-min while strolling in her garden at Javasu. After a series of nautical adventures on board the corsair she jumps ship near England and swims ashore bereft of possessions or identification. The East India man obtained an ethnography of Javasu. Caraboo's mother blackened her teeth with a betel nut, painted her face and arms, wore a jewel at her nose and a golden chain over her left temple; but Caraboo's father, a strict Chinese, would not suffer his daughter to indulge in these barbarous body ornaments. Her father was white-skinned, an official and a commander of troops who was borne aloft in a palenquin by commoners. His soldiers salaamed to him right hands to right temples. This last fact was judged a verification of Caraboo by the Malay expert because the right hand salute was peculiar to the Malayan peoples. He had laid his own trap in giving Caraboo an alternative between a right hand and left hand salute; she happened to choose the right one. I doubt the wrong choice would have deterred him.

Javasu also had its complement of cannibals who cut off the arms and legs of captives and roasted them as they danced before their murderous gods. Caraboo's own mother worshipped idols—Caraboo pointed out one such in a book—and threatened Caraboo with hellfire when she preferred to venerate Allah Tallah, a more abstract deity. And so on.

The fabric is a patchwork of customs stitched randomly together, some finely threaded, others randomly sewn. It follows the outline popular with gentleman ethnographers of the nineteenth century, based on the belief that primitives live amid a crowd of customs they blindly obey. To list the customs under topical headings is to describe what there is of primitive culture. Caraboo's interviewer not only extracted a list of customs from their imaginative interaction but in the process gave them the correct intelligible order so that Eyenesso's small beginning and Caraboo's compliant miming turned into a "culture". The illusion gained mass regularly in conformity with the rules governing any knowledge of a foreign land. Caraboo had the advantage of seeming the source of this construction when she was really on the periphery working along with everyone else. Every affirmation, contradiction or paradox augmented the whole.

Caraboo, the Princess Caraboo now, was hardly passive. She entered into the invention of her own past as adroitly as her perceptions would allow her. She evinced "much pleasure" upon seeing a Chinese chain purse and a rose-colored scarf which she wore alternately in Chinese and Javanese fashion over her long hair, twisted on a skewer. Presented with a piece of calico, she assembled a "Javanese" dress, which she wears in a large engraving included in Bates' tract: voluminous sleeves reach almost to the ground but are confined at the wrist, the waist is gathered by an extremely broad embroidered band, with embroidered fringes also at the bottom of the hem, around the bosom and part of the sleeves. The dress calls up the flamboyance of Gypsy costume in its spread and color, enhanced by Caraboo's awareness that Orientals prefer wide sleeves, probably gleaned from prints. Anything Oriental arrested her attention, fans, puzzles, India ink, green tea. She took to keeping time with knots on a string, like the quipus of the Incas of Peru, and wrote with a reed on a leaf in a script that, from the samples copied by Bates, resembles crippled Arabic letters emerging from a chaos of scribble.

Caraboo was circumspect about her speech and always used the same word for the same thing. "Samen" was "heaven" (?); "kala" was "time" (good Sanskrit!); "mono" stood for "morning," "anna" for "night" (close enough to English or French); "no bo" was "no good" (French enough), and, wisely, she used "zee" for "tea" (the same word, modified by local phonetics, is nearly universal in Asia and Europe). The Gypsies had made their contribution to Caraboo's vocabulary too: "mosha" for "man;" "raglish" for woman, and a whole spectrum of terms for currency units, including "bob" for "shilling." This term, which really means "five" in Romani was making its way into British slang via thieves' cant. Caraboo was like the Gypsies, remembering words and customs from every source she touched and gathering them before the eyes of her confused hosts.

Even Caraboo's slips were contrived to be plausible in a genuine Oriental. There was a conspiracy in the Worrall house to surprise her speaking English. The servant woman with whom she bedded lay awake at night listening for any English words she might pronouce in her sleep; Mrs. Worrall, out driving late with the drowsy Caraboo, suddenly addressed her, trying to provoke a spontaneous reply in English. Caraboo endured all this petty torture. One day in the midst of a game one of the Worrall children accused her of cheating and she exclaimed, not so rashly, "Caraboo no cheat." The child rushed to its mother with the news, but to little effect since Caraboo had been among English speakers long enough that any failure to absorb some English would have been suspect. The imposture was not just plausible but dynamic. Caraboo was "adapting."

The longer Caraboo remained at the Knole the more extravagant her behavior became. Maintaining the cloud of mystification that enveloped her needed more than a repetition of past performance, each new distraction, more bizarre than the last, concentrated all gazes on her but kept them from penetrating too far by the confusion caused. For example (Bates 1817: 13),

> During her stay she used to exercise herself with a bow and arrow, and make a stick answer to a sword on her right shoulder. She oftentimes carried a gong on her back, which she sounded in a very singular manner, and a tambourine in her hand, the sword by her

side and a bow and arrow slung as usual, her head dressed with flowers and feathers, and thus she made it appear she was ready for war.

And a bellicose sight she must have been.

According to Bates, this imaginative posing began to excite new suspicions about Caraboo's authenticity. I surmise, however, that Caraboo had found a place in the Worrall household and that she was neither fully believed nor fully disbelieved. As a sort of exhibited nonesuch she attracted much attention from the right people, self-appointed orientalists and curious gentlemen who upraised the Worralls with their notice. Although Bates deplores the sideshow character of this interest it made Caraboo into an object outside the confines of truth or falsehood, and into an entity worth visiting Gloucester to see. The rise in scientific showmanship for its own sake in the early decades of the nineteenth century, a phenomenon from which Caraboo, along with mummies, chimpanzees, tropical ferns, orchids and a host of other imported attractions all benefited, was the consequence of popularization and the growth of Empire. Like these other showpieces she was living evidence of the outside world suddenly become rational and tamed, but still possessing its compelling strangeness and brought to England to display that strangeness. Caraboo's popularity, then, was not the result of her deception being effective but because her attempts at deception were amusing and bizarre.

The influx of visitors, frauds and genuine scholars, provided a plethora of new material for Caraboo to assimilate; she grew brazen in her adaptations. A gentleman came with a "crease" (*kriss*), a Javanese dagger, and offered it to Caraboo, who seized it and thrust it through her belt, wearing it on the right side. This impressed the gentleman, for all Javanese natives wear that implement of war on the right. Caraboo's inability to speak Javanese puzzled him, though. And a small drama she enacted was quite distressing. When given the *kriss* after the gentleman had discoursed on its uses to the assembled guests Caraboo immediately ran to the plant vase, crushed some leaves between her fingers and, after rubbing the juice on the blade, touched its point to her arm and mimed the act of collapsing. Unfortunately members of the party recalled that Caraboo was in the room while the specialist explained that the Javanese often envenom the *kriss* blade with toxic plant juices in order to dispatch an enemy with even a small knick. The Princess was too precipitate in this one instance, or she was just obliging the Worralls and their guests by giving a mime version of native custom.

Caraboo ignored the suspicions and made every detail of her daily existence speak in her favor. She conducted fasts, prepared her food in a singular way and even erected a small shrine made out of odds and ends in the main garden. Not only was she abstemious and pious, as a princess should be, she was chaste. On finding one day that she was alone in the house except for male servants she hurriedly made for the highest tree and stationed herself among its upper limbs, bows and arrows ready against the expected onslaught.

The Worralls persisted in sending samples of her writing and speech to learned authorities; but the experts at India House and Oxford were in consternation. That the script and language were an anomaly they had no doubt but imperfect knowledge about the more restricted tongues of Asia made them hesitant to pronounce the whole production a fraud. Less circumspect was a local luminary named Dr. Wilkinson, who announced in a letter to the *Bath Chronical* that upon examining Caraboo he had found her to be not Javanese, Malayan or a total fraud, but Circassian—with what cogency can be seen from an extract analysing the name of Caraboo's erstwhile country (Bates 1817: 22):

> The part Java, of the name Javasu, in Circassian, may either signify a surface of anything, or the second person imperative mode of the verb to drink; the latter part, su, signifies water in Tartar.

Princess Caraboo of Drinkwater, no title to be slighted.

With the procrustean skill born of an irresistable insight, Dr. Wilkinson reduced the entire corpus on information on Caraboo to the Circassian standard. He was the victim of the contemporary pot-pourri view of cultures: Caraboo was identified by the greatest degree of coincidence between her evinced behavior and the recorded inventory of customs belonging to some people. It was precisely this fatuity among the over-informed and under-practised cognoscenti that Dickens satirized when he had Mr. Pickwick learnedly remake a milestone into a Roman monument. Had there been a branch of the Pickwick Club in Bath Dr. Wilkinson would have been nominated for membership.

Caraboo herself, having so flummoxed the good doctor, was in need of his professional attentions. Even before she became Princess Caraboo she had agreed with a sea captain for passage to America. One day she fled the Worrall house, returning the next day exhausted and lugging a bundle of clothes. As she slipped into febrile delirium she explained that she wanted to bury the clothes that they might be safe from the Macrattos, or savages.

Actually, as the Worralls discovered afterward, she had picked up her trunk of clothes at an inn, where she left it before the entire adventure, and went to Bristol to board ship for America. She had saved the five pounds fare the captain wanted, but found that his ship had already parted. Dispatching the trunk to her father she took some clothes and returned to the Worralls.

Her physical collapse nearly led to death. While she was conscious one of the attending physicians saw his opportunity and remarked gravely in her hearing that she would soon perish, then turned with delight at seeing the marks of terror on her face.

Caraboo saw that her mistakes had been too many to be allowed and on recovering her strength fled again, this time to Bath. "It is one of the mysteries of nature," says Edith Sitwell in her sketch of Caraboo (1971),

> that the Princess of that far and savage isle must, undoubtedly, have known, by the instinct that wild people possess in such acuity, that Bath was at that time the centre of fashion.

Mrs. Worrall went in pursuit, and found her seated in the parlor of a fashionable house surrounded by a bevy of personages all playing court to her. Mrs. Worrall's advent did not discommode Caraboo, who quickly fell on her knees and made such a display of supplication that she further charmed her admirers. But it was too late.

Oddly enough Dr. Wilkinson's letters to the *Bath Chronicle*, the most spectacular testament to Caraboo's success, led to her undoing. A Mrs. Neale, reading the paper, saw in Wilkinson's mysterious Circassian the tatterdemallion beggar girl who had visited her rooming house near Bristol. The lady hastily sent word to Mrs. Worrall who, firm evidence in hand, staged a confrontation with Caraboo at the home of a friend.

Caraboo did not consent to becoming Mary Baker again with good grace. Faced with Mrs. Neale's statement she muttered "Toddy, Moddy Irish." But Mrs. Worrall was not to be put off any more, and demanded that she speak proper English as everyone knew she could. Under the threat of being brought before Mrs. Neale herself for an even more degrading scene Caraboo broke down and began to narrate a life she had lived in Bombay and France. This too proved against her, she was finally wrestled to the extremity of recounting her unglamorous history, not without, however, an embroidery around the edge.

The hoardes of curiosity seekers were now replaced by crowds of witnesses who stepped forward and identified Caraboo as the girl they had encountered here or there along the road. The vague areas in her own confession sharpened, and while some parts remained fuzzy the outline was clear and the judgement made. Mary Baker had masqueraded to "impose" (that is the word Bates blamingly uses) on the charitable. Any gloating in the Worrall household over the wages of sin was soon, however, replaced by dismay as the queues of witnesses turned into longer queues of curiosity-seekers. Caraboo was interrogated by magistrates, exhorted by ministers, delineated by painters and felt over by phrenologists. "Some pitied her, some condemned her and others upheld her." The ministers found her heart cold to the call of faith, but the phrenologists were rewarded with an excellent specimen and published letters in local newspapers elucidating the impostor's aberrations in craniological terms. Poets cried out her graces in heavy couplets, not neglecting a touch of satire or a pronouncement on the credulity of man.

Caraboo's comic fame was becoming unpleasant to a quantity of people, especially those who had conversed with her in oriental languages. Funds were quickly found to fulfill her greatest wish, a voyage to America. Little is said of Caraboo's own reactions after the forced unmasking. If she relished her criminal fame as much as she exulted in her exoticism she was probably crushed by the demand that she leave for America; threats of legal action had to be made before she would comply with the wishes of her benefactors.

As she boarded ship for America she prophesied that she would return to England one day in a carriage with four horses. Bates only shook his head. "Poor, visionary girl" he exclaimed at the end. Still, like many others, he wondered how an "illiterate girl, unaided by education" could confound so may intelligent people, so many "people of quality" for so long. He did not wonder long enough to examine the premises of education or even quality which would lead to conflating the false with the genuine. Instead he occupied himself with another character, a swindler and escape artist named Frederick Moon whom he nostalgically called in a later tract "Companion for Caraboo."

Caraboo's story does not end with Bates for with her departure the narrative moves into another medium as light from water into glass, and is deflected entirely. On September 13, 1817, a while after Caraboo's departure, a letter appeared in the *Bristol Journal*. It was a precis of another letter which had recently been received from Sir Hudson Lowe, an officer attached to the garrison guarding the exiled Napoleon of St. Helena (text in Sitwell 1971: 211-13). Sir Hudson told of watching a single boat rowed by a young lady enter the harbor. The "female of interesting appearance" who sprang from the craft introduced herself as Caraboo, Princess of Javasu, and stated that she was in transit to Philadelphia under the care of some missionary ladies but had escaped to visit St. Helena and the exiled Emperor.

> Sir Hudson introduced her to Bonaparte under the name of Caraboo. She described herself as Princess of Javasu, and related a tale of extraordinary interest, which seemed in a high degree to delight the Captive Chief. He embraced her with every demonstration of enthusiastic rapture, and besought Sir Hudson that she might be allowed an apartment in his house, declaring that she alone was an adequate solace in his captivity.

Caraboo convinced the St. Helena community that she was conversant with the Malay language, with Chinese and Indian politics; and she so rose in the favor of Napoleon that he determined to divorce Marie Louise and marry Caraboo. Thus two of the great legends of the age (as far as Bristol was concerned) Caraboo and "Boney" were united in a touching if far-fetched embrace.

Notes and Queries, the busy forum of arts and letters, had just a small fragment to add to Caraboo's later life. In 1865 an answerer noted (7: 196-97) that she had, after years in America, come back to England—though without the coach and four. She settled in London and among the other shows charged admission for a glimpse of her renowned person. After business slackened she took a husband and passed the rest of her life as a purveyor of medicinal leeches—an ironical occupation. The answerer was William Bates, the son of Walter. The father's literary romance with the "fair deceiver" had passed to his son.

Caraboo's end, in a fiction and a memoir, was the end of grand masquerade. Others have disguised themselves since her day, and have lived fictional lives but because of the narrowness of the niches remaining they have had to be cold, professional and exact, filling only the empty spaces in the knowledge of their victims. No one, unless feigning madness, would expect to deceive by inventing a language or a culture without some considerable acquaintance with existing languages and cultures. Caraboo remained a colored tatters on the stark, scientific branches; others pursued their apartness differently.

References

Bates, Walter.
    1817 *Caraboo: A Narrative of a Singular Imposition, Practiced upon the Benevolence of a Lady Residing in the Vicinity of the City of Bristol by a Young Woman of the Name of Mary Willocks, alias Baker, alias Bakerstendt, alias Caraboo, Princess of Javasu*. Bristol: J.M. Gutch.

Bates, William.
    1865 [Note], *Notes and Queries*, 3rd Series, 7 (March 11): 196-97.

The Gentleman's Magazine.
    1764 [Notes], 34 (August): 394 and (November): 543.

Goldsmith, Oliver.
    n.d. *The Citizen of the World*. London: Baynes and Son.

Sitwell, Edith.
    1971 *English Eccentrics*. Harmondsworth, Middlesex: Penguin.

VI

British Arabesque:
The Montagus, Lady Hester Stanhope and Lady Jane Digby

Islam was never very far from Europe. The Prophet Mohammed saw in Christ and other Christian figures the forerunners of his own Message; for centuries, up until the expulsion of the Moors from Granada in 1492, an Islamic civilization had flourished on the Iberian peninsula more or less tolerating Christians on the assumption of common heritage and infusing Europe with ideas and technology which had been lost since the time of the Greeks. Though Europeans never regarded the Muslims as better than infidels and their Prophet as an arch-impostor whom Dante, expressing the common opinion, cast into the infernal Circle of the Deceivers, nonetheless they could not help accepting the gifts so freely offered, and could not avoid feeling a taste for things Islamic as the former threat grew more distant.

One sensibility associated with Islam and its followers was arabesque. Usually it manifested itself as delicately knotted visual patterns, suffused with flowers and leaves, in fabric, woodwork and stucco. But arabesque might describe a phrase of music, an architectural folly, a poem or even a life. An exact definition in any medium is impossible; an arabesque is only known by the response it evokes. It is a European affectation that refers itself back to the Near East, gaining from that reference that tang of spiced strangeness each civilization must somewhere provide. Arabesque is Europe coming upon itself in Arab guise and being histrionically surprised at the sight.

Of course one of the delights is total imitation. Take for example a group of Turkish carpets owned by the Duke of Buccleugh and kept at Boughton House. Two are dated, 1584 and 1585, and three have the arms of Sir Edward Montagu on the border. Connoisseurs long assumed these were genuine Turkish carpets imported by Montagu. A closer examination of the fabric gives the lie to this opinion; the carpets are English by warp structure and dyes-indeed, the weavers initials appear amid the matrices. The closer the look the clearer the real identity. The custom of attributing Near

Eastern origins to certain patterns made it easy to mistake the conception for the fact, the Turk for the Englishman, the Englishman for the Turk.

The precocious deceitfulness of these carpets resonates over the centuries. Over 150 years after their date the name Edward Montagu is connected with another arabesque, more fantastic than the carpets but less artfully contrived because woven on the shifting weft of human experience.

In 1716 King George I, Protestant successor to Queen Anne and secure on his throne after the defeat of the Jacobite rebels, appointed Mr. Edward Wortley Montagu "Ambassador Extraordinary to the Grand Seigneur." Mr. Montagu along with his wife, Lady Mary Wortley Montagu and their young son Edward, were to bear the new King's salutations to his brother monarch. Together they made their way to Vienna and from there overland to the Sublime Porte. Lady Mary, better known as a commentator on her age than as an ambassador's wife, etched out the sights en route in letters to a variety of correspondents, including her then-admirer Alexander Pope. She dabbled in local practices, conversed with local sophisticates and, for a lark, got herself into Turkish dress. In a letter from Adrianople (April 1, 1717) Lady Mary wrote to her sister the Countess Mar asking for society gossip (Montagu 1906: 115-16).

> Pray let me into more particulars, and I will try to awaken your gratitude, by giving you a true and full relation of the novelties of this place, none of which will surprize you more than a sight of my person, as I am now in my Turkish habit, though I believe you would be of my opinion, that 'tis admirably becoming—I intend to send you my picture; in the meantime accept of it here.

Lady Mary proceeds with the details of her costume and with an ironic account of its advantages for Turkish women; its expansive quality, supplemented by the customary muslin veil, permits them a "perpetual masquerade," in which, as in all masquerades, there is a refuge for trysts and intrigues (Halsband 1956: 80; Barry 1928: 128). By her own telling Lady Mary only went abroad in her Turkish character once, to visit some baths, and even there the solicitude of the attendants told her she was recognized.

A salacious fable extends her adventures *à la Turque* far beyond this modest excursion. Curious to see the inside of the harem Lady Mary was surreptitiously conducted there, says the fable, but once arrived she learned that all female visitors to the place must yield to the sultan's pleasure (Anonymous 1777: vol. 1: 19).

> Whether the lady made a virtue of necessity, and submitted with a good grace to what she had no power to prevent—whether she affected to expostulate-yielded with reluctance, or was compelled into a compliance, we cannot pretend to assert...

The product of this union with the Grand Turk was, we are led to believe, Edward Wortley Montagu. Since Edward was four years old at the time of his parents' stay in Constantinople his harem conception is unlikely. The anonymous, and apocryphal, biography of Edward from which this story comes needed, in the light of Edward's later predilections, to provide some link between him and Turkey. Lady Mary's curiosity and her Turkish gown were a good excuse.

The "predilections" which required explanation become clearer by another, less fabulous relation. Lady Mary, in deep dread of smallpox, had her son "engrafted" while in Turkey. That is, he was innoculated with some disease-bearing matter to induce a lesser case of the disease and bring immunity from grave visitations. The adult Edward, when he was not stretching the credulity of his hearers by repeating the tale of his mother's harem visit (of which he was the original source), would remark more conservatively that this immunization had "infused something of Turkish blood into my English veins" (Curling 1954: 35).

For whatever causes he believed or told Edward Wortley Montagu grew up to exceed by far his mother's own museful venture into Turkish dress. From the earliest possible moment he displayed an intractibility that exasperated his father and only a little amused his mother. He was a prodigy, though in an excessively comprehensive way for not only did he excell at his studies, whenever he chose to study, but he discovered the delights of female companionship in his early teens and after that point was rarely without a wife. Edward's amorous conquests earned him the title of the "British Don Juan," and his biographies, even the serious ones, contain long inventories of his brides and lovers. Were he nothing but an eighteenth century roué he would have found ample territory at home, but Edward was lured eastward, or he was driven from England.

He trained for eccentricity at Oxford, where he engaged in the study of Arabic, Turkish and Persian. He fled school periodically, to flex his discontents and masquerades. In 1761, after years of vexing his parents, relatives and various wives Edward left England bound for the Near East. He stopped in Venice long enough to cut a figure with a newly affected turban crowning his increasingly bewhiskered face. Thence to Alexandria, where he eloped with the wife of the Danish Consul. He absconded with her across the

Sinai Desert not failing, in his progress, to compare his movements with those of Moses and to compose an account of his observations to be read before the Royal Society.

His new wife was Catholic and preferred that Edward also look to Rome so obedient to her will he returned to Italy and converted, leaving her closeted away in a Syrian convent. The idea of having a harem obviously relaxed Edward, for instead of returning to his votary mate in Syria he made his way to Egypt and there whiled away his time in scientific and antiquarian researches. He excavated the base of a Roman commemorative pillar and determined its construction; he added his views to the body of opinion on Egyptian hieroglyphics and he composed a learned paper in Turkish on the cause of earthquakes. This capstone to his orientalist-scientific attainments convinced him he was ready for the object of his life. Bypassing Syria he travelled to Constantinople and in full Turkish garb petitioned the Grand Turk for an audience. His failure was a body blow to the growing romance of his Turkish identity, but it did not defeat him entirely.

He retrieved his wife from Syria and brought her to Rosetta, Egypt where he constructed a Turkish-style household to contain his fancy and give room for his studies in Turkish and Arabic. The brief idyll was shattered when Edward, obedient to his pattern, eloped with an Arab lady. He apostasized to Islam, had himself circumcised and projected a pilgrimage to Mecca. This final thrust collapsed in exhaustion. Edward Wortley Montagu went back to Italy, to Venice, the city where his mother had lived out her last years, and he built another Turkish domicile but without even one of his wives. He became a resident spectacle, an Englishman who lived after the manner of the Turks, performed his ablutions, said his prayers and entertained numerous visitors with his dinners and conversation. His judgements of men and events were solicited for their alluring eccentricity rather than for any incisiveness. When his correspondent Sir William Watson told him of Omai's visit he replied that the Polynesian was no doubt more civilized than anyone he might encounter in London. When Montagu died in 1776 he left an "Abyssinian" son among a number of other children and a legend that keeps on dimly uncurling in the chronicles of peculiar lives.

There are cultural traditions in marginality just as there are traditions in normalcy. Edward Wortley Monatgu was the initial charge of a movement that communicated itself from person to person over the next few hundred years, a flight away from things British and into the curves and turns of the

Near East. Montagu began his flight early but it did not gain its levantine direction until late in his life, though he had made preparations all along. Only in the last few years did he experiment with constructing a Turkish self, unsuccessfully in Turkey, temporarily in Egypt and with finality in Venice. His Turkish character resulted from a lifelong inquiry into Turkish culture, and was most satisfyingly played before a European audience, as evidence of how well Edward had mastered the art of being "Turkish." Edward Wortley Montagu was the Midlands loom charming oriental patterns out of English wool for the delight of learned connoisseurs.

The next British arabesque was no less fine-threaded than Edward Wortley Montagu, though her exhibit was less accessible and even more a defiance of her conventional antecedents.

Lady Hester Stanhope was born in 1776, the year of Montagu's death and since she believed in reincarnation, or at least in incarnation, that may be significant (Newman 1862:130-202). She was the daughter of Charles, third Earl of Stanhope, whose contribution to her make-up assured some aberration. The Earl was renown as inventor and revoutionary. He invented a coal transport steamship that consumed as much coal as it could carry, prompting T. Baker, the epic poet of steam, to celebrate the contribution in a passage which confounds the ship, Lord Stanhope and a duck. In order to demonstrate conclusively the worth of his fireproofing compound the Earl positioned a party of unwitting friends on the roof of a house and burned the structure beneath their feet—fortunately the compound was effective. However, he did initiate modern print stereotyping with his design for a versatile iron press.

During the French Revolution he shocked his peers by siding with the revolutionary riffraff, democratically removing the family escutcheon from the coach and dinner service. The Terror soon made "Citizen Stanhope," along with many less ostentatious British friends of the Revolution, repent of their support.

Despite his libertarian politics, the Earl was such a martinet at home that his children slipped away as soon as they came of age. Lady Hester found a haven in the house of her mother's brother, William Pitt the elder, Lord Chatham. As Lytton Strachey instances at the beginning of his splendid brief biography of Lady Hester (1922: 297-307) she was accurately fixed in the Pitt lineage by the curve of her nose. During Pitt's last glorious years as Prime Minister Lady Hester was at the center of his menage; she organized entertainments, planned the running of the house and distributed political patronage all from the same anomalous position. Pitt tolerated the brashness of his niece, reprimanding her only when she sallied too far in her mockery. For her part Lady Hester modeled herself after her uncle in both dignity and fluidity of character.

Shape-shifting, both light and purposeful, seems to have been a part of the Pitt household spirit. Lady Hester's niece and biographer, the Duchess of Cleveland, quotes a passage from William Napier's *Life of Pitt* in which the Prime Minister is first playfully battling Lady Hester and others in a cushion fight, suddenly alters his mood to extreme gravity as he receives government dignitaries, then returns to his fun once the visitors have parted (Cleveland 1895: 50). Lady Hester was characterized as an "excellent mimic" of the mannerisms of others, a talent which she preserved into her old age (Cleveland 1897: 40). Having observed the number of forms a human being, albeit a political human, could take Lady Hester was ready and able to assume different shapes herself.

Pitt's death, in her 27th year, ended her apprenticeship. Typical of that society and time the demise of the patriarch terminated the communal order surrounding him and left unmarried females stranded. Lady Hester had been too independent to submerge herself in the subordinate obscurity of marriage hence she was uprooted and flung out into the world. Her father had disowned her and Pitt's heirs would not provide for her but luckily the great man had foreseen the effects of her contrariness and made a deathbed request that she be given a Parliamentary pension for life. She took a small house in London and tried to replicate there the former happiness, but everything was scaled down and warmed over. Then came the news that General Moore, her most passionate admirer, together with her brother, had died in some colonial war. She withdrew to a hut in the Welsh countryside, supposedly to mourn but in truth because she could afford no better. Her past had been too brilliant and her fall too great for her not to appear merely pathetic to those whose attendance she once commanded. The few who saw her remarked on her degradation.

England being intolerable, Lady Hester left, as it turned out forever, in 1810. She moped about the Mediterranean calling in at Malta and hatching a scheme to steal into France and catch a glimpse of Napoleon, but the plot was quashed by Stanford Canning, then British Minister to Malta, who had little use for the Stanhopes or the Pitts.

Malta did render her an intricate blessing in the form of Michael Bruce, a lover, companion and boost to her flagging pride (Bruce 1951). She suffered a "mental crisis" of unspecified character in coming to grips with the considerably younger Bruce, but was soon sufficiently stable to head with him toward Egypt, then in the hands of the British. Even during the Napoleonic Wars tourism to the Land of the Pharaohs was booming; each year artists, archaeologists, historians and dilletantes of every description surged down the Nile to make their sketches of the Pyramids and scratch their names on the flanks of the Sphinx.

Lady Hester's part was not, however, so happily served. Their ship capsized in a storm off the Isle of Rhodes, en route to Alexandria; they clung to a barren rock watching the ship sink with all their possessions. Rescue was long in coming, tortuous and expensive when it did. She eventually secured passage to Rhodes and even more eventually to Alexandria. The disaster was catalytic, a final break with her old life which literally tossed her into a new being. First she changed clothes (Letter to Murray Jan. 12, 1812; Cleveland 1897: 93).

> Everything I possessed I have lost; had I attempted to save anything, others would have done the same, and the boat would have sunk. To collect clothes in this part of the country to dress as an Englishwoman would be next to impossible; at least it would cost me two years' income. To dress as a Turkish woman would not do, because I must not be seen speaking to a man; therefore I have nothing left for it than to dress as a Turk...

And she goes on, describing the costume in considerable detail, much as Lady Mary Wortley Montagu had done in her letter to the Countess of Mar—only Lady Hester is describing a man's costume.

Though Havelock Ellis later counted her among the eonists Lady Hester's "male" dress was in truth very close to acceptable standards for females in Europe. The billowing gowns, cloaks and pantaloons that comprised Lady Hester's new wear, wrote her personal physician Dr. Meryon (Meryon 1845: vol. 1: 99):

> Although it was in fact that of a Turkish gentleman, the most fastidious prude could not have found anything in it unbecoming a woman, except its association, as a matter of habit, with the male sex.

The Turks were known as a luxuriating and effeminate people; they were the metaphor of soft sensuality (but also of grotesque brutality) in literature and painting. In the sartorial realm they gave Europe a new type of leisure dress: Turkish trousers and dressing gowns were casual wear for people like Franz Liszt, Honoré de Balzac and George Sand. But Lady Hester, and though

Dr. Meryon does not admit it the rest of her household including Dr. Meryon himself, adopted Turkish clothes as regular wear. "We all mean to dress in future as Turks" (Hamel 1913:122); she wrote in a letter to General Oaks, Dec. 19, 1811. The sexual dimorphism of European clothes was banished and everyone in her party, men and women, now dressed alike.

When she finally did reach Cairo she was well-received. The ruling Pasha was misinformed and thought her more important than she was; he regaled her with a sumptuous meal and humored her with praise for her appearance in this exotic garb. She and Michael Bruce spent not inconsiderable sums of money, over 600 pounds sterling, on additional clothes, the original economic motive for her change having been forgotten—probably because she found that Michael's wealthy father, Crauford Bruce, would defray the expenses (Bruce 1951: 142).

From Cairo she made a progress through major cities, flaunting the contradiction between her person and her dress with the knowledge that this betokened either political or magical power. Warned that no woman should approach Damascus, an especially fanatical place, without a veil she entered the gates astride her horse and unveiled. The populace was cowed and jubilant; she must be at least the daughter of the King of England. Lady Hester reveled in the affection of the unsettled tribes, the Bedouin, and boasted that this unruly, romantic people would obey her every command. As she wrote to her "disagreeable cousin," the diplomat Henry Williams Wynn (Cleveland 1897: 147):

> Going like a thief in the dark, as you did, fearing the Bedouins at the right and left, is abominable. The thing is to look, free as the air around the deserts, to observe something like a flight of crows at a distance—to look properly that way, move your hand, and in one instant see fifty lances spring in your defence; to see them return, exclaiming 'Schab-Friends.'

These words are a manifesto of the British Arabesque, celebrating the open space, lawless regime and sweeping action that the desert of the imagination was thought to offer. In its nearly cinematic picture of the ideal Briton-among-the-Bedouins this passage foreshadows the ultimate mythification of British Arabesque, the film *Lawrence of Arabia* of nearly 150 years later. But there was still much distance between Lady Hester and T.E. Lawrence, particularly the fictional Lawrence.

Confident in her Bedouin cavalry Lady Hester pushed on to Palmyra, a politically and physically impossible trek, and was crowned Queen of the

Desert under an arch (Bruce 1951: 193-8 reproduces Michael Bruce's letter describing the episode).

Queen, not King. Lady Hester was still a woman or, rather, a compromise creature between the two genders. Much later she told the German Prince Pückler-Müskau who had tactlessly asked her if a certain Arab chieftan had been her lover (Cleveland 1897: 297):

> It has often been said of me, but it is not true. The Arabs have never looked upon me in the light either of a man or of a woman, but as *un être à part*.

Her unique, even sacred status (if it was as impressive as she said in her letters) was due to a concerted preservation of this "being apart" quality among her train. She did not need to make any deep inquiry into Arab civilization—she never was a scholar of Arab language or literature—but only capitalized on being an Englishwoman, a strange creature to begin with, who owned up to her strangeness in aspect and action.

She acquired an entire wardrobe of costumes, from Chief of the Albanians to Syrian soldier, Bedouin Arab to son of a Pasha. The clothes were "like something in a play" and "quite ridiculous" but she stayed in them (Letter to Mrs. Fernandez Jan. 22, 1813; Cleveland 1897: 114-15). They gave her mastery, her true self symbolized as clothes can symbolize a self. She resided in them, a female in body (no one ever bet against that though she was, people would say, tall for her sex) and issued her commands from their citadel. She was not in disguise, not transformed into a Turk or an Arab but Lady Hester reinvented in a new environment where she was the person she could be-the person she no longer was in England.

The clothes were a seed of a household, for it was a matter of course that Lady Hester would seek to crystallize a domestic arrangement after the model her father had provided and the affable circumstances she had experienced while living with Pitt. As she relaxed into her clothes and fame covered her she scouted about for a location from which her presence could extend to its natural limits. For a space she rented a monastery in Lebanon from the Greek Orthodox Patriarch. Then she invaded and installed herself in another monastery, Mar Antonius, traditionally forbidden to women. Treasure-hunting, a popular preoccupation which united thaumaturgy with dogged searching of the desert, filled her hours and won her the collusion of the Turkish sultan. But she was too much in the thick of events she was unable to manipulate. In 1817 she moved to an abandoned monastery high in the Lebanese mountains. It was a perfect setting for the life she craved, remote, desolate, frequented only by the Bedouin who idolized her.

This was the terminus of Lady Hester's flight. At Djoun she constructed an establishment which, though tiny, encircled her entire domain. She stopped there for the rest of her life, less mobile but willing to receive visitors from Europe. Michael Bruce and Dr. Meryon had left her, though the latter returned periodically to collect materials for the biography he was secretly compiling to expose his imperious mistress. Lady Hester's letters continued, but with diminishing number as she became inextricably ensconced in her hermitage. "The nun of Lebanon" she called herself part whimsically part longingly in a letter to Michael Bruce, but her isolation was only the outside.

At Djoun she expanded her costume to a locale and within it accomplished the domestication (or householdization) of the orient in an English country house that surpassed anything in her native land. The servants, from Lady Hester's maid down to the stable boys, were required to wear Arab clothes and assume Arab names, those who were not Arab already. Dr. Madden, a visitor to Djoun in 1827, remarked (Madden 1829: vol. 2: 253)

> The only European at Djoun is Miss Williams Lady Hester's maid whom I have not seen, for the laws of the harem are observed as strictly there as in the Turkish capital.

The "laws of the harem" did not apply to Lady Hester herself who was master of the settlement and by nature exempt from any such imposition, but any female on the premises, including Dr. Meryon's bride during their stay, had to retire in Turkish costume (Meryon 1845: vol. 2: 146-49).

The fittings of the house were in keeping with Lady Hester's conception of Arab decor, rugs, low tables, tapestries. When Lamartine, the French poet and statesman, was lured to Djoun by rumors of the exotic on his tour of Syria (1832) he walked with Lady Hester through "one of the most beautiful Turkish gardens I have ever seen in the Orient." He fashioned about her, in his *Souvenirs, Impressions, Pensées et Paysages* an Arabian Nights rhapsody, admitting Greek mythology in his sobriquet, "Circe of the Deserts," since she captured men in her refreshing bower and transformed them by her spells (Lamartine 1859: vol. 2: 180-81). Alexander Kinglake, who came a few years later with letters of introduction from members of Lady Hester's family, punctured this starry sphere in his enormously popular travelogue *Eöthen*. After being regaled with cuisine "of the oriental kind," Kinglake was ushered into Lady Hester's room, and found her seated on a common European sofa which she occupied after the usual manner, her feet on a footstool (Kinglake 1908: 67). She was not the enchantress Lamartine had promised: yet another Englishman, James Silk Buckingham paid her the backhand compliment that her mode of living had (1825: 410).

> nothing peculiar in it except, perhaps, that it was more rational than the mode observed by the more fashionable of her own sex in particular, at home.

Buckingham, for different reasons, was as disgruntled with the British conventions as Lady Hester, and found in her a worthy rebel.

Lady Hester withdrew into the household ever more deeply until it imprisoned her. Asserting an oriental despotism—the heritage, says a biographer, of her grandfather Thomas "Diamond" Pitt who "ruled those about him with notions of absolutism which are associated with oriental monarchies" (Hamel 1913: 3-4). Lady Hester tried the servants with her idiosyncratic schedule and incessant demands for petty services at all times of night or day. All her guests returned to Europe with stories about the obedience she exacted from underlings and the rigidity of her rule (Meryon 1845: vol. 1: 119-23). A call for a special preparation of tea could ring out at any moment only to be rescinded when the weary maid brought the cup to her room (Hamel 1913:268 has a drawing of her in her "sitting room"). The bell-rope hanging over her bed was being yanked through all her long waking hours, sending ripples of uneasy energy into the solar system and upsetting her satellites in their lazy orbits.

Djoun was geared to Lady Hester's every caprice, and she was prolific of caprices, from more treasure-hunting to bumptious meddling in local politics. One airy crotchet took over her teeming brain and ousted all the rest. In England during her youth a soothsayer named Richard Brothers forecast that she would be a Queen in the East. Within her hermitage she brooded on this prediction and the counsel of Arab prophets she called to her abode. A Mahdi, or Savior, was soon to arrive and Lady Hester, the prophets added, would rule beside him. Some professed to find evidence of the coming reign in sacred books, while others pointed to auguries that adumbrated her special destiny. Lady Hester had long been a subscriber to astrology and other mantic arts which she used to mask uncomfortably penetrating analyses of others. These arts verified for her the Mahdi's advent.

When outsiders such as Lamartine or Kinglake mentioned the Mahdi (probably having been assured of a diverting response) Lady Hester placed all the prognostications before them. Then she conducted the guest through her private garden and into a stable which housed two fine Arabian mares, one of them with a natural back deformity like a saddle. This is in perfect fulfillment, exclaimed the Lady, of the prophecy for the Madhi is to ride this horse into Jerusalem. The other horse was reserved, she implied, for herself, the Mahdi's inevitable consort. Both mares were attended by grooms and though never ridden were exercised and pastured on a piece of ground behind the garden wall. Dr. Meryon asserts that Lady Hester's dreams about the Mahdi were deliberately cultivated by the Arab servants for their own profit-why else would she need two grooms? (Meryon 1845: vol. 1:200-01). She was caught in her own imaginings, obliging the servants to oblige her in a commune of deceits.

Back in England she was the pivot of many another fancy. Even the self-proclaimed messiah and inadvertent social revolutionary "Sir William Courtenay" (John Nicholas Tom) told in his newspaper *The Lion* (April 6, 1833) of how he journeyed through the Holy Land disguised as Hassan Abdullah and attempted to obtain an audience with Lady Hester for confirmation of *his* mission (Mathews 1971: 140). Lady Hester moved further away from England (for which she expressed hatred); away from womanhood (she hated women too, according to Dr. Meryon); away from her friends; and away from the Arab and Turkish officials who had permitted her to act as a minor potentate. Kinglake says she ceased to read books and newspapers entirely in her last years, and pretended to draw all knowledge from the stars: She was "perilously near madness." Lady Hester had created a *folie à menage* and wove the entire countryside into the web but the price was isolation, not even a grand isolation.

Djoun had natural limits in time and space. As Lady Hester grew older it began to wear. Her insistences annoyed everyone. The Bedouin who swore fealty and avenged the murder of a French traveler at her request took to avoiding her, for she had mixed in tribal politics too long. Although she courageously withstood the onslaught of an invading Pasha nothing but further enmity resulted. Her former guests laughed politely from a distance and her servants robbed her. The slightly more tangible prospect of an Irish estate and a larger income supplanted the Mahdi for a while. She harried the Duke of Wellington, Viscount Palmerston and Queen Victoria with letters demanding their assistance in procuring the estate, but finished by selling her pension to satisfy creditors. There were few visitors any more—the American Harriet Livermore who quarreled with her over "sacred mares" and drifted off to the desert to become herself a "prophetess." In her last letter Lady Hester complains "all men have become beasts," and they had. She died alone, unable or unwilling to tug at the bed-rope. A missionary who had known Djoun during the life of its mistress passed that way 18 years later and found it ruined. The artificial vitality that had kept the walls at attention and the garden blooming was gone; it was Circe's island after the death of the enchantress.

Only William Beckford in that resplendent romance *Vathek* conducted an arabesque akin to Lady Hester's realm of clashing tribes, autocracy, magic and destiny. But the Caliph Vathek's prodigality contrasts hopelessly with the actual leanness of Lady Hester's monastery, however rich her imaginings, and may be less of an accurate comparison than the antic Hajji Baba of Isphahan. Lady Hester's was the last inner romance in British Arabesque. After her spareness, complicity and concession ruled.

Lady Hester's immediate successor in the living Arabesque was transitional, with aspects of both the older, romantic variety and the newer, more direct one. Lady Jane Digby (it is still aristocrats) was never deprived of the wealth, connections and admirers which drove Lady Hester into exile. It was an added virtue, beauty exaggerated by her contemporaries into an almost supernatural quality, that led her along her eastward course from husband to husband in a line quite as long as the file of Edward Wortley Montagu's wives. She began in a grim marriage to an English peer but unlike most wives enjoyed his negligence indecently as the mistress of an Austrian prince. In Paris she knew Balzac and in Munich King Ludwig of Bavaria. The rest of her track to the East led past the King of Greece and at its terminus stood Syria and a tribal chieftain named Medjuel, with whom she stayed for the rest of her life. Besides his restlessness Lady Jane had Montagu's facility for languages, and could converse with each of her husbands in his own tongue. Her colloquial Arabic and familiarity with Bedouin life impressed even Richard Burton, whom she knew when he was Consul in Damascus.

Lady Jane lived a Persephone existence, six months in her house near Damascus, six months with Medjuel in the desert. The house was built to accommodate her ambiguous life (Oddie 1936:226).

> The house itself was like its owner, half Arab, half English. The description of it suggests that Jane took over an oriental house and added to it an English wing that was hers, for the main portion of the house was entirely Arab and was furnished quite simply in the Arab fashion. Her own wing consisted of a great octagonal drawing-room, built out of the garden, a room that was furnished, as long ago they had furnished great salons in Mayfair or Munich, the decorative scheme being like that of her house at

Dukades, gilt cornices and ceilings, walls inlaid with mirrors and windows hung with fine damask curtains.

The compromise was practical, and not in itself sufficient. For her six months in the desert Lady Jane lived among the Bedouin and had their regard, not by ruling from a mountain but by active participation in their feasts and wars (Schmidt 1976). When her husband's tribe clashed with enemies she diverted some of her considerable income to purchase modern weapons and joined in the clash herself, jotting notes in her diary that sound in their terseness like the war dispatches of T.E. Lawrence.

Lady Jane never prided herself in being *un être à part*. She had acquired a uniquely assimilated position from her alliance with Medjuel, and assimilated to the extent she wished without any great display of exoticism. Her concession was less a performance than her predecessor's, or it was a different kind of performance geared to living *with* the people more than to living *as* one of them, in the view of others. This submersion into the life of the Arabs for personal reasons, for the sake of information, for political manipulations, was subject to as many variant executions as there were individuals who attempted it. It could form a reborn masquerade played to the hilt for total, though temporary identification or a refusal to wear any disguise at all, but to go among the Arabs as a foreigner and thus a pilgrim.

These outward extremes of British Arabesque, already visible in the history leading from the Montagus to Lady Jane Digby, have a common denominator, nothing which can be readily stated but a cultural air which can be sensed in the travels of the great nineteenth century exponents of the tradition, from Richard Burton to Charles Doughty.

References

Anonymous.
    1777 *Memoirs of the Late Edw. W-ly M-tague.* 2 v. Dublin.

Barry, Iris.
    1928 *Portrait of Lady Mary Wortley Montagu.* London: Benn.

Bruce, Ian.
    1951 *The Nun of Lebanon: The Love Affair of Lady Hester Stanhope and Michael Bruce*. London: Collins.

Buckingham, James Silk.
    1825 *Travels among the Arab Tribes*. London: Longman's.

Curling, Jonathan.
    1954 *Edward Wortley Montagu*. London: Andrew Melrose.

Cleveland, Duchess of.
    1897 *Life and Letters of Lady Hester Stanhope*. London: W. Clowes and Son.

Halsband, Robert.
    1956 *The Life of Lady Mary Wortley Montagu*. Oxford: Clarendon Press.

Hamel, Frank.
    1913 *Lady Hester Stanhope*. London: Cassell.

Kinglake, Alexander.
    1908 *Eothen*. London: Dent.

Lamartine, M. de.
    1859 *Souvenirs, impressions, pensées et paysages pendant un voyage en Orient*. 2 v. Paris: Pagnerre.

Madden, R.P.
    1829 *Travels in Turkey, Egypt, Nubia and Palestine*. 2 v. London: Colburn.

Mathews, Ronald.
    1971 *English Messiahs*. New York: Benjamin Blom.

Meryon, Dr. James.
    1845 *Memoirs of Lady Hester Stanhope*. 2 v. London: Colburn.

Montagu, Lady Mary Wortley.
    1906 *Letters*. London: Dent.

Newman, Norris.
    1962 *The Stanhopes of Chevening*. London: Macmillan.

Oddie, E. M.
    1936 *The Odyssey of a Loving Woman*. New York: Harper's.

Schmidt, Margaret Fox.
    1976 *Passion's Child*. New York: Harper and Row.

Strachey, Lytton.
    1922 "Lady Hester Stanhope. "In *Books and Characters*. New York: Harcourt-Brace.

Pilgrim garb
from Richard Burton's *Personal Narrative*.

VII

Richard Burton in Mecca and Medina

On old maps of the Near East the Arabian Peninsula frequently bears across its center the legend "Arabia Felix," "Happy Arabia"; only beyond the northernmost edge of the Peninsula, on the far side of a mountain range or even past an imaginary body of water does the more truthful designation "Arabia Deserta" appear. The wholesome cartographic repute of Central Arabia was the sole survival of an ancient legend placing the Earthly Paradise, the bountiful garden from which Adam and Eve were expelled, in the least known region. Even by the middle of the nineteenth century the interior of the Peninsula was so unknown that it left cartographers no recourse but to continue an old name in the place of new names or landforms to fill up the embarrassing gap. But white space on a map is as abhorrent to civilization as a vacuum is to nature; the rush of investigative molecules is terrific, and the most savage conditions cannot hold them back for long.

The draw of emptiness was abetted by positive attractions: Mecca and Medina, the seat and the sanctuary of Islam, the objects of pilgrimage were both in Arabia Felix. The Prophet had forever barred infidels from entering their precincts, but that only tempted them to try. Stories of miracles and absurdities of the Muslim faith, mixed in together by the dim medieval reports, added to the lure. If anyone successfully entered the cities before Ludovico di Varthema they did not leave notice. Varthema, a Bolognese, fell in with a band of Mameluke soldiers who were conducting pilgrims to the sacred cities in 1502 (Varthema 1863). His *Travels* are a salty chronicle of haphazard journeys, miserable confinements and lucky escapes at the hands of amorous sultanas. All the time snarling to himself at the "filthiness and loathsomeness of the trumperyes, deceits, trifles and hypocrises of the religion of Muhamet" (in Richard Eden's Elizabethan translation), Varthema was clear-headed enough to watch the sacrifices of the pilgrimage and fanciful enough to see unicorns on the streets of Mecca.

Varthema was followed by a less willing but better informed visitor, the Englishman Joseph Pitts (1704) who, captured by pirates in 1678 and sold as a slave to an Algerian Muslim, lived in Algiers for 15 years learning Arabic and Turkish, absorbing (but never really respecting) Muslim customs. Pitts' master longed to convert the Christian slave to Islam for the atonement of past sins against the faith and he tried every persuasion, first bribery and then the bastinado applied, in the Arab manner, to the soles of the feet. This won Pitts' insincere acquiescence: taken to Mecca by his master he delighted in covertly violating every last prescription of the pilgrimage, and of Islam, eating pork in private, reading his Bible, cursing the prophet as he prayed. After many excursions he slipped away from his master (who had freed him) and escaped to Europe, only to be taken by a press gang on coming ashore in England. But he evaded that final enslavement to be reunited with his father and write his book.

The nineteenth century saw an upsurge of scientific travelers to Arabia Felix. Some chose to dawdle on the fringes of the territory and make what observations were allowed, but those seeking to enter Mecca, if not honestly professing Islam and thus unlikely to report their experiences, were obliged to go completely disguised. The Wahhabi movement, a revitalization which spread among the Bedouin tribes of Central Arabia, urged a return to the simple, militant Islam of the unornamented Koran and, not incidentally, driving out of the Turkish overlords. The Wahhabis did not tolerate Christians. In 1811 Ulrich Edward Seetsen (1854), a Tsarist agent who made the pilgrimage in disguise, was slaughtered in the Yemeni highlands, his books and diaries scattered to the winds. A more careful mock pilgrim, the Spanish Jew Badia y Leblich (1816), possibly a spy for Napoleon, garnered his way to Mecca by dint of his excellent Arabic and princely posing; en route to his second pilgrimage in 1818 he died mysteriously, of poison or of dysentery, but his papers were rescued by Lady Hester Stanhope.

The chief of the disguised pilgrims was the Swiss ethnographer Johann Burckhardt. Burckhardt had already explored the River Niger and followed the course of the Nile from its lower reaches before he crossed the Red Sea and disembarked at Yanbu to take the pilgrimage. A malady contracted at Mecca impinged seriously on his note-taking, yet he was able to transmit to his London publisher the most complete description yet of the pilgrimage practices before dying in Cairo (1817). Burckhardt's success was resented by Muslims; the rumor spread in Egypt that he actually had been spontaneously beheaded in a mosque when it was learned he was an infidel (Kiernan 1937: 241). The disease had killed him, but the warning implicit in the story could not be ignored.

Some thirty years later Burckhardt's adventures (1829) were read with lasting impression by a young officer in the British East India Company, Richard Burton, a member of the alienated British middle class, which produced so many novelists and social critics in the middle part of the century. Burton was not only an outsider and an observer, he was a landless outsider who observed his own nation and other nations with a combination of scorn and anxiety. He was raised largely in France, which gave him too much of a perspective on Britain to accept indoctrination at Oxford. His genius for languages supplemented his anger. The usual antidote for not fitting in at Oxford, a stint in the India service, was the opportunity to master numbers of native dialects and too many native habits, but his ability and knowledge were no substitute for social rank. He rankled as dolts were promoted above him and fools assigned him to unworthy tasks. Desperately ill he left the thankless drudgery of the service and went home, he thought, to die.

His recovery foisted upon him the need for a career. The life review occasioned by his reexamination of the years he had spent in India led him to writing—thick, hodgepodge books which for all their lack of polish showed more dispassionate observation than his more conventional rivals in travelogue writing (Burton 1851). But his memories were not inexhaustible. After four books on India he was eager for more travel.

While in India Burton had undertaken some missions in disguise, a few of them official but most of them amorous, curious or merely playful—he is reticent about details in the books. He went as a Muslim, often a wandering dervish, and discovered that he could be wonderfully convincing in this role. His experiences taught him, from a native's standpoint, how devout the Muslim's really are and how they crave to fulfill the most solemn enjoinder of Islam, to make the pilgrimage to Mecca and Medina. Burton contracted this craving himself, not for any devotion but because he saw in the pilgrimage the truest use of his abilities and the most spectacular announcement of his faith in himself and his own scientific outlook. It was impossible for him to do anything about this in India—he lacked the resources and the Company would not aid him—but his books had won some prestige for him in the Royal Geographic Society. Funds were provided, and he readied himself for the pilgrimage.

Burton's predecessors in British Arabesque, Edward Wortley Montagu and Lady Hester Stanhope, had both planned to make the pilgrimage but never went. Any pilgrimage for them would have been an exhibit, announcing themselves as British at each stop to the accolades of the Bedouin. Burton intended to go in disguise, "like a thief in the night," as Lady Hester might have described it, and with an avowedly scientific purpose. He wanted to determine the exact latitude and longitude of the sacred cities, learn if any true rivers flowed through Central Arabia, fill out Burckhardt's description of the rituals and find if Arabian horses could be made available to the British in India. The proclamation of his visit was reserved for after his return and for the medium of writing.

Burton grew a beard, shaved his head and when ready to board the steamer for Alexandria put on the clothes and style of his "old character of a Persian wanderer, or Darwaysh" which had served him in India. He knew from past experience that the sanctity of the holy man and his eccentricities were broad cover for any infelicities an Englishman might commit. At the suggestion of a friend, however, he switched to the guise of a "Persian Prince" right before embarking. His baggage was remodeled to sustain the loftier rank, and he took ship in style.

At Alexandria the persistence of a dockside beggar convinced him that the Persian prince was an adequate wrapper; the liabilities of the pretense soon caused him to change his mind. Persians were accounted Shi'ite heretics by orthodox Sunni Muslims. To them were attributed all manner of desecrations and impieties, and, as Burton graphically learned much later, they traveled to Mecca greatly at their peril. Burton remade himself into a dervish, or prepared himself to become a dervish in earnest.

Few travelers have had Burton's ear for gossip and his understanding of its uses. He lodged in Alexandria with John W. Larking, a resident who had also afforded hospitality to Burckhardt. Burton noted that the servants of Larking's house accepted him as a Muslim though not so devout as they, with only a few reservations. He was guided by popular sentiments in marking his path toward the pilgrimage. Formally he commenced study with a tutor of the Arabic language and of the Koran; informally he lounged around cafes, baths and bazars picking up the fine points of custom and speech which would be vital to his disguise and arousing confidence of his fellow Muslims by the well-turned (if self-amused) form of his idleness. Having expertise in the art of "physic" he made further contacts receiving patients. This guaranteed him employment at all junctures and access, he wryly adds, to the "fair sex." As proof of his success he was offered the daughter of one old patient in marriage. But "the man wants to wander, and he must do so, or he shall die."

Burton required a Turkish passport before he could leave Egypt. The indignation and delays he endured at the various bureaucratic offices assured him that he was in truth gaining the attention usual for a native, a bitter assurance for the amount of misery it accompanied. The uniform treatment of Burton as a genuine Muslim was counterpoised by his irregular reaction to this treatment, as an Englishman within the effective disguise. Paying a five shilling fee for a certificate of identity from the British Consulate causes him to carp about the pettiness of British exactions from the natives, "the meanness of our magnificance! the littleness of our greatness!" The surly demeanor of a *Kawwas*, or policeman, of whom he is inquiring the procedure for obtaining a visa drives him to the opposite tone. Persistent asking brings only a curse of dismissal from the officer (Burton 1893: vol. 1: 3).

> I then turned away slowly and fiercely, for the next thing might have been a cut with the Kurbaj, and, by the hammer of Thor! British flesh and blood could never have stood *that*.

The dervish can criticize the British bitterly but is himself British when the lines are drawn. There is no inconsistency in that. Burton may speak on occasion as a dervish-pilgrim reacting to the English but he always remains an Englishman who has assumed that role the better to express his views.

The optimum validation of his disguise arrived not in the curse of the Kawwas, but in the curse of an Englishman he jostled on the steamer to Cairo, for this new imprecation proved to him that he had reached a vantage point from which to gaze critically upon natives and English. The English, however, are the beneficiaries of his criticism because they will see it in writing. Burton never ceased to be an Englishman, a superior Englishman able to turn the passenger's curse back upon the English nation two-fold. Solely by perfect disguise could Burton occupy this privileged place. Indeed, the same chapter of the *Personal Narrative* that tells of these curses shows how silly the English look when they haughtily assume native dress, language and customs. Either one is an Englishman completely or is in disguise monitoring natives and English. Burton had no patience with the blank stupidity of either state or the sloppy pretense of half-measures.

The trip to Cairo rewarded the vagabond with a sure friend in Haji Wali whose ironic inquisitiveness pleased Burton. The Haji, a Russian-born Muslim who knew the pilgrimage route quite well, nominated himself as Burton's companion and advisor. Burton had already provisioned himself with some small pieces of equipment—a canteen, an inkwell, and so on—of local manufacture. The Haji recommended other implements a pilgrim would want; he deflated Burton's medical ambitions by alluding to the surfeit of doctors and counseled Burton toward another transformation of identity.

Haji Wali actually believed Burton to be a Persian Muslim and warned him not to carry that character into Arabia where Persians faced beatings and exactions. Burton thereupon dropped the Persian entirely and invented an alternate persona that drew on his India years. He became a Pathan, or Afghan (Burton 1893: vol. 1:45).

> Born in India of Afghan parents who had settled in the country, educated at Rangoon, and set out to wander, as men of that race frequently are, from early youth, I was well guarded against the danger of detection from fellow countrymen.

Meaning, of course, that Burton had the fluency in Persian and Urdu which any other Afghan he might meet along the pilgrimage route would naturally expect. The Pathan really was Burton himself remodeled in Muslim clay since he really was born in one country (England), educated largely in another (France) and was sent out early to wander the earth. The new Burton just had the peculiar property of needing a huge outlay of knowledge and wit to be normal among the Muslims—he had to run in order to stay still. The older Persian identity clung to him like the "shirt of Nessus" while he was in Cairo. His arrival in the robes of a Persian was remembered and transmitted down the line; he compounded the initial misjudgement by registering for theological studies in the Shafe'i school, which was commonly used as a concealment by Shi'ites when among orthodox Muslims. He elliptically refers to drawing his knife every time an "offensive hint was thrown out." The odious attribution pursued him even into Mecca.

The infamy of being a Shi'ite under wraps was far less awful than the truth if divined. Burton had taken every precaution to hide his trail from England and his English "flesh and blood," but there were some acts the Englishman must perform disguised or not. Note-taking was their chief.

In Cairo Haji Wali forecast that Burton's writing in public would awaken antagonisms among the pious Muslims on the Hajj. The orthodox teacher, Shaykh Mohammed, with whom he studied the Koran after withdrawing from the Shafe'i teachers was even more pointed (Burton 1893: vol. 1:72).

> 'Thou art always writing, O my brave!' (this is said on the few occasions when I venture to make a note in my book), 'what evil habit is this? Surely thou hast learned it in the land of the Frank. Repent!'

Burton never repented. Earlier European pilgrims to Mecca had failed to bring back accurate descriptions because they feared the consequences of conspicuous note-taking. Burton would not allow himself to be cowed by superstition or by wariness of other people's superstition, and return with a depleted account because furtive scratches were all he could muster. The challenge to his writing was a challenge to the sovereignty of English civilization.

The first serious obtrusion of his English preoccupation through his Muslim facade was during the first leg of the pilgrimage, the trip from Cairo to Suez thence to Yanbu. Burton had hastily departed from Cairo because of a rather indiscrete drinking bout with an Albanian captain. Drinking spirits, not to mention intemperate rowdy drinking is an anathema to orthodox Muslims; the "staid Indian doctor" had been seen partaking of the forbidden drink, and this did great damage to his reputation for sobriety. He saw signs of the episode's ill results all along his path; the porter at the gate, convinced he was a Persian heretic, would not even utter the customary valediction for pilgrims when Burton passed. Along the road to Suez Burton's servant absconded with his baggage and he arrived in the port of departure robbed and bedraggled from an 84 mile camel trek.

Burton learned that a Hindu servant answering the description of the runaway had arrived at the Caravanserai in Suez, lodged some baggage in a room which he then locked, and parted for festivities on a boat. No inducement could force the porter to allow Burton entrance. While awaiting either the Indian's return or a chance to petition the local Turkish governor for permission to gain forceable access to his goods Burton fell in with a group of Mecca and Medina natives. Deducing that Burton was a "great man under a cloud" (a suspicion Haji Wali had earlier expressed) or at least well-to-do, the men elected themselves Burton's companions. The wisdom of cultivating this entourage did not escape Burton: he would need their protection along the route, their instructions while in the pilgrim cities and the aura of legitimacy their respect would confer. He forged a bond with the lot of them by tendering loans of rather modest sums, princely by their impoverished standards, taking sundry items by way of collateral and agreeing on repayment at usurious rates—a neat profit, though he intended to forgive the whole on collection day, and thus win greater glory still.

This deft investment of the Royal Geographic Society's funds repaid Burton immediately by giving him the dignity of a patron. His clients accorded him precedence in all matters, in truth pressed precedence upon him, and made him the oracle of their party. The clever (an partially unwitting) juggling of the Arab social order to situate himself advantageously nearly wrecked his disguise. While he was away appealing to the governor for the recovery of his belongings the servant returned, unlocked the door and admitted his master's followers, who did not hesitate to rifle the baggage for evidence of Burton's exalted origins. They were unearthing the sextant when Burton returned (Burton 1893: vol. 1: 168).

> My friends had looked at my clothes, overhauled my medicine chest, and criticised my pistols; they sneered at my copper-cased watch, and remembered having seen a compass at Constantinople. Therefore I imagined they would think little about a sextant. This was a mistake. The boy Mohammed, I afterwards learned, waited only my leaving the room to declare that the would-be Haji was one of the Infidels from India, and a counsel sat to discuss the case.

The "boy Mohammed" had, when Burton first encountered him in Cairo, shown "signs of over-wisdom." This youth of 18, a Mecca native was familiar with the English from trips to India and was returning home from a visit to Constantinople when he attached himself to Burton. The apprehensive pilgrim purchased an *ihram* or pilgrim's cloak for Mohammed and cured one of his friends of ophthalmia but the boy parted quickly afterward leaving his address in Mecca. Burton's reunion with the boy outside of Suez reawakened old anxieties; he bribed him with the largest sum loaned to any of his companions. But that did not prevent Mohammed from making his charges when the sextant was produced.

> Fortunately for me, Omar Effendi had looked over a letter which I had written to Haji Wali that morning, and he had at various times received categorical replies to certain questions in high theology. He felt himself justified in declaring *ex-cathedra*, the boy Mohammed's position perfectly untenable. And Shaykh Hamid, who looked forward to being my host, guide, and debtor in general, and probably cared scantily for catechism or creed, swore that the light of Al-Islam was upon my countenance, and, consequently, that the boy Mohammed was a pauper, a 'fakir,' an owl, a cut-off one, a stranger and a Wahhabi (heretic), for daring to impugn the faith of a brother believer. The scene ended with a general abuse of the acute youth, who was told on all sides that he had no shame, and was directed to 'fear Allah.'

The proceedings were narrated to Burton by Omar Effendi whom he accidentally encountered in Cairo after the pilgrimage was over. The Effendi did the "gentlemanly" thing and though he had every reason to suspect Burton of being the false pilgrim mentioned everywhere in Cairo made no accusations. At the time of his trial Burton did not realize how close he had come to an exposé, and how marvellously well his largesse had worked. He only had to deal with the sextant.

> I was struck with the expression of my friends' countenances when they saw the sextant, and, determining with a sigh to leave it behind, I prayed five times a day for a week.

Burton rapidly resorted to prayer in satirical thanks for deliverence and genuinely in assertion of his piety to offset the possession of an impious instrument. By Burton's own estimate this was the worst threat to his disguise in the entire pilgrimage.

The discretionary junking of the sextant embarrassed him scientifically since he was unable to take the bearings of Mecca as accurately as expected. He rejoiced in the security it afforded him once on the pilgrim boat, however, and joined in with the others to fend off some Maghrabis who aspired to capture the pilgrims' comfortable spot. This phase of solidarity with the Arabs put him in a melancholy humor when he watched the flag of the British Consulate recede in the distance; he regretted that he was banned from the society of other Englishmen, which he preferred to his present companions no matter how comradely they might seem. Even while writing his travelogue in England he recalled the isolation.

The halt at Yanbu separated him from poignant reminders that he was a sojourner from his own people and threw him into heightened cognizance of his hostile surroundings. The physical presence of the English and their institutions had reminded him of his true self: he was an Englishman commenting upon humanity in general. Being injected into the pilgrimage he no longer preserved this balance, nor could he rely on his fellow-countrymen for asylum if he did slip up. Burton's devil-may-care tone masks (sometimes incompletely) a growing uneasiness with this condition. He would like to appear fully self-confident and always the master of himself, a British Everyman among heathens. Yet the frail barrier of his costume alone shielded him from the wrath of violated Islam.

When Burton refers to his anxiety in the *Personal Narrative* it is almost always for rhetorical effect, and not as if it really affected him emotionally. Remarks about British reserve are probably in order but whatever their validity as generalizations they would only cloud the fine detail of Burton's personal experience. At one overnight stop near Yanbu Burton's alias was "severely tried" by the persistent company of a bonafide Pathan.

> ... he could speak five or six languages, he knew a number of people everywhere, and he had travelled far and wide over Central Asia. These fellows are always good detectors of an incognito.

Burton sidestepped the Pathan's probing questions about his place of birth by declaring that as a dervish he had disowned name and country. When the man insisted on a straight answer Burton asked him to guess; and to the flustered pilgrim's joy "he claimed me for a brother Pathan." Following effusive exchanges Burton fortified the man's conviction by offering to arm his friends and take after the Persians who had mistreated his "brother Pathan." The dread of discovery resolved itself into hearty common cause with an intensity that need no longer lie hidden.

In Yanbu proper Burton found himself in another situation which he accepted as a test of his authenticity. The room where he stayed was occupied by the families of Omar Effendi's brothers, "broad-shouldered, large-limbed men distinguished only by a peculiar surliness of countenance." He read in the fierceness of their glances a mistrust, and in their careful survey of his ablutions and prayers to watch for errors. He won their indifference by exercising the nonchalance of a True Believer. Burton cannot be blamed for hypersensitivity; all of his actions were a performance and these actions he felt justified in performing more to a particular audience because his anxiety had settled in them. That he was joyed at the Pathan's recognition and calmed at the brothers' neglect is the only admission of his state of mind when the events actually happened. We readers appreciate his anxiety only because he had skillfully put us in his place and left us to respond in our own way until he summons us back with his own admirably nonchalant way of extricating himself from a tense situation.

From Yanbu began the overland phase of Burton's pilgrimage to Medina and Mecca. Strangers, he learned probably to his amusement, were advised to disguise themselves as Arabs in order to avoid the capitation tax levied upon outlanders by the settled tribes of Central Arabia. This entailed wearing Arab garb and speaking nothing but Arabic. Burton subversively modified his new outfit to suit the peculiarities of his mission as note-taker (Burton 1893: vol. 1: 234-41). The Hamail, a small Koran usually carried over the left shoulder by pilgrims, was on Burton a hollow box with three internal compartments. In these compartments he placed the paper, pens, ink and drawing materials that remained to him.

The Bedouin were even less tolerant of writing than the urban Muslims, and more likely to do violence to a person caught in the act of placing "enchantments" on their country. A German traveller had lost his entire sketchbook and nearly his life when he was detected at work; others were not so fortunate. Only horoscopes, charms for prosperities and genealogies are fit cause for taking pen in hand among these excitable people. Burton did not relish being caught in the act or even with the tell-tale implements, hence the fake Hamail.

Other measures included a long, thin diary custom crafted in Cairo to fill a breast pocket and the provision of empty metal tins in the medicine chest to hold the pieces of sketches which Burton cut up (and numbered for reassembly). But he would not bend back all the way: a few times along the way he exhibited samples of English writing to his companions explaining that it was "derived from Solomon and Alexander, the Lord of the Long Horns." Their ignorance promised him leeway.

The dialectic of caution and effrontery, of danger and security is so much at the center of Burton's disguise, and the rhetoric of playacting his way through all events so complete that the real instances of entering into the spirit of the pilgrimage stand out in full relief. During the march from Yanbu to Medina he kept to his routine; he snickered at the folly of his companions, made note of historic landmarks and (in spite of an earlier resolve) he persecuted one of the party for the repayment of a loan—he did not want the unsavory repute of being a permissive creditor. The Bedouin were predacious and the misery of travel great. Yet at the summit of an embankment from which the pilgrims caught their first glimpse of the Holy City they stopped their beasts "as if by word of command" and lifted their voices in picturesque exclamations (Burton 1893: vol. 1: 280):

> 'O Allah! This is the Harim (sanctuary) of Thy Apostle; make it to us a Protection from Hell Fire, and a Refuge from Eternal Punishment! O open the Gates of Thy Mercy, and let us pass through them to the Land of Joy!'...

Burton was caught off guard by this sudden enoblement of his comical comrades, and he was honest enough to admit it in a paragraph that is his own exclamation at the sight of Medina.

> Such were the poetical exclamations that rose all around me, showing how deeply tinged with imagination becomes the language of the Arab under the influence of strong passion or religious enthusiasm. I now understood the full value of a phrase

in the Moslem ritual, 'And when his [the pilgrim's] eyes shall *fall upon the Trees of Al-Madinah*, let him raise his Voice and bless the Apostle with the choicest of Blessing.' In all the fair view before us nothing was more striking, after the desolation through which we had passed, than the gardens and orchards about the town. It was impossible not to enter into the spirit of my companions, and truly I believe that for some minutes my enthusiasm rose as high as theirs. But presently when we remounted, the traveller returned strong upon me: I made a rough sketch of the town, put questions about the principal buildings, and in fact collected materials for the next chapter.

The transitions in the paragraph are remarkable, from an objective statement about "those Arabs" to a gloss on ritual to personal relief at the prospect to participation in the Arab enthusiasm and finally back to the steadiness of objectivity and note-taking. He rose up with them on a plane of common joy but catching himself relaxed into measurements which were his ritual acknowledgement of the spot's importance.

Burton was welcomed in Medina by Shaykh Hamid, a companion who had preceded the main party there to ready his house. He was given room, food and, with minor interferences, the solitude which he missed. The business of religion was not left aside for long and he followed the customary rites under the guidance of Shaykh Hamid, first a visit (meritorious, but not of the pilgrimage) to the Prophet's Mosque and its adjoining sanctuaries. This was the culmination for which he had endured; he did not omit a prostration or a prayer, nor did he omit taking them all down for inclusion in the printed *Personal Narrative*. The combination of a bantering tone that reminds the reader Burton never takes any of this too seriously with solid detail forms the crux of Burton's description. The steps of the pilgrimage come in their order, but no longer with the infusion of anecdotes or self-revelation that highlighted the beginning passages. In the pilgrimage city Burton is an Englishman with access to the facts and he will examine them as they go by with remarks on history and nature. Burton's Medina is no exotic or even fascinating place; it is a cluster of informative observations that answer to the criteria of ethnography and of sightseeing.

The inquirer after Burton's method of maintaining his disguise or even his feelings about being in disguise will be disappointed in the pilgrimage chapters. He is unassailable. Though he remained minutely sensitive to interactions among people and to his own best part this comes out only in silhouette behind the mosques and tombs. He did not submit himself to exposing the frailties and the trivia which might compromise him as a thoroughly *accurate* narrator. Arab guise matters no more.

He did employ the various scenes of the pilgrimage to digress on aspects of belief and superstition which had connections in his own experience. The visitation to the Tomb of Hamzah presented him with a curious ceremony that was a point of departure for a discussion leading far from the topic at hand. Admission to the mosque containing the tomb was a privilege specially accorded "Turkish pilgrims." The keeper removed from his pouch a mass of keys and, directing Burton to stand away and not look, opened the mosque door with a tremendous clanging of locks and bolts. The rationale given was that the spirits of the martyrs often gather in the chamber of the mosque and must be averted to the profane intrusion that they might sequester themselves. The precaution "sounded like poetry if not sense" to Burton, who marvelled at the imagination of the Arabs. On second thought he recalled numbers of similar phantasms who haunted Europe and the civilized superstition of the spiritualists; the men of Medina are "as wise, and the superstition as respectable, as that of others." No concession to superstition in itself, but an allowance for differences which do not fall into hierarchy. The remark is, however, more a condemnation of superstition from Burton's scientific standpoint than it is allowance for cultural equality. Burton could afford to be tolerant from his superior position.

The trip to Mecca in completion of the pilgrimage required another desert passage. Burton attached himself to a caravan under official escort which cleared the progress through lines of robbers and Bedouin. The fascination of the nomads caused Burton to compile, while taking appropriate care to not be noticed writing, a full description of the desert tribes. Within sight of Mecca the pilgrims gave themselves over to the same ejaculations Burton had heard before Medina, but without his joining them. His time in Mecca seems more clipped and matter-of-fact, as if he is exercising his faculties only for the gathering of facts which his reading of Burckhardt and other travelers taught him to anticipate.

The boy Mohammed offered the promised hospitality and was his cicerone for the visits. The Ka'abah required immediate attention for Burton had much to see. After circumambulating the entire shrine he and his companions rammed their way through a crowd of beggars and pilgrims to kiss the Black Stone (Burton 1893: vol. 2: 169).

> After thus reaching the stone, despite popular indignation testified by impatient shouts, we monopolised the use of it for at least ten minutes. Whilst kissing it and rubbing hands and forehead upon it I narrowly observed it, and came away persuaded that it is an aerolite.

There then follows a petrological discourse on the opinions recorded by other pilgrims of the stone's composition.

This was the most perfect desecration of Burton's entire pilgrimage. Outwardly an Arab greedily venerating the holy object he was in fact an Englishman bent upon telling what category of minerals could be invoked over the stone. One is the same as the other, but Burton's readers were bound to think his approach more respectable than that of the Arabs.

On his next visit to the Ka'abah, after other duties, he finished his reduction of the place to positive analyses. But an old fear loomed. This time Burton sought access to the cubicle of the Ka'abah; this was only granted after an inquisition by the attendants in charge. Burton had not been subjected to this kind of evaluation for a while, but he satisfied the questioners with his background and was given leave. Once inside he found the place a metaphor of his real condition (Burton 1893: vol. 2: 207-08).

> I will not deny that, looking at the windowless walls, the officials at the door, and the crowd of excited fanatics below—
>
> 'And the place death considering who I was,'
>
> my feelings were of the trapped rat description, acknowledged by the famous nephew of his uncle Perez. This did not, however, prevent my carefully observing the scene during our long prayers, and making a rough plan with a pencil upon my white Ihram.

The same turn from thoughts of terror, quite acute in the infidel who had traspessed upon the holiest precincts of Islam, with a quote from Byron, to the sang-froid of recording the state of the pavement and walls, the texture of the curtain. No orthodox Muslim of Burton's time, visiting there, would have bothered with such things but he might have tried, as Burton did later, to procur a sample of the cloth that covered the Ka'abah.

Nothing, Burton says in a sweeping sentence, is so simple as the interior of the Ka'abah. The stark plan which he copied under such risk lies on the page of his book in evidence. The material nature of the place and the shiver it gave him are the complement of his message; a few prayers said and he was done with it all. He was not gifted with responsiveness to the genuine pilgrims, or with a talent for seeing that the *magnum mysterium* of the Ka'abah lay in the simplicity of the setting. The architectural muteness was destined to be filled by the believer. As Burton notes, "all pilgrims do not enter the Ka'abah."

> Those who tread the hallowed floor are bound, among many other things, never again to walk barefooted, to take up fire with the fingers, or tell lies. Most really conscientious men cannot afford the luxuries of slippers, tongs and truth.

This is a folk-wise generalization that earns a nod from everyone but speaks part truth. Pilgrims surely had these restictions in mind when they did not enter, but they were also carrying the emptiness of the Ka'abah one step further in not seeing it at all—a mystery remained at the center of their faith. Burton, bent on literal exactitude, did not grasp the individual sentiments that consecrated the unprepossessing visible space.

The episode in the Ka'abah brings Burton's shallowness into focus. Burton's adventures, his resolute exploring and his Dickensian sketches of human beings in society are delectable, but the reason and experience of the pilgrim are absent. From reading Burton one must take it for granted that all pilgrims are high-blown fanatics without any inkling of what his contemporaries would call "religious sentiment." He forgot, as Chaucer never did, that in the midst of their manias and confusions pilgrims are all clinging to something they assume to be a common faith. Outside of a feeling for poetry Burton was not willing to allow the Arabs any deep emotional nature. His description of the pilgrimage is correct in its information but devoid of true empathy—and this distorts the information.

Since this is not a study of the pilgrimage but of Burton's disguise and his experience within it the substance ends here. After Mecca he returned to Egypt via Jedda. Only one incident deserves a mention. While he was on the boat to Cairo he spotted some acquaintances from the India service and wore his Muslim robes to deceive them. Only this time he disclosed his identity and the men saw coming forth from the shell of a miserable Arab Richard Burton, or "Ruffian Dick" as they called him.

Burton was a truly successful impostor and it would be denying him credit truly his to say that he was anything but a great explorer. The term "explorer" must, however, be redefined here to cover the social and cultural worlds. Burton traversed his share of unmapped ground, but his flooding rivers, mountain passes and steaming jungles were all in the lives of other men and in the realms of custom through which they were joined. His risks on this terrain were as great as any pioneer, as the *Personal Narrative* shows.

His traveling and exploring were the reflex of his alienation from the society and culture of his fellow English. He rejected his nation's conventions which preserving in high degree its values, hence his paradoxical longing for the company of Englishmen while his disguise had succeeded in deceiving both English and natives. The disguise was the expedient of social exploration and the materialization of his rejection of the typical English life. He had, after all, failed as an East India officer and as a writer, and he saw in this failure an inability to fit into English society at home or abroad. Yet he succeeded as a Muslim where he was deficient as an Englishman, and won the desideratum of a hajji's robes. Returning to India where he would rejoin his regiment (the entire pilgrimage was accomplished on leave) he wore the robes and turban but did not pretend to be a Muslim. He was an English hajji, a proper Englishman because he had been the very image of a pious Muslim without being absented from his English self.

He rapidly composed the *Personal Narrative* in Cairo and Bombay sending it on to his London publisher but not himself returning to England where his exploits were known and much praised. The wanderer was firm upon him; again in his disguise he explored Somaliland in Africa and penetrated the "forbidden city" of Harar. But he had outgrown the disguise. The affronts he met were too great to tolerate as a white-skinned hajji, a Turk the Somali thought, and he revealed himself to the ruler of Harar as an Englishman. He capitalized on his personal danger from fanatics even more than in Arabia for he was an Englishman unmasked in a xenophobic city— perhaps the plight of all English in their colonial enterprises.

After his "first footsteps in East Africa" Burton's stature as an explorer was certified. He was assimilated into English society in the marginal class of foreign adventurers and was now able to raise financing for large expeditions, the unlucky search for the source of the Nile, and find a readership for his descriptions even of regular tours, his jaunt across North America. He abandoned disguise entirely and explicitly. In his book on the Mormon "kingdom" of Utah he gazed with his usual sardonic wit on the career of the Mormon Prophet Joseph Smith. Sham and disguise, he said, have no ability to alter the course of human events but, pesonally, there is (Burton 1968: 452)

> the hourly pleasure taken by some minds in finessing through life,
> in concealing their real selves from the eyes of others, and in
> playing a part till by habit it becomes a nature.

Disguise itself had given way to a devilish ambiguity about disguise. Burton, soon Sir Richard Burton and Her Brittanic Majesty's Consul in Damascus, was satisfied at least with the ambiguity.

Burton was not unusual in disguising himself among the Arabs—many of his contemporaries did likewise—but he was out of the ordinary in proclaiming his disguise. In a way his entire journey was a perfection of that disguise, which was complete in his being a *hajji*. Other travelers were far more reticent about owning up to the use of masquerade; in their writings the edge of uneasiness always so close to Burton's flesh is abstracted and evaded. The implications of disguise, metaphoric and actual, are not directly evident, but the response to certain situations among the Arabs and other Near Eastern peoples has elements of similarity between Burton and otherwise vastly dissimilar contemporaries, similarity which can only be ascribed to the conditioning of British culture.

A good example of a traveler-in-disguise "vastly dissimilar" to Burton is Robert Curzon, self-avowed bibliomaniac, hunter after illuminated manuscripts in the monasteries of the Levant and reluctant heir to Gilbertian title of Baron Zouche. Curzon was a member of a small body of British connoisseurs who had the means to pursue their taste for hand-printed books by collecting in the wilds of Egypt and Ethiopia. It was, of course, a polite form of pillage; but one cannot be stern with Curzon for very long. He was earnest in his credo that the books he purchased from the often cunning monks were thus rescued from disintegration in the moldy vaults of the monasteries, and he was generous with the fruits of his labors, as the Coptic manuscript collection of the British Museum attests.

The disparity between Curzon and Burton is plain even from the motives for writing down his experiences. Years after he had returned from his manuscript-hunting he chanced to be leafing through some of his prizes alone in his country-house when the thought came to him that the "scenes and recollections" of the chase would be well set down. The unpretentious volume that was born from this inspiration is suffused with the atmosphere of that aristocratic vocation, the hunt: Curzon trails his quarry across the desert, up the sides of unscalable mountains and into the depths of monastery cellars. His dickering with the monks, ingratiating himself with the abbots, vignettes of monastery politics are as engaging as anything in travel literature; his trip over the mountains of Albania under the protection of (unknown to him) notorious bandits, is a classic in the annals of good-natured naivete.

Visits to Monasteries in the Levant contains only offhand signals of its author's disguise, and alludes to his comprehensive knowledge of Near Eastern languages and literatures strictly in his evaluation of manuscripts, which he could read better than the monks in some places. The allusions are engrossing (1850:142).

> As I was desirous of seeing the shrine of the heads of Hassan and Hussein in the mosque of Hassan En, a place of peculiar sanctity in Cairo, into which no Christian had been admitted, the Pasha sent a chaoush with me, who concealed the head of his staff in his clothes, to be ready, in case it had been discovered that I was not a Mohamedan, to protect me from the fury of the devotees, who would probably have torn to pieces any unbeliever who intruded into the temple of the sons of Ali.

This passage is dropped in the middle of a section on the officers of the Pasha and is intended to illustrate the functions of the chaoush, "the same as those of a chamberlain with us." Curzon was obviously in disguise but more than a little jittery about treading where no Christian had before him; the Sultan's officer, his badge of authority veiled not to advertise the uniqueness of this party, was Curzon's safe conduct were the populace aroused by the sort of solecism which Burton sometimes feared. He gives no sequel; presumably the masses did not descend upon them, for if they did it is doubtful that the chaoush would have afforded much protection.

An expanse of personal experience is writ small in these few sentences; Curzon did not hope to be passed as a Muslim; he trembled over being decried as a *non*-Muslim. Seventeen years later Burton visited the Hasanayn and the neighboring Azhar Mosques (where Burckhardt was reputedly beheaded) and found them "remarkable for nothing save ugliness," though granting the Hasanayn stateliness. He epitomizes the religious and educational activities of the Azhar Mosque categorically; his analytic eye was cast over the precincts without special protection and without trepidation. His disguise effected confidence enough in Cairo. This is not to say that Curzon was cowardly; he simply was not engaging in the positive act of disguise, just the negative act of notice evasion, and he substituted the chaoush for assertiveness he did not have. The will to power is common to both men, Burton's in the form of scientific self-perfection, Curzon's in the form of government protection obtained through British influence upon the Pasha.

Normally Curzon did not go about in full disguise; he seems only to have worn Arab costume for the comfort, and allowed himself to be known as a Frank. The Frankish habit of writing and sketching was no great threat to his well-being since he practiced it openly among people who were amused rather than antagonized-by contrast to Burton's Bedouin (1850: 213).

Some of the Copts, whose curiosity appeared to be insatiable, had followed us to these quarries, for the mere pleasure of staring at us. One of them, observing me make a sketch, came and peeped over my shoulder. 'This Frank,' said he to his friends, 'has got a book that eats all these stones, and our monastery besides.' 'Ah!' said the other, 'I suppose there are no stones in his country, so he wants to take some of ours away to show his countrymen what fine things we have here in Egypt; there is no place like Egypt, after all. Mashallah!'

The real contrast is not between the intolerance of the Bedouin against the affability of the Copts; it is between the stupidity and ignorance Burton professes to find among people who cannot tell English letters when they see them and the quaint chauvinism of Copts conferring among themselves about why these Franks sketch even the stones of the quarry. Burton and Curzon each chose people who reflected his own temperament; the kind of humanity they found in Bedouin or Copts was the humanity they had gone among these people to locate. They might have seen it in themselves or among their fellow countrymen but it never would have appeared so small and deviant as removed into others.

Curzon's Arabesque is rounded out in an incident which curves into another in Burton so closely that they both seem variants of the same tale (1850: 237).

It was curious to observe the different effect which our approach to Jerusalem had upon the various persons who composed our party. A Christian pilgrim, who had joined us on the road, fell down upon his knees and kissed the holy ground; two others embraced each other, and congratulated themselves that they had lived to see Jerusalem. As for us Franks, we sat bolt upright on our horses, and stared and said nothing; whilst around us the more natural children of the East wept for joy, and, as in the army of the Crusaders, the word Jerusalem! Jerusalem! was repeated from mouth to mouth; but we, who consider ourselves civilized and superior beings, repressed our emotions; we were above showing that we participated in the feelings of our barbarous companions. As for myself, I would have gotten off my horse and walked barefooted toward the gate, as some did, if I had dared: but I was in fear of being laughed at for my absurdity, and therefore sat fast in my saddle. At last I blew my nose, pressing the sharp edge of my Arab stirrups on the lank sides of my poor weary jade, I rode on slowly towards the Bethlehem gate.

The risk of facile comparison with Burton is greater here than before, but it is striking that Curzon could not bring himself to concert with the

Christians before Jerusalem while Burton could unaffectedly join Muslims singing the praises of Medina. The main restraint on Curzon—the censorious looks of his English companions—was not applicable to Burton and in fact Curzon's wording implies that he regretted not having the *freedom* of the simpler, uncivilized Christians who were free to give vent to emotions which he honestly felt. The detritus of the noble savage mentality circulates in this passage, among the much realer sentimentalism which Curzon apprehended was the sole uplift his Christianity could provide on the borders of the holiest city. He avoided the condescension which the nobel savage theme normally implied, and deplored his own subservience to convention and the rule of proprieties.

But Burton, a wild man in the mind of his colleagues, would under the same circumstances probably have acted the same way as Curzon, unless exhibitionism dictated otherwise. One of the reasons for his escape to Arabia (and everywhere else he escaped to) was extricating himself from the lumber of convention that weighted him more heavily than most people. His *Personal Narrative* was a drama of escape which made him a hero when it was read but would have made him into a renegade had he acted that way with other Englishmen around. There is evidence that though he flaunted his foreign perversions he did not invite the label of renegade any more than Curzon did; both men were in the same cultural mainstream, punctilious Englishman while "in society."

This contrast of styles within the same ambient milieu bespeaks the nature of British cultural identity, and shows how disguise (and refusal to disguise) were both defined within the same larger field of culture. The personal style of Burton as of Curzon is backlighted by that brilliant source, and disguise appears as one person's method for being in his own way identical to someone who did not practice disguise so utterly. British Arabesque patterns are each of a kind when inspected piecemeal and up close, but congeal into sameness when looked upon as whole patterns.

References

Brodie, Fawn.
    1971 *The Devil Drives*. Harmondsworth, Middlesex: Penguin.

Burton, Richard.
    1893 *Personal Narrative of a Pilgrimage to Al-Madinah and Mecca*. 2 v. London: Tylson and Edwards.

    1968 *The City of the Saints and Across the Rocky Mountains to California*. ed. by Fawn Brodie. New York: Knopf.

Curzon, Robert.
    1850 *Visits to Monasteries in the Levant*. London: John Murray.

Kiernan, R. H.
    1937 *The Unveiling of Arabia*. London: Harrap.

Charles Doughty
from Doughty's *Travels in Arabia Deserta*

VIII

British Arabesque:
Doughty and Lawrence

In the Preface to the third edition of the *Personal Narrative* (1879) Richard Burton rushed to defend his predecessor in the disguised pilgrim tradition, Ludovico Varthema, against the preacherly arraignment instituted by G.P. Badger. Badger, the Government Chaplain in the Presidency of Bombay and a stay-at-home Arabist, had edited a scholarly translation of Varthema's *Travels*, and being who he was, used the Introduction as a lectern (Burton 1893: xxvii).

> This is not the place to discuss the morality of an act involving the deliberate and voluntary denial of what a man holds to be truth in a matter so sacred as that of Religion. Such a violation of conscience is not justafiable by the end which the renegade (!) may have in view, however abstractedly praiseworthy it may be; and even granting that his demerit should be gauged by the amount of knowledge which he possesses of what is truth and what is false, the conclusion is inevitable, that nothing short of utter ignorance of the precepts of his faith, or a conscientious disbelief in them, can fairly relieve the Christian, who conforms to Islamism without a corresponding persuasion of its verity, of the deserved odium all honest men attach to apostasy and hypocrisy.

The exclamation point after the "renegade" was not in the original but was interpolated by Burton in quoting the paragraph as a banner of his own pain; the word he had done most to avoid was pinned upon Varthema and, by extension (Burton could not ignore the drift of the words) upon himself.

In a strict sense Badger was correct; by the ethical standards of the Anglican Church, a creed was a constant and could not be feigned. One only was a Christian or a Muslim or a Buddhist when one held to the outward identity under all circumstances. Otherwise the rituals were shame, theology a fiction and the martyr just fools killed for no reason. Badger was not unreasonable, he was just narrow in his reason.

Burton's was the latitudinarian response (Burton 1893: vol. 1: xxi).

> The reply to this tirade is simply, 'Judge not; especially when you are ignorant of the case you are judging.' Perhaps also the writer may ask himself, Is it right for those to cast stones who dwell in a tenement not devoid of fragility.

Burton had mellowed with age; his former headlong blistering attack was reduced to innuendo. His disavowal of disguise, established some years earlier, did not extend itself to the admission that he was wrong in ever falsifying his religion, and he defended his famous expedient rather weakly. It was a matter of knowing the urgency of not appearing Christian in certain parts of Arabia.

Badger, inexperienced in travel, could be shrugged off with no more than that reason, however another critic of disguise was not so simply dismissed. William Gifford Palgrave, "the author of *A Year's Journey through Central and Eastern Arabia*" was not, following the etiquette of literary invective, named by Burton in the combative Preface, but Burton's animadversions warranted a heartier reply than Badger's. In the midst of his narrative, published first in 1865, Palgrave paused to point his finger at Burton (without actually mentioning Burton's name) by the assertion that "passing oneself off for a wandering Darweesh, as some European explorers have attempted to do in the East, is for many reasons a very bad plan" (Palgrave 1865: vol. 1: 258-59).

> To feign a religion which the adventurer himself does not believe, to perform with scrupulous exactitude as of the highest and holiest import, practices which he inwardly ridicules and which he intends upon his return to hold up to the ridicule of others, to turn for weeks and months together the most sacred and awful bearings of man towards his Creator into a deliberate and truthless mummery, not to mention other and yet darker touches— all this seems hardly compatible with the character of a European gentleman, let alone that of a Christian.

This was a heady draught for Burton to swallow because it repeated Badger's blame in the company of yet harsher criticism, even with an infusion of acid for Burton's by then infamous studies of sexual customs ("yet darker touches").

Palgrave, as Burton and every other reader of exploration literature knew, dwelt in the most fragile of tenements to be casting stones. He was an English Protestant of Jewish descent (his brother compiled the celebrated *Golden Anthology* that bears the family name) who turned Jesuit and proselytized for his new church in Arabia disguised as a Syrian doctor.

Plagrave played the Moslem among Moslems, but later somersaulted back to Protestantism once again—as complete a tour of religions that could be accomplished West of China. Naturally Burton enshrined each of Palgrave's faults in a nugget of venemous prose.

Besides various kinds of hypocrisy, Burton urged against his opponent the charge of lying. The *Year's Journey* is a glowing, heroic account of desert adventure more brightly toned that Burton's most romantic pages. Palgrave crossed scorched earth, frolicked with the Bedouin and faced down a scheming native prince, ever forthright as a true Englishman should be. This truth to a respected stereotype was too faithfully exhibited in Palgrave: his adventures were outrageous and his facts, when checked, unreliable. As information about Central Arabia became more lucid Palgrave's reputation as a poseur grew; a twentieth century explorer, St. John Philby (1922: vol. 2: 117-56), took the time to trace numbers of his geographical claims down to their false origins. Recent attempts at rehabilitation remain unconvincing (e.g. Allan 1972:169; 266-68). Burton, in his reply, cited Palgrave as "little worthy of trust."

More's the pity, because Palgrave's travel was the last strange flower of the tradition that had bloomed in Burton. The conflict between the two men—chastising each other but not themselves for voyaging in disguise—indicates the disrepute into which disguised travel had fallen late in the century, and the moral qualms it caused its most confident practitioners. Disguised travel did not end because of Palgrave's falsehoods; his falsehoods were the sign of its decadence. Truth, quite simply, should not wear a mask.

Straightforward, unmasked visitors to Central Arabia had existed alongside their stealthy brothers from early times. The crude Elizabethan Tom Coryat bragged that he had denounced the Prophet himself from atop a minaret and went unharmed; a troop of Crusaders enlivened by the prospect of gold clustering Mohammed's tomb, landed on the coast and approached within one mile of Medina before being routed. There were many other stories of good Christians miraculously preserved after revealing themselves as Christians in the center of Mecca. By arms or by religion an infidel could survive in Arabia.

Even in the years when disguise was the dominant conveyance and proven effective by Badia y Leblich and Burckhardt an ingenuous traveler like Captain G. Foster Sadlier (1866) could bumble across the entire peninsula dressed as an East India Captain and not speaking a snatch of Arabic or giving a damn about the natives. Sadlier, whose journal was not published in its entirety until fifty years after he had made this crossing, the first ever by a European, had been sent on a crackpot mission by the East India Company and was passed from shaykh to shaykh like a ticking bomb from east coast to west. Colonel Pelly (1866), Palgrave's prime detractor, wore Arab dress when he caravaned through Central Arabia in 1865, but he left no doubt he was a Christian and making astronomical observations. The evidence that disguise was needless mingled with the sentiment that it was immoral.

The condemnation of disguise was more an alteration in style; it was one arm of culture change that led to prizing the blatant, procalamatory presence among other peoples over the guileful adaptation. The changeover from colonialism to imperialism was its political-economic manifestation: the British colonies were unified into the British Empire which rationalized all nations under the British flag into one administrative whole. Evangelical missionaries brought their own violent assertions to a hostile world and anthropology, a newly invented scholarly discipline, classified cultures according to their advancement toward an apex filled by Victorian England. The culture which had demonstrated its supremacy in conquest need not go masked among lesser peoples. But if disguise was everything from traitorious to unscientific the absence of disguise and the announcement of identity to the natives was not the shout of victory for Christ and nation that theorists thought. There were possibilities for pathos and dark victory that no one ever would have imagined, or having imagined would have wished for himself.

Charles Doughty was one of those distant beings who never seems quite aware of what he is doing in the world until the end, when the plan is unfolded and there appears completed a pattern invisible to all but him. Doughty was a gifted wanderer, more a wanderer than an explorer, and his success lay in the quality of his wandering, not the land it covered. Doughty's book, *Travels in Arabia Deserts* was printed in 1888 but the journey it describes had taken place twelve years earlier. The book was nine years in the writing, a journey longer than the one it recounted. Few bought the book and still fewer read it through to the end; only a small company of discerning reviewers expressed any satisfaction with the 900 pages of print interspersed with maps and dry sketches. Thickness, however was not the only reason for the book's limited readership: Doughty had set out to reinvigorate English prose by reinventing Elizabethan English. To many readers this preoccupation made *Arabia Deserta* seem involuted, a trial for an attention span already taxed by length.

Doughty wrote at the time of many similar experiments, notably those of the Pre-Raphealite Brotherhood, in returning to a pre-modernistic inspiration, before machines, before newspapers, before linear perspective. But while William Morris and others trying to write medieval epics ended by creating stilted, dull pieces Doughty fashioned a new prose most eminently suited to the experience it described.

Doughty idolized Chaucer (not exactly an Elizabethan) and Spenser. His prose does bear a formal relationship to the language of Elizabeth's reign (Taylor 1939), the first great age of discovery in England. However Doughty speaks of discoveries no longer commercial; his New World has no plantations and gold mines. It is more barren and personal, like the landfall of a Drake or a Raleigh grown introspective. *Arabia Deserta* is the discovery of Arabia as a species of self.

Doughty's one sentence on the "art of travel" announces him to the tradition of undisguised travel with marvelous brevity (Doughty 1921: vol. 1: 95).

> As for me who write, I pray that nothing be looked for in this book but the seeing of a hungry man and the telling of a most weary man; for the rest the sun made me an Arab, but never warped me to Orientalism.

"Orientalism," in Doughty's archaic usage means absorption into the ways and beliefs of the Orient. Burton and Palgrave were Orientalists: Doughty was not. Throughout his two years voyaging in Arabia he pretended to Islam only once, and this to his mortification. He never mimed the act of conversion. He was always a Nasrani, Christian and British, in the face of whatever threats or insults were offered: "It is lawful to kill a Nasrani;" "With a Nasrani who need keep any law?" (Hogarth 1904: 272). Rarely did he bend enough to cease declaring his identity in the open. He was a voice in the desert.

Doughty attired himself in Arab dress and spent some time among Syrian Christians—but even then he remembered how little good a native Christian identity had done those Christians during the Damascus massacre of 1860. The massacre haunts the pages of *Arabia Deserta*, and image of Doughty's susceptibility and the Muslim's intolerance.

Despite the Arab dress Doughty did everything he could to evince his participation in all the significances of the term "Nasrany." He joined the pilgrimage caravan in Damascus, bringing with him his copy of the *Canterbury Tales* but he found his companions not nearly so rollicking as

Chaucer's merry souls as they neared the holy area and realized there was an infidel in their midst. Deposited at an outpost he taxed the officials there with requests to be taken to archaeological monuments so that he might make copies of inaccessible rock inscriptions. He made no secret about taking notes or sketching; he "did nothing covertly" (Doughty 1921: vol. 1: 33n). Thus he was buffeted among the villages, an outlander and an infidel who had no respect for Islam, that "thin-witted religion."

Arabia Deserta is a long jeremiad of the varying ill-treatments and accidental agonies Doughty met on his erratic wanderings. He was robbed, pummeled, stoned, ridiculed and abandoned. Towns expelled him and the Bedouins only laughed, saying he belonged to a religion of murderers and miscreants whose members deserved no better than death. Only on occasion did he find a deliverer (Doughty 1921: vol. 1: 198).

> In an evening I had wandered to the oasis side; there was a flock of village children soon assembling with swords and bats followed my heels, hooting 'O Nasrany! O Nasrany!' and braving about the kafir and cutting crosses in the sand before me, they spitefully defiled them, shouting a villainous carol, 'We have eaten rice with the halib (milk) and have made water upon the salib (cross).' The knavish boys followed ever with hue and cry, as it were in driving some uncouth beast before them, until I came again to the town's end, where they began to stone me. There was a boy among the troop of dastardly children who ever stoutly resisted the rest, and cursed with all his might the fathers that begat them, with great tears in his eyes he walked backward opposing himself to them, as if he would shelter me with his childish body; so I said, 'See, children this is weled el-halal (son of righteousness), think rather to be such, every one of you, than to despise the stranger, the stranger is the guest of Ullah.'

The advancing hoard of children restrained by only one higher spirit is Doughty's Arabia. If it be objected that there is no terror in the mockery of children Doughty's precise situation should be recalled; he was alone and defenseless. He carried a carbine and a revolver but he gave the carbine away and was loath even to show the revolver except in the direst emergency. His tormenters were unruly and passionate in even the pettiest matters, and would begin a murderous assault for no reason. An officer in a border fort beat Doughty and offered him the supreme insult of plucking his beard because he imagined Doughty had slighted him in a distribution of gifts. Children they may have been, but with the horrifying destructive power of children unrestrained.

Unrestrained, but also unmotivated. Up against Doughty's reiterated complaints of violence are his equally frequent denunciations of the torpor of intellect afflicting those of the Faith: "the Moslem religion ever makes numbness and death in some part of human understanding" (Doughty 1921: vol. 2: 21). The common religion fails to unite the Arabs into any effective political entity nor can it encourage them, as they slumber under its narcotic, to meditate on ways of easing their hard existances. The merchants and Prince of a plague-ridden village did not even contemplate importing direly-needed grain from a distance and the people died by multitudes.

The counterpoint of irrational excitement with mindless stagnation forms the main theme of Islam as Doughty perceived it. Yet Islam is not alone; it resonates with other religions of the world (Doughty 1921: vol. 2: 389-400).

> The Moslem, as the rest of mankind, are nearly irrational in matters of faith; and they may hardly stumble in a religion which is so conformable to human nature.

Islam is only truer to human madness than other religions, but cannot finally be separated from them in general. Doughty's sufferings were the work of other humans, not of Muslims.

The malignant tendencies of Islam and of religions as a whole are not inevitable—it is the Parable of the Sower once again (Doughty 1921: vol. 1: 599).

> Religion, when she possesses the better mind is amiable, humane and liberal; but corrupting in envious disgraced natures needs must give up some baneful breath of self-loving and fanaticism, which passes among them for laudable fruit of the spirit that is of their religious patriotism.

As he found many of the latter type in Arabia, he also found a few of the "amiable, humane and liberal" former. He found some who doubted the more absurd propositions of Islam and taught a revelation joining together Judaism, Christianity and Islam (Doughty 1921: vol. 2: 400).

Among those Arabs given to a "lower" practice of Islam Doughty found a "natural religion"; hospitality. He often relied on the rights accorded guests and he lasted because of this reliance, though he was sometimes even denied the least welcome in households that held the rules of hospitality inapplicable to a Nasrany. Many hosts felt an extreme conflict between religion and hospitality, and this drew an almost comic path for Doughty as he solicited aid. Doors were closed and then opened; food was offered to him and then pulled from his grasp. The few men who mastered their compunctions and helped Doughty became his benefactors in large ways. He remembered these people long after his departure and attempted to compensate them for their trouble.

Mostly, however, he had to deal with brutal everyday men. His manner invited martyrdom; he eschewed violence of any sort and even answered curses with reasoned arguments, accepting whatever pain and discomfort the Arabs were minded to bestow upon him. When a thieving sherif, who had deprived him of all his belongings, strode up to him Doughty realized that

> there was but a moment, I must slay him or render the weapon, my only defence, and my life would be at the discretion of these wretches.

He handed the man his revolver and suffered the lesser consequences. At any point the negligent blows of the Arabs could have become deliberate and their anger lethal but, through luck and sheer courage, Doughty was never fatally hurt. His lack of disguise or pretense made him susceptible, a potential martyr to the things he openly professed, but it also conferred upon him an afflatus of righteousness. Khalil, the "Righteous one" or the "honest one," was that name commonly given, and by which he was known among the Arabs years after his wanderings were over. In this character he was simultaneously an outcast and a saint—people had no categories for compassing him—the mistreatment and hospitality resulting from their genuine ambivalence about the man.

Doughty's displacement, his incipient martyrdom, was not the result of religious fervor. At no time did he try to convert anyone to Christianity. If they were bad Muslims they would also have been bad Christians. Doughty only defended Christianity when it was affronted, and then as an element in his own identity. His label of Nasrany was a cultural complex of which Christianity was but a part. It was equally important that he was British, and most important that he was not a Muslim. His voyage was indeed a voyage of negation wherein all that he was stood in denial of all that surrounded him, and reached out selectively for the few common elements.

The strange appeal of the book's every episode lies precisely in this struggle of an individual will against the juggernaut of an entire nation which he has aroused by his posture of defiance. His curiosity animated him to slightly to move this way and that, but mostly his motion was obliged by the gargantuan (and stupid) energy of what his essence itself opened. By letting everything be known and not restricting it consciously to religion Doughty in himself brought British civilization into direct confrontation with Arab civilization. His martyrdom was potentially a cultural martyrdom; his fascination that of the lone individual against the aggressive corporate whole.

D.G. Hogarth, Doughty's biographer and major historian of the exploration of Arabis, analyses the "spiritual atmosphere" of *Arabia Deserta* (Hogarth 1928: 133).

> The transcendental effect is not produced by the glorification of Kahlil and certainly not by any suggestion of saintliness, but by the extraordinary impression conveyed of the plight of a being of a higher world who finds himself alone in another and lower. His incongruity, with its constant menace of peril, is accentuated by his mind's solitary continuous and implacable reaction against the religious and social system which had him at its mercy. As has been said already his was a racial and cultural rather than a religious reaction.

Everyman and Christian of *Pilgrim's Progress* combined in Doughty to make a modern hero whose personhood is tied up in the "higher world," that is, the superior values of English civilization. Constancy more than the things to which he was constant held him together and gave him the presence of mind to experience life in Arabia as an outsider and to gather a vast potpourri of information on Arabia while seeming to be at variance with every fact he collected. Although Hogarth is correct in denying that Doughty's was a religious reaction the total effect of his existence among the Arabs has an ethical tenor which might cause a superficial reader of *Arabia Deserta* to conclude that Doughty is merely a Christian. This is, of course, reinforced by the inclining of the entire narrative toward some future martyrdom, but Christianity or even religion is too crude a rubric to write over Doughty's experience as an undisguised greater being.

Late in the narrative, for example, Doughty was in the town of Boreyda accompanied by his protector Kahtany Jeyber, "the mild Bedouin nature sweetened in him his Kahtany fanaticism." (Doughty, unlike other travelers, found the Bedouin preferable to the townspeople.) Jeyber was reproached for bringing the Nasrany out into the streets of the town, and placed Doughty in his quarters to wait their departure the next day (Doughty 1921: vol. 2: 529).

> The mid-day heat was come; and he went to slumber in a further part of the waste building. I had reposed some while, in my chamber, when a creaking of the old door, painted in vermillion,

startled me!—and a sluttish young woman entered. I asked wherefore had she broken my rest? Her answer was like some old biblical talk; *Tekhalliny anem fi hothnak?* 'Suffer me to sleep in thy bosom.' —Who could have sent this lurid quean? the Arabs are the basest of enemies—hoped they to find an occasion to accuse the Nasrany? But the kind damsel was not daunted; for when I chided she stood to rate the stranger; saying with the loathy voice of misery, 'Aha! the cursed Nasrany! and I was about to be slain, by faithful men; that were in the way, sent from the Emir, to do it! and I might not now escape them.' —I rose and put this baggage forth, and fastened the door. —But I wondered at her words, and mused that only in the name of Religion (O Chimaera of human self-love, malice and fear!) I was fallen daily into such mischiefs, in Arabia. —Now Jeyber came again from napping; and his harem related to him the adventure: Jebyer left us saying he must go to the Emir.

A rock-throwing mob stormed Jeyber's gate and was only held back by the eloquence of his two wives ("the hareem") until Jeyber returned with the Emir's command for the mob to desist.

This misadventure reads like a temptation of St. Anthony from a medieval hagiography. Only the saint defeated his tempters and dispersed or converted them, or he suffered. Doughty, cowering behind a barred door too believably to be saint-like, depended upon a pair of sequestered women to quell the fanatics outside, blamed in himself the mischiefs done in the name of devotion. Even the temptation itself was transposed into the devious campaign against the Nasrany and was not just an invitation to unclean indulgence. The spiritual and ethical problems of the saints only appear to afflict Doughty, and his resolution alone appears to be saintly. His peril, although constantly on the verge of translation into religious metaphor, was religious on the surface and by resemblance to religious motifs—and in no other way. Doughty's antagonism was to the social groupings of the Arabs and their collective symbols (which include Islam). Doughty's rejection of the Arabs was much more elaborate than their rejection of him, for they only saw (according to Doughty) his disdain for Islam while *he* skipped over the crust of their society repulsed by a myriad of evils.

Doughty conceived of Arab society as a Darwinian state, "nature red in tooth and claw," in Tennyson's common phrase, though he never would have accepted that characterization himself. The amount of fighting, murder, thieving and chaotic upheaval in the daily life of the Arabs is appalling, even more so when they reached out for Doughty. His anti-disguise was a refusal to be sunk into this pit of animal passions ungoverned by laws justly applied. His vision is prevented only by his sensitivity to the many facets of Arab humanity from degenerating into a colonial adminstrator's view of a society needing civilized intervention to set it straight on the road to progress. But Doughty was never that elementary about himself or the people who loved and hated him.

An overview of Doughty's wanderings cannot have a form any more specific than an assessment of his manner of *not* being one of "*them*," whereas the study of a disguised explorer must concentrate on the particulars of his disguise. To follow Doughty through each bend and course of his movement is purposeless; the "sketch map itinerarium" he drew for his speech before the Royal Geographic Society is laced with curving lines which must lead to distraction any systematic mind. Lined up against explorers with goals Doughty seems arbitrary. For the reader of *Arabia Deserta* the absence of goals and the intrigue of details is its greatest virtue. Precipitating from this seemingly amorphous whole is the consistent negating of Arab culture which invests Doughty with the equal but opposite affirmation of being ideally British against the detestible environment.

Had Doughty died by Arab hands perhaps he would have become a lesser version of General Gordon, the martyr of Khartoum, who died battling insurgent Muslims after disdaining an offer of clemency in exchange for his apostasy to Islam. Gordon, beseiged by the troops of the Mahdi, the millinarian leader of the Muslims in West Africa, publicly trampled the *ihram* which the leader had sent to him (Strachey 1918: 285). Doughty was writing *Arabia Deserta* during these events and may well have reflected on the similarities between his experience and the trials of Gordon as reported in the newspapers.

The personal similarity between Gordon and Doughty lay in a common ground of intractability, Gordon's defended from a fortress and Doughty's from within himself. Gordon had organized and led a Manchu army against the T'ai P'ing rebels in China, and during that time had a conversion experience which left him a firmer but idiosyncratic Christian. Other than the epithet "Chinese Gordon" he was poorly rewarded for his services; back in England he spent years of obscurity studying his Bible and supervising the construction of coastal forts. The summons of the Egyptian government to administer the Sudan and defeat the Mahdist rebels drew him out of retirement; on the way to Egypt he detoured to ramble about the Holy Land and see the sacred places on an informal pilgrimage. His downfall at Khartoum—he had held out longer than anyone predicted—was the result of misfortune and the refusal of Gladstone's government to send relief.

Chapter Eight: Doughty and Lawrence | 133

Posthumously he became the paragon of heroic resistance to inferior and savage peoples in the name of civilization; the expedition finally sent was an army of vengeance that mowed down the rebels with the newly invented needle guns.

Doughty was ignored as thoroughly as Gordon on his return to Britain and he was never apotheosized. The ideal cultural identity which he shook in the faces of the Muslims was in itself just an oddment to the British; it never came to the dramatic fruition of slaughter by savages. The various royal societies scorned him and his erratic travels; he could find no one to publish or even accept as a donation his arduously accumulated copies of Semitic rock inscriptions. These snubs did not forestall his treasured project, the composition of *Arabia Deserta*. After years of slow labor the book emerged. Publisher after publisher rejected it as poorly written. When Cambridge University Press finally did accept the book it took years of chaffering and revisions before it saw the light. Doughty valued his style much more than his matter and blocked the reasonable suggestions of editors (Fairley 1927: 11). The Press lost a considerable sum on the original printing.

Arabia Deserta had a slightly better career in the literary world than its author had in Arabia. Many reviewers liked the adventures but deplored the heavy-footed language. Richard Burton, miffed at Doughty's omitting to mention him even once (he mentioned Burckhardt twice), took *Arabia Deserta* apart over the course of two articles in *The Academy* (Hogarth 1928: 129). Doughty's stubborn Nasrany annoyed Burton: Doughty, he said, had earned his hardships. Burton himself had escaped from the Damascus massacre (along with Lady Jane Digby) by slipping off in disguise; why did Doughty question its value?

Another luminary of Arabia exploration, Wilfred Scawen Blunt, was praiseful. He and his wife Anne had covered part of Doughty's route not long after Kahlil had left the country and Anne Blunt had published a slow-paced account of their journey in 1881. They went in Arab dress but not professing Islam and, apart from a few "unpleasant" incidents were undisturbed while making their observations and setting down their notes, which the Arabs by then considered a type of British ritual (Blunt 1881). Blunt saw Doughty's Arabia and he heard the voice of his prose, calling *Arabia Deserta* "the best prose work of the XIXth century." Burne-Jones, the painter; Robert Bridges, the Poet Laureate and William Morris all read the book with delight. They were, however, a small company against the gray crowd that ignored Doughty.

Doughty lived out his remaining years (he died in 1922) authoring epic poetry and drama, a continuation of the speech of the primordial Briton who uttered *Arabia Deserta*. *The Dawn in Britain* was the national history of this Briton stretching from the Celt and Romans across a long history. Much more followed this, texts for the self as embodiment of the nation, but Doughty's contribution to British Arabesque was over. The ends unwound elsewhere.

Late in 1909 Doughty received a letter from a young Oxford undergraduate who had consulted him the previous year about a walking tour of Crusade fortresses in northern Syria. Returned from the tour and full of desert impressions Thomas Edward Lawrence requested a meeting with the great man with a nervous dignity that must have made Doughty smile ever so slightly. "I am more interested in the author of *Dawn in Britain* and *Arabia Deserta* than in the traveller;" and this gained him an immediate interview. Lawrence's don at Oxford, D.G. Hogarth, also wrote to Doughty recommending the young enthusiast as a "boy of extraordinary aptitude for archaeology and a wandering life among the Arabs," and as one who "knows *Arabia Deserta* nearly by heart" (Hogarth 1928: 174-75).

There is no record of this noteworthy meeting but one imagines that the Golden Bough of Arabia exploration was delivered up to Lawrence. He was corresponding regularly with his new mentor directly thereafter and on his spying-archaeology mission to Carchemish he ran errands for Doughty, carried letters and presents to Arabs who had befriended him years earlier. Lawrence contemplated a sojourn into Central Arabia; he discussed with Hogarth and Doughty a plan to accompany the Soleyb, a tribe of itinerant tinkers, to the Center. The tribes' unwholesome practice of ingesting raw gazelle meat discouraged him, and they did not venture far enough into the Peninsula. When Lawrence did enter Arabia it was under far different circumstances.

The legend of T. E. Lawrence is still in its formative stages. He was a war hero in the desert struggle against the Axis-aligned Turks by grace of his own bravery and good newspaper coverage. Then he was neglected and debunked until the publication of *The Seven Pillars of Wisdom* cast him as a literary hero. He locked himself into obscurity thenceforth released only by his death. Since then almost every year introduces a new Lawrence. He is a ready blank into which our aspirations can be filled and found to be adventures. When, if, Lawrence is ever mythified Doughty and the whole tradition of the British Arabesque will play no part in it. Few biographers

Chapter Eight: Doughty and Lawrence | 135

acknowledge Lawrence's debt to Doughty (or even know who Doughty was) and none acknowledge Lawrence as the most visible representative of post-disguise travel in Arabia.

Had World War I never ordered a military task for Lawrence he might well have gone on a Doughty-like exploration of Central Arabia and died or survived with the same air of quiet martyrdom. In joining Feisal, son of the Sherif of Mecca and military leader of the Arab insurgents against Turkish rule, Lawrence was given an opportunity to exercise the nationalistic component of his heritage from Doughty, bringing the Arabs to a higher level of their own national consciousness through his own sacrifice. Lawrence knew at the beginning of the campaign that the Arabs had been sold short by the British over the conference table and were made promises never to be delivered. But he acted like Doughty too, more a child of the ideals of the nation and its culture than the tool of sordid politicians. The moral cleanliness Lawrence found in the desert permitted him to act in response to a British tradition divorced from the councils of diplomacy and policy while serving them in a very practical way. Lawrence perpetuated a British presence in Arabia which had been maintained by individuals in a tradition that changed in tune with British culture but was not before now strongly influenced by policy.

Lawrence himself was quite consciously an emissary of Doughty's strain of the tradition. He called *Arabia Deserta* "a Bible of sorts," meaning that it was a vedemecum for action as well as belief. He clearly etched out the divergence of Doughty's rejection from Burton's adaptation and with a moral flourish set his mark alongside his master's pattern (Lawrence in Doughty 1921:17).

> We export two chief kinds of Englishmen, who in foreign parts divide themselves into two opposed classes. Some feel deeply the influence of native people, and try to adjust themselves to fit its atmosphere and spirit. To fit them selves modestly into the picture they suppress all in them that would be discordant with local habits and colors. They imitate the native as far as possible, and so avoid friction in their daily life. However they cannot avoid the consequences of imitation, a hollow, worthless thing. They are like the people but not of the people, and their half-perceptible differences give them a sham influence often greater than their merit. They urge the people among whom they live into strange, unnatural courses by imitating them so well that they are imitated back again. The other class of Englishman is the larger class. In the same circumstances of life they reinforce their character by memories of the life they have left. In reaction against their foreign surroundings they take refuge in the England

that was theirs. They assert their aloofness, their immunity, all the more vividly for their loneliness and weakness. They impress the peoples among whom they live by reaction, by giving them an example of the complete Englishman, of the foreigner intact.

Lawrence, writing these words in his Introduction to the 1921 reissue of *Arabia Deserta*, had ample reason to include himself along with Doughty, the Blunts and Gertrude Bell in the "second cleaner class." He was penning *Seven Pillars* at this time and could not help but reflect on the conformity of his activities to the standard he lauded. Lawrence, however, inherited Doughty's austere integrity with a twist and a hit; already in this passage it is apparent that he regards "imitation" as an alternative rather than as an unqualified blasphemy. Lawrence's very different personality and the state of war that lashed his Arabia prevented him from being so clean as Doughty. Doughty was a watcher and a recipient, Lawrence had to be an actor and an influence.

Lawrence was cognizant of the paradox of fulfilling his mission to rouse and guide (and civilize) the Arabs from within Doughty's pilgrim character (Lawrence 1966: 4).

> I was sent to these Arabs a stranger, unable to think their thoughts or subscribe their beliefs, but charged by duty to lead them forward and to develop to the highest any movement of theirs profitable to England in her war. If I could not assume their character I could at least conceal my own and pass among them without evident friction, neither a discord nor a critic but an unnoticed influence.

Via Doughty, Lawrence seems to have come round to Burton, to an integration of both approaches. Lawrence's "concealment" was not that elementary, nor was it ever as totally self-confident as Burton's disguise or Doughty's rejection of disguise. The discord between the two alternatives subjected Lawrence to a personal paradox which martyred him more fully than Doughty and filled out in him the pattern of a modern anti-hero just traced in his predecessor.

The Seven Pillars of Wisdom is the crystal of this paradox, but unstable: the penetrating blow shatters it. Less destructively entered are the "twenty-seven articles" published in the *Arab Bulletin*, August 20, 1917, wherein Lawrence generates the rationale of his concealment as a series of numbered imperatives (Garnett 1963: 136-42).

Chapter Eight: Doughty and Lawrence | 137

He begins conditionally. If you are to succeed among the Bedouin (and them alone, these rules are not for other groups) these articles are his "personal conclusions." However,

> Handling Hejaz Arabs is an art, not a science, with exceptions and
> no obvious rules.

The technical form of rules conveys the discipline of an art, mostly a theatrical art.

Handling the Arabs, says Lawrence, comes from knowing how to handle oneself. Lawrence is a gradualist in both, as the first article shows.

> Go easy for the first few weeks....When you have reached the inner
> circle in a tribe you can do as you please with yourself and them.

The strongest motif is asserted at the outset; behavior is calculated only in terms of its effects on the Arabs. The central position, a location from which behavior can be effective, must be reached before right behavior can happen. It is a voyage across wild terrain to a social place where each gesture has an influence.

Lawrence mandates knowledge as the primary perfection: "Learn all you can about your Ashraf and Bedu." The person mastering this social knowledge must begin a program of self-effacement in the simultaneous practice of command and obscurity. Sufficient knowledge will lead to a state where the advisor merges himself with the Arab commander while building the commander up to a size which can accommodate a concealed advisor. This connection, which is Lawrence's chief method of tying himself to the "inner circle," has the character of symbiosis, though an uncharitable critic might call it parasitism. Optimum attachment consists of absorbing the outward self into the Arab leader's figure while personal (that is, national) intentions and the will to pursue them remain intact. Far from being totally submerged in the Arab leader Lawrence's intentions become the leader's intentions. The interloper reshapes both himself and his Arab leader into instruments of the same will.

The Sherif is cultivated as the best natural agent for leading the Arabs and as the most easily touched link in the leadership chain. He must be respected and honored. "Call your Sherif Sidi (My Lord) in public and in private" for this will put to rest uncertainty about who is in charge. There is a real danger that the Sherif will, whatever the precaution, realize that his advisor is a manipulator, or that his followers will fall off when they see their leader controlled by an outsider. Suppressing the appearance of guidance while exercising it with the utmost refinement is the advisor's most binding duty.

This means avoiding what the Arabs consider unmistakable postures of command and acting in all things outside the circle of notice. Never lay hands on an Arab; do not try to do too much of anything with your own hands. These and a number of other prohibitions check "natural" inclinations of British officers when harried by the inertia of Arabs. Lawrence counsels consistency with the role adopted next to the Sherif. There is only a narrow band of liberty for the release of prejudices and preferences, and this fluctuates according to principles that seem irrational.

After these negative injunctions keeping the British self from disrupting an Arab situation Lawrence issues a positive article. The agent should "wear an Arab headcloth when with a tribe." This is better than a hat which the tribesmen will ridicule. But having allowed the headband Lawrence balks. Instead of suggesting full Arab disguise (or dress) as might be expected from Lawrence of Arabia, the Lawrence of the article decrees that "Disguise is not advisable." Having moved in close to the Sherif, identified the areas of assimilation and swept away offensive mannerisms Lawrence is willing to don an Arab headband and be quit of the matter.

Lawrence's injunction against disguise derives from his concern for safety. There is danger in loosely worn Arab dress.

> They make no special allowances for you when you dress like them. Breaches of etiquette not charged against a foreigner are not condoned to you in Arab clothes. You will be like an actor in a foreign theater, playing a part day and night, and for an anxious stake.

Lawrence's apothegm on dress divides the undisguised advisor from the disguised one; on the one side you are free and on the other you are under duress. Dress imitates committment to a way of life and a responsibility never to deviate from the native custom. So far Lawrence keeps to Doughty's prescription but at the nexus of his firmest adherence he changes abruptly.

> Complete success, which is when the Arabs forget your strangeness and speak naturally before you, counting you as one of themselves, is perhaps only attainable in character; while half-success (all that most of us strive for; the other costs too much) is easier to win in British things, and you yourself will last longer, physically and mentally, in the comfort they mean. Also then the Turks will not hang you, when you are caught.

Chapter Eight: Doughty and Lawrence | 139

Lawrence's message, deeply tinged with irony, is that disguise is only for superior beings who are able to endure the anguish of the costume, the "skin of Nessus" as Burton himself described it. Suffering is the price for fitting successfully into the ranks of the Arabs because the adoption of "character" makes you into a living contradiction. Only bitterly unique individuals can bring the character to a useful life among the Arabs, individuals like Lawrence who can make the sacrifices. He treats the performance as role-playing ("like something in a play," said Lady Hester Stanhope) but without the frivolity associated with the theater. Lawrence's adaptation is total self-abandonment into the world of discipline to be bound by the arbitrary customs and the minds of other men.

The final articles reiterate that this agonizingly perfected character does not mean assimilation into the Arabs as one of them. Lawrence advises unremitting study and emulation of Arab ways for those who have chosen the difficult path but never releasing his identity to the Arabs. The dress and customs are his own personal attributes worn as a Britisher recognized by the Arabs as one of them. Advising against costume while he himself entered it with dramatic effect singles Lawrence out from the rest of humanity, elevates him in his pain.

Lawrence was by nature a confined and punished being. His confinement and punishment needed a ritual shape and a grand finale. The articles are a rehearsal for sacrifice which, though they are addressed to "you" can only be completed in Lawrence himself. Lawrence is the victim who has suffered for you, even as you, among the Arabs. All that he recommends is turned on its head in himself, bound over as a hostage to complete success.

After it was all over and Lawrence had tried to live as Doughty did in the desert, endured privation and torture worse than torture to serve his nation more actively than Doughty ever could after that Lawrence was not quite sure he had obeyed his own rules.

> In my case the efforts for these years to live in the dress of Arabs, and imitate their mental foundation, quitted me of my English self, and let me look at the West and its conventions with new eyes: they destroyed it all for me. At the same time I could not sincerely take on the Arab skin; it was affectation only... Sometimes these selves would converge in the void, and then madness was very near, as I could believe it would be near the man who could see things through the veils at once of two customs, two educations, two environments.

The external facts of disguise or non-disguise, assimilation or aloofness were not kept external for Lawrence as they were for Burton and Doughty. By taking the disguise he wore seriously, as an extension of an inner self which must also exist, Lawrence smashed the barrier which generations of travelers had raised between the Arab shell and the British interior. The two selves raced in a maddening whirlpool, never halting to be integrated into any one consistent self. Lawrence demonstrated in himself what the previous travelers had feared when they masked as Arabs but held Arab civilization in contempt. The protective assertion of British civilization was abandoned by Lawrence. He had no place either in Arabia or England.

At the end of the war Lawrence's inability to forge any commonwealth among the Arab tribes he had brought together for fighting left him stranded. R.V.C. Bodley saw him at the Paris Peace Conference and described his unhappy existence there (Bodley 1944: 4).

> He moped as he wandered about the gilded halls of the Hotel Majestic in his faded Arab head-dress while out of the corners of their eyes the Colonel Blimps watched him suspiciously. 'There goes that crazy chap, Lawrence,' they muttered into their mustaches. 'Gone native, you know, actually slept in the same tent as a Bedouin. Damned disgrace. What's England coming to!' And Lawrence had no comeback. He had done something which would live through the ages as one of the world's great stories of adventure. He did not realize this himself. If he had he would not have mentioned it. He never mentioned anything he had done.

When Bodley in a conversation with Lawrence mentioned that he was planning a career in politics Lawrence grew furious and shouted, "Go and live with the Arabs!" which Bodley did for some seven years, adopting Islam and the nomad life completely. While he was in the Sahara (then the more stylish desert) Bodley savored the freedom and cleanliness of the nomad life, and when he returned to England with an Arab friend he found himself classed as a "freak" along with Lady Hester Stanhope and Richard Burton. The distinctions which Lawrence clearly perceived between Englishman and Arab were lost to Bodley. The superficial "adventure story" aspect of Lawrence's life in Arabia was all that Bodley gathered from the sad spectacle of a man who was out of his element at a Peace Conference. Lawrence's isolation was to Bodley nothing but heroic-and this heroic challenge to convention Bodley chose to copy.

The remainder of Lawrence's life could be interpreted in the same way: he was too unconventional to live in British society. Yet contrary to expectations he never returned to Arabia, for he was no more at home there than in England, and perhaps even less welcome. *The Seven Pillars of Wisdom*, though intended as Lawrence's *Arabia Deserta*, did not win the approval of Doughty, who saw an early version before his death. The adventure in the book made it more popular than any other book in the British Arabesque traditions and resulted in the dismissal, common in popular literature, of the book's context. The deeds of Lawrence of Arabia, primped and perfumed, became the stuff of an Arabian romance not very different from the fantasies of earlier times. Lawrence's finding his place as the last practitioner of undisguised travel, and his anguish at seeking simultaneously the complete success of disguise are lost in the oversimplification and most people assume, as Bodley did, that harking to the command "live with the Arabs" is as simple as going into the desert and falling in with a wandering tribe. No amount of retrospective reshuffling can alter the inside of Lawrence's experience and the cultural past to which he was responding.

He only lasted a brief while longer. As if bowing to the legend he hid himself in the R.A.F. training program and there as a Corporal Shaw he underwent a new schedule of transforming discipline. As before he wrote of the discipline but was no longer buoyed by the adventure. Lawrence ended on a country road, a martyr to his motorcycle and two awkward delivery boys. The growth of the British Arabesque pattern stopped then, at the innermost tip of the tightest spiral.

References

Blunt, Anne.
> 1881 *A Pilgrimage to Nejd*. 2 v. London: John Murray.

Bodley, R. V. C.
> 1944 *Wind in the Sahara*. New York: Coward-McCann.

Doughty, Charles.
> 1921 *Travels in Arabia Deserta*. 2 v. in one. New York: Random House.

Fairley, Barker.
> 1927 *Charles M. Doughty*. London: Cape.

Hogarth, D. G.
1904 *The Penetration of Arabia.* New York: Stoker.
1928 *Charles M. Doughty.* Oxford: Oxford University Press.

Lawrence, T. E.
1966 *The Seven Pillars of Wisdom.* New York: Doubleday.

Palgrave, William Gifford.
1865 *Personal Narrative of a Year's Journey through Central and Eastern Arabia.* 2 v. London.

Pelly, Lewis.
1866 *Journal of a Journey from Persia to India...Also Report on a Journey to the Wahabee Capital of Riyadh in Central Arabia.* Bombay.

Philby, H. St. John.
1922 *The Heart of Arabia.* 2 v. London: Constable and Co.

Sadlier, G. Foster.
1866 *Diary of a Journey Across Arabia.* Bombay.

Strachey, Lytton.
1918 "The Death of General Gordon." In *Eminent Victorians.* London: Chatto and Windus.

Taylor, Watt.
1939 *Doughty's English.* Society for Pure English Tract No. 51. Oxford: Clarendon Press.

Varthema, Ludovico di.
1863 *The Travels of Ludovico di Varthema.* Hakluyt Society, 1st Series, vol 32. London: Hakluyt Society.

A NARRATIVE OF THE LIFE OF

MRS. MARY JEMISON,

Who was taken by a party of French and Indians at Marsh Creek, in Pennsylvania, in the year 1755, and carried down the Ohio River when only 12 years of age, and who continued to reside with the Indians and follow their manner of living 78 years, until the time of her death, which took place at the Seneca Reservation, near Buffalo, N. Y. in 1833 at the advanced age of 90 years.

CONTAINING

An account of the Murder of her Father's Family, who were taken captives at the same time with herself, but who were Tomahawked and Scalped the second night of their captivity; her Marriage to two Indian Chiefs, with whom she lived many years, and both of whom she followed to the grave

TO WHICH IS ADDED

An account of her conversion to the Christian Religion a few months before her death:—Her ideas of the Christian Religion and views of herself previous to her conversion, as related by the Rev. Mr. Wright, Minister at the Seneca Reservation, where she died.

ROCHESTER:

PRINTED BY MLLER & BUTTERFIELD.

1840.

FAC-SIMILE OF TITLE-PAGE OF 1840 EDITION

(Actual size)

Facsimile of the title page of James Seaver's *The Life of Mary Jemison.*

IX

The Captivity of Mary Jemison

Every civilization has boundaries and beyond its boundaries savages, convenient beings who set in relief all that is best and worst about the civilized state. When America stood on the boundary of European civilization the savages were Indians, that extremely varied group of peoples explorers had mistaken for inhabitants of the East Indies. These Indians were rude, uncouth and fascinating, fit to decorate a court or be aped in a masquerade. The American settlers could not be so light-hearted. Any moment the savages might fall upon them as they hacked their orderly trails into the American wilderness.

The Indians had the contempt born of small familiarity. They were black sorcerers in league with the Devil or degenerates who had lost the word of God and never heard the message of Christ. Some thought they might be redeemed from their savagery if educated and read the Gospel in their own tongues. But civilization had to be imposed on them with more energy than the colonists generally had.

There were a few Indians, like Squanto the savior of the Puritans, who dwelt in white men's houses and begged to be taken up into white men's heaven when they died. Boundary paths lead in both directions and in the earliest years more white people traveled to the Indians than the other way around. It was the custom of the savages to abduct children or young adults in the place of their own people who had been killed by the whites. This humane custom gave evidence of mercy which the whites were loathe to concede and of a far more upsetting fact: the captives sometimes preferred to remain with their captors even when openly ransomed. Those who were brought back to civilization after long residence among the Indians were often difficult to acclimate and might flee back. Civilization was not always the most attractive, or the most potent possibility.

Captivity was unnerving to the individual captive and to society at large, for it posited just this conclusion, that savage life is no worse than civilized life and may replace it in civilized people. The literary genre known as captivity narratives was a reassurance that the Indians after all were demons and white captives longed for rescue (Washburn 1974). Though arising from Old World prototypes it was the first genre to develop in the

New World. Its line of development was independent of the captivity experiences themselves, and threaded through a history of purposes from religious tracts, to anti-Indian propoganda to dime novel plots (Pierce 1947).

Cabeza de Vaca's 1542 *Relación* heads off the form's long history in both North and South America. Not until 1591 did the English captivity narrative come into being with Job Hortop's *The Travails of an Englishman*. The more famous initiation was, however, in Captain John Smith's *Generall History* of 1642. The Captain modified portions of his *True Relation* (1608) to tell readers how the comely maid Pocohontas threw herself down upon the recumbent Captain's neck to preserve him from the beheading her father, the sachem Powhatan, had commanded. Mary Rowlandson's *Soveraignty and Goodness of God* printed in Boston, 1682 (Vanderbeets 1973) was the first full length captivity and perenially one of the most popular. Mrs. Rowlandson, a grown woman with children, was abducted into the forest by marauders under the command of "King Philip" (Metacomet), a Wampanoag Indian who, though baptized, had run afoul of settlers over land rights and reverted to his foul warlike habits. The captivity lasted only eleven weeks and did not transform Mary Rowlandson into anything other than a more virulent despiser of Indians. When she put her tribulations on paper a few years after her redemption she alternated between pouring invective upon the Indians and citing Bible quotes as evidence of God's higher plan in causing the savages to test the resilience of her faith. The second edition was crowned with an exhortatory sermon by Mary's husband, the Reverend Rowlandson, which illuminated the divine purpose in Mary's captivity. The pamphlet saw well over thirty editions in America and in England, probably because it made religion exciting.

The long train of eighteenth century captives were, like Mary, sinners in the hands of an angry God and his lusting Indians. Soon the publishers and printers of the new nation realized that the market for stories of captives was not exclusively due to the meditation on the wondrous scheme of God's grace they offered. Fiction was disreputable; the captivity was a means of marketing thrills under the label of tract or documentary. Captivity narrative style moved toward highly melodramatic tales in which torture and the reactions to torture proceeded improvingly amid atmospheric details of Indian tribal rites. Professional writers took over the composition of the narratives and finally fabricated whole narratives to slake the thirst for horrors.

In 1720 W.R. Chetwood, envying the success of Daniel DeFoe's fictitious pirate foisted *The Voyages, Dangerous Adventures and Imminent Escapes of Captain Richard Falconer* upon a receptive American public, with the Indians as the chief menace. Charles Brockden Brown led his somnambulist Evan Huntley into a Gothic Indian captivity. But popular taste was best appeased by the discomfiture of beautiful young women in the forest wilds and it was they more than males who held literary attention. Unfortunate, pining Maria Kittle shared the distress of many a sister captive when she was spirited away from her murdered family by a band of lubricious Indian warriors who luckily never had their way with her.

Women were the most sentimentally appropriate captives. Frail, swooning they nonetheless struggled pathetically against the Indian captor. Every white person knew the unbridled lust of the savage regarding the defenseless white woman. She was civilization incarnate, what the savage longed to possess for reasons unclear to his dim mind, yet a thing which he would cruelly destroy in his efforts to embrace. In Gothic, sentimental and romatic dress the woman laments as the towering black form engulfs her (vid. illustration in Barber 1816).

The double-dealing, vengeful Huron Indian Magua of James Fenimore Cooper's *The Last of the Mohicans* is the dreadful stereotype of the Indian captor. Magua connives to get Cora under his power as retribution for her father's humiliating him, but he is far from insensitive to her charms. He will have his love and his revenge at any cost, and only relinquishes both when he and his captive die as pursuing rescuers near. Cooper was unusual in giving his Indians any slight complexity of emotion; he was true to the captivity genre illustrating the hopelessness of a white woman left to the Indians.

Cooper's rewriting of the typical female captivity uncovers an element of sexual fantasy in these tales. The envisioned onslaught of a bestial rapist who crushes his victim in one furious act is a common fantasy. The female captivity narrative was one of the few literary forms in the eighteenth and nineteenth centuries expressing sexual fears and desires that showed weakly and with excessive apparatus in the novels of seduction, *Clarissa* and the rest. The Indians were not gentlemen; they were devoid of the soft words and shadowy promises of the polished rakes.

In the Indian captivity narrative Americans experienced an ever-present cultural anxiety, the savages, in the potent emotional language of assault, resistance and mastery. The reality of the Indian threat, the abruptness of the attack and its overwhelming destructiveness made the Indians a metaphor of sexual aggressiveness and their assault on white women a vehicle for sexual imaginings. The Indians are the psychosexual savage in every person; their victims, especially when seen as women, are the psychosexual victims in everyone. This is not just a Freudian cliche. There are political, social and cultural messages simultaneously borne, given impact and deferred by the emotional language of the captivity narrative. The narrative tremulously tells of attack and concessions between Indians and whites which symbolize a range of conflicts that filled (and fill) American life. They permit these immediate conflicts to be displaced from the here and now to a time and place of Indian savagery. Mastering and being mastered can be obscenely enjoyed in a realm of feeling very like, but far distant from, everyday life. Captivity novels are pornography of the past.

On November 19, 1823 Dr. James Seaver of Pembroke, New York sat carefully writing down the words of an aged woman. Dr. Seaver, disadvantaged in his practice by crippling rheumatism, had been induced by some friends to record the life story of this woman, Mary Jemison, an Indian captive who had passed her entire lifetime among the savages. Seaver was enthusiastic. He had already achieved some local reputation as an epigrammist; his humorous little poems "expressing lofty sentiments and touching human foibles" were often found in upper New York state literary magazines. Mary Jemison was his first biographical subject and she merited clinical attention.

Mary was illiterate, hence Seaver had complete sway over the written form of her narrative. In his preface to *The Life of Mary Jemison* Seaver voiced his conception of biography (Seaver 1942: iii).

> ... a telescope of life through which we can see the extremes and
> excesses of the varied properties of the human heart.

The "extremes and excesses" are a source of precepts about human nature. Dr. Seaver's biography is of the approved moralistic type which exemplified the rewards of goodness and the punishment of evil in the lives of paragons and blackguards.

Mary Jemison is an excellent opportunity for indulging in both sides of this characterology; Seaver found the fruits of both good and evil abounding in her life. The dynamics of her change from white woman into Indian were still more exemplary, for in them Seaver found a model of "what changes may be effected in the animal and mental constitution of man." Dr. Seaver's physic trained him to observe human beings across the Cartesian division into mind and body and to consider acute anomalies in mind or body as revelation of the physical or intellectual fabric. Mary's case history enlightened him to the frightening changes which occur in any human being subjected to degenerate conditions.

Medicine in Seaver's time was overwhelmingly environmental; malaria was thought the result of exposure to swamp air; madness was induced by living in morally imperfect surroundings. Thus Seaver believed that civilization weakened and then evaporated from a civilized person placed in savage surroundings. This had been a moral axiom—the pervasiveness of sin in sinful surroundings—ever since the Middle Ages; with Seaver it became both medical and anthropological. Mary Jemison was not unique: she was an example of what might happen to any of us under the same circumstances given our malleable bodies and minds.

Seaver was quite aware of the form the captivity narrative should take, but he injected his own conception of a captive life into its framework. His insight was not psychologistic; he was not concerned with Mary's inner life. He probably did not believe she had one. For him the captivity narrative showed the permanence of certain moral traits *in spite of* the mandate for change in the environment. Mary Jemison's *Life* was Seaver's instrument for vindicating the ancient belief in fixed personal quality over the mutability imposed by differing environments. In other words the captivity narrative form called up in Seaver the opposite of his stated medical bias. The underlying epigram is that good and evil will out whatever the situation, though the situation may hamper or abet the consequences. Mary's captivity attracted Seaver because the Indians seemed to bring out moral character uncompromisingly.

Mary Jemison tells the story in the first person. Her "I" is full of others, the doctor, the captivity conventions, and it invites many more. For the time being Seaver swears to report everything as he heard it; for any errors he begs the reader to blame Mary Jemison.

Mary Jemison was a child of nine when the Indians (the tribe is not specified) descended upon her family's farm near Philadelphia. The savages were accompanied by several Frenchmen, this being the time of the French and Indian Wars. After killing some of the men the Indians carried off Mary, her brothers, sisters, parents and the members of another family who sought refuge with the Jemisons. An engraving from the 1840 edition of the *Life* illustrates the scene as the reader should see it (Seaver 1840: Title Page). The figures are in a clearing before a pioneer cabin. A few trees stand over the house. A scalped corpse lies stiff on one side amid the tree stumps of the clearing. Laden with booty, the Indians are driving their prisoners before them. They are like animated plants with crowns of leaflike feathers sprouting from the centers of their heads. The men are being led off at gunpoint by the two Frenchmen; Mrs. Jemison and her brood of children, miniature adults, march before tomahawk carrying warriors at center. Some of the figures, Indians and a few children, look out toward the viewer as though he had just happened upon the scene and startled them into rigidity. Mary, clad in a white gown, is escorted off to the right by a savage who clasps her right hand while she buries her face in her left. This is the typical scene of captivity par excellence: the dark savage grinning his moon-face out of the page, grasps the sorrowing white woman and possesses her.

The Indians moved quickly. At the first rest stop Mary and a small boy from the other family were given a pair of moccasins and separated from the others, who were massacred and scalped with devilish efficiency. The Indians drove further into the forest. At the next stop Mary was obliged to watch them cure and stretch her family's scalps. Mary endured all this passively; the remote scientific attitude grafted on to her by Seaver ever allowed her to notice particulars of the flight, how the Indians distracted pursuit by setting the grass where they had tread back in place. Seaver's Mary studied the occasions of her own grief.

The Indians dyed her face and hair red then incarcerated her in a French fort. Her brief and painless imprisonment there ended when she was handed over to a pair of squaws. They transported her past more tableaux of Indian cruelty, scalps, arms and legs and heads hanging from trees, to a Seneca Indian village, where she was dressed in new, Indian clothes. The unusual behavior of the Indians had her convinced she was designated for new atrocities until she was reassured that all was part of an adoption ritual; she was the replacement for the brother of the two squaws who had died on the battlefield. The affability of her two Indian sisters calmed her. Provided with an Indian name (Dikewamis, Seaver 1942: 137; or Deh-ga-wa-mis, 832-33) and given chores in her sisters' house, she settled into the routines of life.

Seaver does not provide Mary Jemison with a complex narrative of personal adjustment to Indian life. Her adaptation spans only paragraphs, and includes nothing but the symptoms of her conformity to Indian customs (Seaver 1942: 39).

> Being now settled and provided with a home, I was employed in nursing the children, and doing light work in the house. Occasionally I was sent out with Indian hunters, when they went

but a short distance, to help them carry their game. My situation was easy; I had no particular hardships to endure.

She was still not reconciled to her captivity, however easy her work, and she maintained the English language in secret.

> My sisters would not allow me to speak English in their hearing; but remembering the charge that my dear mother gave me at the time I left her, whenever I chanced to be alone I made a business of repeating my prayer, catechism, or something I had learned in order that I might not forget my own language.

Although she lost the ability to read English, and never regained it at least she could still speak English when Seaver set down her life because of this rote practice.

After one year of this existence, doing light work in the house and repeating catechism on the sly, Mary was taken to Fort Pitt where they were negotiating a treaty with the British, and shown to the white people there. The captors obviously thought that Mary was sufficiently adapted to their customs and would not want to return—but they were mistaken in her case. The two sisters had just spirited Mary away from their camp when a party came out of the Fort to rescue Mary (Seaver 1942: 43).

> Although I had then been with the Indians something over a year, and had become considerably habituated to their mode of living, and attached to my sisters, the sight of white people who could speak English inspired me with an unspeakable anxiety to go home with them and share in the blessings of civilization. My sudden departure and escape from them, seemed like a second captivity, and for a long time I brooded the thoughts of my miserable situation with almost as much sorrow and dejection as I had done those of my first sufferings. Time, the destroyer of every affection, wore away me unpleasant feelings, and I became as contented as before.

The vicissitudes of Mary's adaptation can be summarized in the aphoristic final line of this paragraph. The trend is toward losing all former usages and becoming content with her lot in life. But already conflicting concepts arise; the environment surrounds and permeates Mary but an inner light fueled by civilization (English) and religion (the catechism) will not be extinguished. Mary's salvation against the onslaught of total savagery is assured; she will remain civilized though Indian in form.

Her marriage to a Delaware Indian, Sheninjee, was decisive. Her sisters insisted and "with a great deal of reluctance" Mary wed the Delaware according to the Indian custom, which was very much at variance with the white idea of a correct ceremony. Shininjee was a good man but for all that an Indian, yet again "strange as it may seem, I loved him!" A child was born and died leaving her almost fatally ill, then, the narrative moving swiftly here, three years later another child was born, and survived. Mary was tied to the Indians (Seaver 1942: 55).

> I had then been with the Indians four summers and four winters, and had become so far accustomed to their mode of living, habits and dispositions, that my anxiety to get away, to be set at liberty, and leave them, had almost subsided. With them was my home; my family was there, and there I had many friends to whom I was warmly attached in consideration of the favors, affection and friendship with which they had uniformly treated me, from the time of my adoption. Our labor was not severe; and that of one year was exactly similar, in almost every respect, to that of the others, without that endless variety that is to be observed in the common labor of white people. Notwithstanding the Indian women have all the fuel and bread to procure, and the cooking to perform, their task is probably not harder than that of the white woman, who have those article provided for them; and their cares certainly not half as numerous, nor as great.

Mary was truly habituated to the life of the Indians, that is, she joined them in the community of labor and in carrying out those functions which would be expected of a woman in any situation. The cyclical schedule of agriculture made life uniform and predictable from one year to the next; Mary was mesmerised by the usual events. The main characteristic of her womanly temperament, placidity and contentment, matched the calm setting of her life with Sheninjee on the Ohio. Only the canker of memory wormed into her happiness, not the memory of once being a white but of the family she had lost. Her loyalty to her Indian family presupposed an innate virtue which will not allow her to abandon all thoughts of her mother, father and siblings. Her Indian family substituted for them to an extent—she named her first son after her father, and they all bore the name Jemison—and she lived as a wife and mother as she might have in a civilized community. With what she had she always came as close as possible to the ideal toward which her inalienable virtue inclined her.

The subject of Indian cruelty adds another dimension to this moral universe. Mary exclaims that the Indians are a kindly, peaceable folk and only indulge in the torture and mutilations for which they are known when they have captured enemies. She herself was lucky to be adopted, since execution was the sole alternative. As she, her husband, her Indian sisters and brothers were traveling up the Muskingum River to visit their mother they came across a party of Shawnee who had murdered several traders and were disfiguring a young white man. Aghast at the sight, Mary pleaded with the Indians to release their prisoner, which they did after a small delay. She was not alone in compassion; her Indian mother (the mother of her sisters) on hearing that one of the sisters wished to attend the execution of men taken in a raid on Fort Niagara delivered an oration against bloodthirstiness and persuaded the sister to remain at home.

Normally the Indians (like Mary) were "content," and refrained from warlike outbursts. The introduction of spiritous liquors, of money and its ills excited them to irrational actions. Wherever civilization reached the Indians it did them no good; they were best left children of nature with no excitant to the atrocities they were capable of performing.

The commencement of a captive redemption program was the start of civilization's corrupting influence on the Indians. Mary felt the brunt of it herself: a Dutchman named John Van Sice chased her so that he might capture her and pocket the redemption money at the Fort. She outran him and concealed herself for several days. The chiefs agreed, on her return, that she would not be taken to the Fort without her own consent but later one of them, and "old King," openly conspired to gain Mary's ransom for himself. Shinenjee, her husband, was away trading (she learned soon after he had died); her "brother" swore that he would kill her before allowing her to be taken. She had become a marketable commodity, endangered among the Indians and unwilling to return to the whites. She hid herself again. The old King, after a perfunctory search of her house, gave up and conducted the captives he had to the Fort.

The Revolutionary War proved an even more severe incursion of white vices. At first the Indians promised the rebels they would stay neutral; the British Commissioners tempted them to reverse their decision and for payment combat the Americans. Venality won the day, and the Indians went to war, though they suffered from the campaign of General Sullivan in their area. Mary had no part in the war itself. She had remarried and given birth to more children. The world was in tatters about her, and the customary quiet of Indian life was undermined by the white men's quarrel. She saw certain people who typified virtues and vices, acting out their ends of the struggle in small dramas. The Indian Little Beard, fighting for the British, secured his own brother, a scout for the Americans, in an ambush and after lecturing him on the profits of war dispatched him with a tomahawk. Another Indian taken at the same time Little Beard released, saying that his war was with

Chapter Nine: Mary Jemison | 153

white men. The warrior Cornplanter invaded a frontier cabin and carried off an old man named John O'Bail. Along the trail Cornplanter faced the captive and pronounced himself O'Bail's son by a squaw, from a dalliance of many years earlier. He treated his father honorably, offering to provide for his old age among the Indians or send him back to the whites as he chose. O'Bail chose to return.

In contrast to this almost Roman nobility among the Indians (with an equally Roman refusal to be swayed by loyalty to kin when greater issues are at stake) the white men whom Mary observed were riddled with moral defects. They entered the Indian environment to release their indecent passions. Ebenezer Allen, a Tory who fled Pennsylvania for some dubious reason after the Revolution, resided on Mary's land, Gardow, near the Genesee River. During the war he had pillaged with the Indians; there was a tale of his entering a cabin at night, decapitating the man and tossing his head to the wife on her bed then bashing their infant's brains out on the door jamb. He left the woman amid this carnage; he regretted the episode later. The Indians along the Genesee had not yet made peace with the Americans so Allen procured some wampum and presented it to the commander of an American fort as a token of peace. This outraged the Indians but they had no recourse but to honor the bogus treaty. Allen went off and returned with some trade items: he planned to use the artificial cessation of hostilities to begin a profitable exchange of goods. Instead he was pursued by the Indians and sought the protection of generous Mary.

The Tory's ruling passion had already been revealed in an adulterous relationship with the squaw of a white man who also lived on Mary's property. When that had a violent conclusion—the woman had to flee to the all-sheltering Mary for refuge from her offended husband—Allen took an Indian woman to wife. Not satisfied with her he married a white woman and brought her home. The narrative then describes the fluctuations in Allen's polygynous household, which reached four wives at one point and never contained fewer than two. He even murdered one woman's aged husband to obtain her for the harem which, Mary interjects, was not devoid of civil strife. Allen discarded the squaw when he moved to a town in Upper Canada and when he died, as a final affront to womankind, he left all his property to only one of his two surviving wives.

As Allen is assigned to the circle of the lustful Simon Gurty, another renegade, belongs with the vengeful. In 1782 Mary's second husband, Hiokatoo, was part of a band that captured part of an American regiment, including its leader Colonel Crawford (Seaver 1942: 109).

Gurty, but a short time before this had been a soldier in the American army, in the same regiment with Crawford; but on account of his not having received the promotion that he expected he became disaffected—swore an eternal war on his countrymen, fled to the Indians and joined them as a leader well qualified to conduct them to where they could satiate their thirst for blood upon the innocent, unoffending and defenceless settlers.

Crawford, who had commanded an American army against the Indians, was condemned to death by burning. As the preparations were being made Crawford addressed the most pitieous pleas to Gurty but was met with unconcern. As the flames rose around the Colonel he entreated Gurty to end his misery with a bullet but the white savage only stood aside with a "demonic smile," declaring that he had waited long for this revenge. Crawford's fellow prisoner, Dr. Night was luckier: he clubbed his guards, scalped them and made his escape. Viciousness engendered viciousness.

After the hostilities were formally ended between the Americans and the Indians the anguish of war was succeeded by the further encroachment of civilization on the Indians' idyll. Land, which was owned by the Indians now by legal titles, enmeshed both Indians and whites in arguments over its possession. Mary was given title to a large tract along the Genesee through the good offices of her brother and of a famous orator, Farmer's Brother, who won the council over to Mary's case against the weighty opposition of Red Jacket. The acreage was eyed by land speculators; Mary's illiteracy and her openhandedness made her as easy mark. A man claiming to be her cousin by a father's brother who had emigrated from Ireland years after her father intruded himself upon her hospitality and by various deceitful methods tricked her into signing over 400 acres of her property, which he sold for a pittance. Following the cousin's departure a lawyer and one of her tenants conspired to deprive her of much more land using as bait her lack of a clear right to citizenship. Not being a citizen she could not own her land free of entailments. At the end of the process Mary was left with a parcel about one mile by two miles—but she was content. The price of the land, whenever it was sold, was by her will to be divided among all members of the Seneca nation, "without any reference to tribes or families." There at least she had the last word.

In the matter of her family, virtue did not hold against the ravages of vice so well. Thomas, her son by Sheninjee, drank heavily and had altercations with John, the eldest son by Hiokatoo. Thomas disapproved of John's having two wives (Seaver 1942: 132).

Chapter Nine: Mary Jemison | 155

> Thomas considered it a violation of good and wholesome rules in society, and tending directly to destroy that friendly social intercourse and love, that ought to be the happy result of matrimony and chastity.

Thomas' catechismal argument against polygamy was probably improved by Seaver's report; John responded only to the censure it contained. Thomas, who became abusive when inebriate, had taunted him with nicknames like "witch," since childhood. He had even raised his tomahawk against Mary and had struck Hiokatoo, who at 103 years of age was not fit to defend himself. One day in 1811 the drunken Thomas found John alone in Mary's house and the two began to dispute. John grappled with his brother, dragged him out the door and murdered him there with a blow to the head. Mary soon afterward returned to find the lifeless body of her son. His death occasioned a moral.

> As he was naturally good natured, and possessed a friendly disposition, he would not have come to so untimely an end, had it not been for his intemperence. He fell a victim to the use of ardent spirits—a poison that will soon exterminate the Indian tribes in this part of the country, and leave their names without root or branch. The thought is melancholy; but no arguments, no examples, however persuasive or impressive, are sufficient to deter an Indian for an hour from taking the potent draught, which he knows will derange his faculties, reduce him to a level with the beasts, or deprive him of his life!

Seaver's conclusion about human nature had a happy example: the savage nature is unchained by alcohol, the environmental factor draws out what is already there.

John was acquitted of any responsibility for the crime by the tribal council; but the community ostracized him. Jesse, Mary's youngest son by Hiokatoo, a carefree, industrious young man who was Mary's favorite became the focus of John's resentment. Again strong drink precipitated the deadly encounter. John, Jesse and their brother-in-law George Chongo were laboring together and drinking. At the end of the day Jesse and Chongo fought with each other and Jesse won, leaving Chongo in a stupor by the road. John pulled a knife and after being provoked by Jesse stabbed him repeatedly. John evaded retribution once again but like Abel (whom he resembles in a way that seems more than incidental) he went marked. A few years later he had a forewarning of his own death; shortly thereafter he was slain in another drunken disagreement.

156 | *Lives Between Cultures*

The vortex of alcoholism and violence having sucked up all three of her sons Mary, 75 years old when John died in 1817 and long since deprived of Hiokatoo, was dependent upon her three daughters, one of whom lived with her husband in Mary's house, the others with their families 80 rods to the north and south. When Seaver interviewed her she had 39 grandchildren and 14 great-grandchildren "all living in the neighborhood of Genesee River, and at Buffalo." With a few valedictory remarks on Mary's fortitude and another tirade on the evils of alcohol the narrator ends his career through Mary's life. That she never succumbed to degeneracy of her circumstances but was constantly afflicted with its results speaks for her unalterable goodness and for the ineradicable evil of others.

Dr. Seaver, his epigrams brought to life in Mary, died four years after the publications of the *Life*, in 1827. Mary still lived, and in 1831 moved to the Buffalo Creek Reservation, where she occupied a miserable hut. The only visitors to leave a record of Mary's last days were the condescending missionary, Reverend Asher Wright and his wife. Mrs. Wright was called to Mary's bedside: Mary, a confirmed pagan and a critic of Christianity, was filled with mortal doubts about not having kept her promise to repeat the catechism made to her condemned mother over 80 years before. She heard the reading of the Scripture and, according to Reverend Wright, "gave as satisfactory evidence of conversion as could reasonably be expected from a person in her circumstances." Mary was always being taken by force.

Mary Jemison's captivity did not end with death. First she was buried beneath a marble slab in the Seneca Mission Burying Ground, near Buffalo. Red Jacket, who had opposed her land grant with all of his eloquence, was buried nearby and the place was called after him. "Remorseless relic hunters" chipped away at Mary's stone; the grave mound collapsed and the "onward march of improvement" was bringing the city of Buffalo close to the spot. Red Jacket's remains were taken away to Forest Lawn Cemetery in Brooklyn. Mary remained in the decaying churchyard at the mercy of her admirers, only a fragment of her marker to tell the spot.

In 1874 her grandson James Shongo directed the exhumation of Mary's body, lest the location be lost completely (*Buffalo Courier* March 10, 1874; Seaver 1942: 232).

> Every piece of the decayed coffin and the minutest particle of its contents, including the earth itself, were reverently and carefully lifted up, commencing at the foot of the grave, and placed in the same relative position in a new coffin; the undertaker using for

this purpose a broad shovel. The new coffin, of solid black walnut, elegantly mounted in silver, rested close beside the grave.

The bones were partially disintegrated, but the cranium and jaw were whole and permitted phreonological conclusions:

> The shape of the chin betokened firmness, and the intellectual and moral faculties, as indicated by the location and size of the various organs of the brain, were largely developed.

And besides these clues of bygone mental prowess some few shreds of Mary's beauty remained in the earth, "a few soft, silken, yellow curls." The residue of her body symbolized the perfect being she once was.

The writer of these lines, Dr. William Pryor Letchworth, listed the rest of the coffin's contents with the slight scent of necrophilia common to Victorian mooning over the beloved dead. He recalled Mrs. Wright's mention of that last "bit of fair white skin" near those last blonde hairs and he imagined the small, well-shaped feet that left but a few delicate bones in Mary's buckskin moccasins. Everything, the broadcloth, the embroidery, the ribbons, was silken and ethereally fine. At the center of the grave was the only hard, definite object: a porcelain bowl with the remains of some food and a wooden spoon which the Indians had given Mary to provision her on the road to the "happy hunting-grounds."

Letchworth was a businessman who making his fortune early in life retired to travel and engage in philanthropy. He had been drawn to the scenic and historical merits of some property along the Genesee, including parts of Mary's former grant and he purchased a large section in 1859. Twelve years later he purchased and moved to his land an Indian Council House which had sheltered Mary during a stop on one of her flights; the next year he sponsored there an Indian Council which brought several of Mary's descendants to the Council House. Thomas Jemison, a grandson, planted a black walnut tree grown from a nut produced by the tree that shaded Mary's grave in Buffalo.

The exhumation of Mary's grave was Letchworth's project, though he fastidiously consulted James Shongo at every step. A new grave had been readied for the remains on Letchworth's grounds; after a brief service inside the Council House the coffin was opened and Thomas Jemison took a lock of his grandmother's hair, then it was enclosed in a stone sarcophagus and interred in its resting place to the north of the Council House, beneath the recently planted walnut tree. On the same day a descendant of Red Jacket planted a black walnut tree to the west of the Council House and a descendant of Captain Brant, a Christianized Indian and the first Native American Freemason, was aided by ex-President Millard Fillmore in planting yet another black walnut, completing whatever directional diagram Letchworth had in mind.

The composition was finished when Letchworth was given a log cabin from the Gardeau Reservation. Constructed by Mary Jemison for one of her daughters the building was threatened with demolition where it stood. Letchworth moved it to his park and situated it on the other side of the grave from the Indian Council House. But there was still one part missing.

In 1910 Letchworth placed on the marble shaft over Mary's grave a bronze statue of the "white woman" carrying her infant daughter. The statue was fashioned by H.K. Bush-Brown, in accordance with "all possible information respecting the personal characteristics of Mary Jemison" obtained by Letchworth over the course of years (Vail in Seaver 1942: 240).

> The features of Mary Jemison were modeled from those of a girl who was of Scotch-Irish ancestry and who was about the same age as Mary Jemison when she arrived at the Genesee. The face of the babe, showing the distinct Indian cast of features, was modeled after a life study of an actual descendant of Mary Jemison. The dress represented in the statue is similar to that worn by Shosonean women and perhaps other western tribes. As Mary Jemison commenced her journey from Ohio she possibly wore a dress of this character.

It was pronounced "historically correct" by Arthur C. Parker, New York State Ethnologist and "as a work of art" it was approved by a committee of National Sculptors Society. Three months after the statue was placed Letchworht died, bequeathing the land and Mary Jemison to the Scenic and Historic Preservation Society as a public park.

Not everyone was able to assemble full-sized structures to fulfill a Jemison dream, but other Jemisonians (as they actually called themselves) could at least tend the words of the *Life*. Mary's history passed through the hands of a line of distinguished editors and accumulated accretions of notes as it went. Ebenezer Mix, who was an "encyclopedia" of land grant lore in the Genesee Valley put Mary's life in the proper cartographic context: Lewis Henry Morgan, authority on the Iroquois and pioneer social evolutionist, appended details on Indian lore and affixed a list of Indian place names. Letchworth edited five editions over a period of thirty-five years bringing together more random bits on the experiences and person of his heroine.

Charles Vail surappended another set of notes and a bibliography of all known editions up to 1918; later editors pasted more on the shrinking body of the *Life* until the 1942 edition, a complete Mary Jemison icon with the bronze statue embossed onto the cover, was published by the Scenic and Historic Preservation Society.

And those who did not pour their time into the *Life* wrote from the sides their own, derivative *Lifes*, wrote novels, poems, romances on the "Golden Squaw," wondered, like Elmer Adler, the most persistent accumulator of "Jemisoniana" about the "persistent reblossoming of Mary Jemison" as if she were finally an Indian fertility spirit of the Corn Mother type. One writer, resenting the long dominance of Rochester-Buffalo in the production of Jemison studies, reminded the world that Mary was captured in Pennsylvania: he issued *The Red Lily of Buchanan Valley* from his White Squaw Publishing Company in Adams City, Pennsylvania. The captivity continues; the captors change.

References

Barber, Eunice.
    1816? *Narrative of the tragical death of Mr. Darius Barber, and his seven children...*

Bleeker, Ann Eliza.
    1797 *The History of Maria Kittle in a Letter to Miss Ten Eyck.*

Calloway, Colin C.
    1989 "Simon Girty: Interpreter and Intermediary." In *Being and Becoming an Indian: Biographical Studies of North American Frontiers.* ed. by James A. Clifton. Chicago: Dorsey. 38-58.

Heard, J. Norman.
    1973 *White into Red.* Metuchen, N. J.: Scarecrow Press.

Panther, Abraham [pseud.].
    1787 *Account of a Beautiful Young Lady who is taken by the Indians and Lived in the Woods Nine Years, and then was Providentially Returned to he Parents...* Middletown, Connecticut.

Pearce, Roy Harvey.
    1947 "The Significance of the Captivity Narrative."*American Literature* 19: 1-20.

    1965 *The Savages of America.* Baltimore: Johns Hopkins University Press.

Seaver, James E.
    1942 *The Life of Mary Jemison.* New York: American Historic and Scenic Preservation Society.

Van Der Beets, Richard.
    1973 *The Indian Captivity Narrative.* Knoxville: University of Tennessee Press.

Washburn, Wilcomb.
    1974 *The North American Indian Captivity.* New York: Garland.

X

The General and the Indian: Ely Parker

Ely Parker was born an Indian, heir to a sachemship among the Iroquois. He was descended from one of those unlucky chiefs who had visited England in 1766 and his line led through such illustrious warriors as Captain Brant and Red Jacket, Mary Jemison's sometime neighbor. His pedigree, according to his nephew and biographer, Arthur Parker, was truly aristocratic (A. Parker 1919: 7).

> ... the special honor that we wish to give him is that he is the only American Indian who rose to national distinction, and who could trace his lineage back for generations to the Stone Age and to the days of Hiawatha. First and last he was an Iroquois.

In between, however, the question of his identity was harder to decide.

Parker served as a staff officer under Grant during the Civil War. He wrote out the copy of the articles of surrender signed by both Grant and Lee receiving the honor, the legend goes, because Grant's aide-de-camp was too nervous to hold a pen steadily. After the war Grant appointed Parker as First Native American Secretary of Indian Affairs, a post which Parker held for two years through much political turbulence, finally resigning after being tried and acquitted by a congressional committee on charges of peculation.

Parker seemed unique (and dangerous) to his contemporaries because he was a leader among Indians and whites at the same time. Forward-looking, able to appreciate the white man's "superior" ways, yet remaining an Indian, Parker's life appeared to be the best compromise an intelligent Indian could make. He used his eminence in the white world to defend his own people, to keep them from being victimized by the ravenous land speculators who peopled the fringes of all Indian territory. Parker was a hybrid: he derived his empathy from being an Indian and his efficacy from being a white. He acted as both simultaneously, or so it seemed to his admirers. And he was effective enough to raise up formidable political foes when he tried to rectify frauds during his tenure in the Office of Indian Affairs

Parker married a white woman and lived after the fashion of whites. The expenses attendant upon the "fashionable wife" were among the reasons (Resek 1960: 120) Parker's enemies advanced for his habit of taking bribes (A. Parker 1919: opp. 202), that and his "conviviality." An 1879 photograph shows him seated on the lawn of his Fairfield, Connecticut house, a two-story Carpenter Gothic, his dogs around him, his wife and a friend in crinolines playing croquet beneath the elm trees. Inside the house were curios of Parker's military career and Indian heritage, photographs taken of him standing next to Grant, old swords, a tomahawk once owned by Red Jacket, and an Iroquois sachem's regalia. This was the envelope of his life, outwardly late Provincial Victorian, inwardly ersatz white-Indian, temperate and well-proportioned but with local flair, a Carpenter Gothic.

The white man and the Indian in Parker were publicly reconciled in one image which played on the surface of Parker's life: the image of the Good American. The passage quoted earlier concludes:

> In any sense or viewpoint he was an American. There is a sense in which he was the first American of his time and an embodiment of all the heroic ideals that enter into our concept of American manhood.

What truer American than an Indian who has become accomplished in the learning of the white man and has turned all his vigor, drawn from the rich American earth, to the white ideal? All of Parker's spirit, or the spirit of Parker-as-Indian, was transmuted into "American manhood." His Indian virtues were the virtues of American males in general. He was a Civil War hero, not just a Seneca Indian. His Indian qualities ornamented his American heroism, and his Indian origins were just verification of his true Americanness. He was an Indian because he was an American, and because he had lent himself to the cause of all Americans, freedom.

According to Parker's fellow officer Captain Beckwith when General Lee entered the parlor of the McLean House at Appomattox and saw Parker there he (Beckwith 1905: 5)

> was dismayed and would have drawn the color line but for Gen. Grant's quick perception and assurance that his military secretary required no apology, since his right to American citizenship antedated by many generations their own, long before Plymouth Rock loomed up in the world's eye.

164 | *Lives Between Cultures*

The mythic time of the Lee-Grant meeting contained a moment for declaring to all history that Ely Parker was more American than two of the most renowned Americans. His right to the title stemmed from a fundamental conjunction between American history and Indian history in which American history consumed Indian history. The Indians were Americans before the Americans.

Indians were, however, second-class Americans, not even that. Parker was a special individual who according to Captain Beckwith in his funeral oration achieved eminence through "superior mental faculties." Normally no Indian would ever be able to match this level of accomplishment. Parker learned to speak the English language without an accent; he understood the niceties of social intercourse even to the point of playing the gallant in a youthful escapade. He could write a carefully phrased communication to a lady with attention to the rules of the genre, and more than one acquaintance chimes in with praise for his handwriting. His Indian background and war experiences always supplied matter for polite conversation and his skill as a raconteur and public speaker (oratory being an Indian specialty) was mentioned with enthusiasm by friends. He had all the attainments needed to prove that a well-behaved, intelligent Indian could also be a good American, so long as he was content with being one in history alone.

Indians were Americans, but Americans might be expected to have a little Indian in them. One day when Parker was in Albany, New York with a delegation of Seneca he met a Rochester attorney named Lewis Henry Morgan. Years before, Morgan, while still a student at Cayuga Academy, set up a fraternal and literary organization called The Gordian Knot. Meeting in an abandoned Masonic lodge near Aurora, New York the members dressed themselves as Ancient Greeks and engaged in philosophical discussions. The Gordian Knot satisfied a need for adolescent fraternalism in the style of the Classical Revival, which was inspiring city names like Utica, Rome, Troy and Syracuse and Greek-Roman architecture in the burgeoning cities. After its members left the Academy, the Gordian Knot persisted. This was probably because Freemasonry, which would have been an important adulthood affiliation for most of these young men, had come under a cloud: political factionalism and the scandal created by a kidnapping had damaged the Masons' reputation seriously and many lodges were abandoned (Cross 1950). The Gordian Knot was a clean alternative and it grew apace with chapters meeting in several cities in the area.

In 1843 Morgan proposed a rededication of the charter. He had discovered that America had her own native Classical Greeks, the Iroquois, who had organized a Confederacy based on democratic principles of their own accord and met to give grand speeches around council fires, summoning visions of a primitive Demosthenes addressing skin-clad Athenians. The "Grand Order of the Iroquois," as the Gordian Knot was renamed, lit its own council fires; the members in tunics, scarlet leggings and leather moccasins made their own stern orations (Stern 1931: 6-16). Morgan was named chief of the Order under the title Skenandoah.

The Masonic interest was not denied: Salem Towne, the author of *The System of Speculative Masonry* was early made an honorary member, and the grades with their rituals resembled the Masonic practice. But Morgan himself had begun to cultivate an interest in the real Iroquois and to turn the organization toward the goal of aiding the Seneca and other tribes in their fight against enforced dispossession of lands. He deplored the "boyish" play of the other members, their indifference when he made his appeals or invited scholars such as Henry Schoolcraft to address the assembled tribes.

Parker dovetailed neatly with Morgan's development; soon after their meeting Parker was initiated (!) into the Confederacy and contributed his expertise to the conduct of ceremonies. After three years clerkship in an attorney's office Parker had just learned that he could not be admitted to the bar because he was an Indian. He intended as a lawyer to combat whites preying on his people; denied that he went back to school in engineering. The Order funded Parker's education, provided a scholarship to put his brother and sister through the State Normal School and established an award to help other Seneca seeking an education. Parker reciprocated by acting as a guide for Morgan on his information-gathering forays among the Seneca. Eventually Morgan and his brother-in-law Charles Talbot Porter, another Order member, were adopted into the Seneca tribe and given Indian names in a ceremony arranged by Parker.

Morgan was repelled by the purile role-playing of the Order and he left it behind him, preferring to play his Indian role on the stage of scholarship. He wrote a series of "Letters on the Iroquois addressed to Albert Gallatin" in 1847 and signed them "Schenandoah" but the letters themselves contain much solid data on Iroquois houses, dress and ceremonies. The gesture was still embedded in the clubbish politics of his youth—the letters were printed in *The American Whig Review*—but Morgan, with Parker's collusion, was occupied among the real Iroquois. He dedicated his *League of the Ho-de-no-sau-nee, or Iroquois*, the founding work of American social anthropology, to Ely Parker; their "joint researches" Morgan liberally acknowledged in the Preface. Morgan's own Indian character left off the tunic and became fully intellectual, wandering among subjects and fully ascending to wider circles of comparison where he was only one member of "systems of consanguinity and affinity" which rounded the entire "human family."

Ely Parker received more modest advantages. Also in 1847 and most likely at the behest of people he had met in the Grand Order, Parker was initiated in Grand Lodge No. 88 of the Freemasons. This commenced a lifelong membership in the lodges which, though it could not help him to the bar, must have proved beneficial in his later career as a civil engineer and military officer. Freemasons were open-minded about initiating American Indians. Joseph Brant was raised into a London lodge in 1776 and back in America was Master of an all-Mohawk lodge. Red Jacket, Parker's illustrious ancestor, was an Apprentice and his nephew Arthur Parker ascended to the 33rd degree.

Parker's Freemasonry was a bridge between his American and Indian features; among the Masons he was both without prejudice to either. There was a group of successful men practicing rituals; they could welcome an enlightened Indian whom they disdained in their places of business. Some Masons even believed that the Indians practiced a primeval Masonry and were naturally attuned to Masonic philosophy (Vanduzer in Mackey, 1966: 102). Parker found an artificial existence as an Indian American among the Masons, and he performed his American role with them as much as Morgan performed his Indian role in print. Only Parker was under greater constraints.

When his Civil War fame made it impossible to ignore him, Parker was relegated to history, and to a perspective on American history. There is no better document of this attitude than Arthur Parker's biography of his uncle. The first four chapters are devoted to forebears who had been important in Indian-white relations. The text concentrates on events which proved them to be genuinely American. They signed treaties, aided with settlers and fought on the American side during the Revolution. Parker's own life is a procession of important happenings having nothing to do with Parker himself. Morgan, Grant, Seward and Lincoln fill the pages; Parker is ousted. He was confined to the public sphere as he had entered it, was only worth notice in proportion to the importance of what he did for and in America.

Parker's lifting himself out of being a mere Indian condemned him to be nothing but a part of American history festooned with the trappings of events. Beneath all the image-making Parker had his own experience, which is all the more difficult to see for the baggage he was made to carry. The success with which his comrades, friends and family ensconced him in a harmless shibboleth silenced him permanently.

Parker's very "Indian" taciturn quality makes it very difficult to understand him beyond his induction into history. For one the documentary evidence of his thoughts and reactions to the world is limited. His "autobiography" (Beckwith 1905: 527-36), vaunted as "perhaps the only autobiography of a Seneca Indian preserved in our literature," is like all other writings about Parker: it is singularly uninformative about Parker himself while providing a wealth of facts on his times, friends and the state of Indian-white relations. It was found among Parker's papers after his death and was probably written as a speech though it was never delivered.

> I am presented to you as General Parker. Well, who is General Parker? He may answer for himself in a very few words. He may answer because there can be no other person who has been longer associated with the general than he who now addresses you, and he thinks and believes that if anyone can speak with authority he can.

Identities are bandied about tortuously in these words; the pronoun "he" designates two people, "General Parker" and "he who now addresses you." The speaker does not wish to coincide with General Parker, but does wish to remain a close acquaintance whose information is genuine yet not personal testimony.

Parker recoils from himself. The rhetoric of Americanism that defined his public life since the end of the Civil War has no place in his self-reckoning. He verbally does what he never brought about in his real life, he marries the General to the Indian and says that he is both, standing in front of an imaginary audience. The coalescence of identities, the dismissal of a simple American identity in favor of the dyad, is the sort of thing Parker may have been allowed only in the fantasy realm of Masonry; that he cast it as a spoken act at the beginning of a speech never finished or given is enough to proclaim posthumously how important this fantasy was, and how unlikely he considered even a symbolic fulfillment.

The remainder of the autobiography is in the first person, and the reader, the putative hearer, knows exactly who this person is. Parker's problem as he wrote was to keep the first person as he had defined him together and consistent. In order to establish the two categories of experience in a stable symbiosis Parker resorted to the realm of discourse that was used to smother his identity, American history, but he read his history with a difference. By the judicious inclusion of anecdotes he deformed history into a shape commodious for both the General and the Indian. The hovering accusation of hypocrisy motivated Parker to steer away from any too convenient melding of the two at any one moment; he caused his audience to see the necessity of both from his youth onward.

An instance of primary importance, Parker tells his listeners, happened when he was 12 or 13 years old. Some English army officers, having employed Parker to attend their horses, mocked the youth's speech and mannerisms. They assumed he was too ignorant to understand their sport. Parker understood, but he excused the officers for their conduct. He had to admit that he was barbarous in appearance and manners; instead of exciting him to revenge the incident stimulated in him a desire for self-enrichment. The General was already stirring, superseding the Indian. And the Indian was at this moment transformed into a performance: otherwise how could he realize the officers were ridiculing him and still project a character which would lead them to believe he was dead to their jokes. The Indian aspect was undermined by what was still just a proposition. Parker decided that he would learn to speak the English language so well he would no longer be restricted to playing a stereotype Indian in the presence of ill-mannered whites. The picture of the whites as the dirty savage addressed them in modulated tones of a graduate must have drawn itself in young Parker's imagination.

Parker entered Yates Academy, where he was the only Indian student,

> having no Indian companionship I advanced rapidly in the use of the English language.

Freedom from his former compatriots allowed him to expand into the social space of the Academy.

> It was a mixed school and the associating of the sexes had a refining and elevating tendency.

Parker was willing to be civilized by the fair sex; he was not the clutching abductor but the candidate, he thought, for elevation up into white society. In the excess of his enthusiasm for the novel possibilities at Yates he flew upward toward becoming the General. Then, suddenly, he "changed his camping ground" to Cayuga Academy. The sense that he was still an Indian, for whom the Academy was a camping ground, enters the autobiography.

Parker does not explain the transfer; he just projects a feeling of restoration to his Indian character, an unwanted restoration. An extraneous source provides an informative digression. On March 24, 1915 the *Buffalo Express* (Parker 1919: 262) published a letter from a Mrs. Louise Batchelder, who had been a classmate of Parker's at Yates Academy. Mrs. Batchelder gives a catty account of Parker's flirtation with a young lady who belonged to one of the "most aristocratic families." Parker

> showed a lack of descretion by falling in love with one of his fairest schoolmates, who, strange to say, seemed to reciprocate his feelings, allowing him to be her escort from lectures and evening meetings.

Encouraged by the young lady's favor Parker made bold to invite her to drive out with him on the Fourth of July, thus not only asserting serious intentions toward her but bringing his indescretion before the entire community. Mrs. Batchelder draws herself up to report his appearance on that day riding through the streets of town in a splendid rig and

> sure enough, Mary was sitting at the side of Parker and the darky driver in front. The young lady soon went abroad for a long vacation.

Mrs. Batchelder cannot keep the snapshot of the Indian, the woman and the Black man together in a carriage on Independence Day from standing out of context on its own—but the forces she articulates kept Parker (and, one imagines, Mary and the "darky") from going any further.

Mary's holiday terminated Parker's aspirations at Yates and though the autobiography says nothing on the subject was probably a major encouragement to depart for Cayuga. There are no records of similar "indescretions" at Cayuga. Parker alludes only to the personal progress which he made at that institution. The progress as he had plotted it was arrested by an impenetrable barrier which rose whenever he wanted to advance far. Everything in the autobiography implies that he was studying to perform the white identity since he had learned that he would never win it entirely. He tested how far he could go before being humiliated back to Indian status.

The next phase of the autobiography is the first assay of Parker's composite narrator. In a long diatribe against the abuse of the Indians by government officials Parker refers to the Indians as "they," not as "we." He has abundant praise for the Indians but he is not joined with them as a victim. When he extends himself into an Indian identity it is with the distinction of a leader, who is mortified because with a few hundred ignorant Indians at my back I can consider myself the head of a strong independent sovereignty and treat with the United States as if I were Russia or Germany or China or Japan.

This is a good portrait of Parker's situation upon graduating from Cayuga, a leader of Indians but not just an Indian, an ambitious white man yet not permitted to practice law. There was no peak which he could occupy without knowing he seemed absurd. Yet a leader he was by birthright and more than an Indian leader he must be.

The Civil War intervened. Parker, who had qualifications as an engineer, offered his services to the Union Army. Seward rebuffed him initially but Parker persisted and was accepted with an officer's rank. The narrator of the autobiography makes it clear that Parker went to war for America; but this really means, in the process of the autobiography, that the artificial conditions of the war encircled Parker with a unique white identity, the General, which was based in the action of white men.

The General takes the autobiography's podium and speaks, proving his deeds in the Civil War through artifacts. I have Grant's hand-written surrender terms; I have a piece of the apple tree under which Lee rested on the road to Appomattox. My cane comes from a branch of the oak tree which shaded Grant as he received the capitulation of Vicksburg. At the end of this recitation the narrator says

> You have now heard how I am a General and now you perhaps know
> as much about General Parker as he knows about himself.

The narrator points to the General, who has done much that is important to Americans.

The General steps forward again and laments that he has no job or pension for all the years he has served the United States. Standing beside the General the Indian lodges his complaint against the government. The Indians are still treated harshly; all the General's good efforts when he was Indian Commissioner have been wiped away. Parker's personal history culminates in this chorus of the two sides he has developed in himself. Their voices are not dissonant with each other; they are harmonious aspects of the same narrator penalized by the same United States government. The two phases of Parker who introduced themselves at the outset now expound for a (presumably) sympatheic audience their mutual traits. Standing just far enough apart to be distinguished they act in concert to show what really comprises Parker and the American, what history had come to in this individual.

Parker could not end the autobiography on this concordant note; the history which rarely allowed a General to be orchestrated with an Indian, a history with the grip of fate, chokes their harmony.

> The Indian may struggle against his doom, but his fate is as irresistible as the waters of the Niagara. I have remarked that in Indian complications the military are generally called in as a last resort. I can safely say that as a general rule this work is not relished by the trained military man.

Here the General testifies to his distaste at supressing Indians like himself: if he and the Indians are to meet in the regrettable state of affairs the outcome can only be distasteful.

Parker visualised the illusory theatrics of bringing the General and the Indian together in his autobiography. In his life one may be symmetrical with the others but the events of that life—events never mentioned—decreed the futility of any compromise in the historical flow that Parker never escaped. This was the tragic chord in all of Parker's experience: the historical context which he had to accept for the fashioning and display of his identities must, whatever their links, foster a fatal hostility between them. As a corollary he was forever debarred from residing in the smiling American everyone applied to him.

This underworld of uneasy halves in potential conflict surfaces in one other body of material from late in Parker's life: his correspondence with Harriett Maxwell Converse. Mrs. Converse was a wealthy poetess and connoisseur of Iroquois lore who had contributed to Parker's charities. Beginning in 1881 Mrs. Converse nurtured a polite literary friendship with Parker, just retired from the Indian Affairs Commission. Parker did not conduct the correspondence exactly as Mrs. Converse wished since many of his letters apologize for failures to visit her when expected or regret not having written more voluminously or more often. Nonetheless Arthur Parker felt that (Parker 1919: 162)

> General Parker never really knew or thought much about his real self until he met Harriett Maxwell Converse.

Parker was 51 years old then, and dejected. Mrs. Converse moved him not so much to introspection—he had done much of that already—but to vocal self-disparagement.

One letter in particular comes to the fore of the entire selection. Mrs. Converse, in an effort to soothe her friend, had heaped him with plaudits; Parker was overwrought, for in his curious (to Mrs. Converse) fashion Parker was genuinely a modest man and his modesty was offended (Parker 1919: 165).

> And why all this commotion of the spirit? Because I am an ideal or a myth and not my real self. I have lost my identity and look around me in vain for my original being. I never was 'great' and never expect to be. I never was powerful and would not know how to exercise power were it placed in my hands for use. And that I am "good" or even dreamed of attaining that blissful condition of being, is simply absurd. All my life I have occupied a false position....

The balance of the letter is a brief autobiography different in tone from the speech. Referring to himself only as an Indian, Parker describes his youthful eminence in the Seneca tribe, his application to the Army and initial rejection by Seward, the call from the War Department, his service in the war and the subsequent period in the Indian Affairs Office. The Civil War is now a "quarrel among white men." All throughout the passage people are constantly proclaiming Parker a "genius," "great," "powerful," "good." His tribesmen declare him a genius at the start; during the war other officers whisper that he must be a genius; both whites and Indians concur he must be a genius when he becomes Indian Affairs Commissioner; and finally the conspirators against him mutter that he is a genius grown too great and powerful. Parker's perfection hounds him; he is tired of being pumped to an inflated greatness and made the spectacle of all good. The letter is an outcry against Mrs. Converse and all the purveyors of simple reputation who gave him his speech.

The simple treaty of "false position" was always ready for Parker's signature; in this treaty the General and the Indian would have joined in the heartless pact of being nothing but a legend. Parker wanted to be an American very much, but not that American.

References

Beckwith, J.
  1905 *Captain Beckwith's Address marking the Grave of Do-Neh-Ho Geh-Wah.*
  Buffalo Historical Society Publication No. VIII. Buffalo: Buffalo Historical
  Society.

Cross, Whitney R.
  1950 *The Burned-Over District.* Ithaca, New York: Cornell University Press.

Mackey, G.
  1951 *Encyclopedia of Freemasonry.* Philadelphia.

Morgan, Lewis Henry.
  1851 *League of the Ho-de-n-sau-nee, or Iroquois.* Rochester, New York: Sage
  and Brothers.

Parker, Arthur C.
  1919 *The Life of General Ely S. Parker.* Buffalo Historical Society Publication
  No. XXIII. Buffalo: Buffalo Historical Society.

Resek, Carl.
  1960 *Lewis Henry Morgan: American Scholar.* Chicago: University of Chicago
  Press.

Stern, Bernhard J.
  1931 *Lewis Henry Morgan: Social Evolutionist.* Chicago: University of Chicago
  Press.

XI

Frank Hamilton Cushing
Among The Zuni

Frank Cushing was known to the Zuni Indians by a name meaning "Many Buttons," from his ornate costume, festooned with rawhide combs and punctuated with many silver buttons. In an engraving Cushing appears in full dress, an ersatz man, his long hair complemented by a very non-Indian mustache, a lone eagle feather protruding from the top of his headband. His pose is—in a contradictory phrase—sensuously martial, right foot forward, left hand on hip, right hand clutching the hilt of an unseen weapon, a sword perhaps. There is fixation about the eyes and a drifting quality to the face, as if he were not quite conscious of his body but had come upon it from behind, like a tourist photographed in a cutout. When Edmund Wilson compared Cushing to Doughty he was not wide of the mark—but the resemblance is in their faces (Wilson 1956: 15). Cushing's "queer dual life" was not Doughty's.

Frank Cushing was born in northeastern Pennsylvania, but his father, who was a country doctor, moved his family to Barre Center and then to Medina, New York. Frank was a delicate, sickly child, one of those children who early abandoned the raucous games of their agemates for lonelier, more imaginative play. As a child he made himself an Indian costume and roamed deep into the night forest, carrying improvised weapons against what he might find there. Manual dexterity which amounted to a genius for craftwork enabled Frank to duplicate the handicrafts he must have observed on the Tuscarora and Tonawanda Indian Reservations, neither very far from Medina.

When an itinerant geological lecturer visited his town Cushing became infected with the fervor of collection, epidemic in the 1860's and 70's. Ward's Natural Science Establishment, located in Rochester, about a day's drive from Medina, was the nexus of a natural history collecting network that spread to the far reaches of the country, and distributed specimens of plant, animal and mineral types to museums and universities everywhere. There is no record of Cushing ever paying a visit to Ward's, but young men of the vicinity with similar interests, for instance Charles Witney Gilmore future Curator of Dinosaurs at the Smithsonian, were lured to this collectors' mecca. Important figures in museum work and natural history—F.A. Lucas, Director of the American Museum of Natural History and William Morton Wheeler, the Harvard entomologist—were trained at Ward's. The Establishment typified the intense collecting activity in the western states (including western New York) in this period. Even as Cushing matured the center was moving westward, and the "dinosaur wars" in which collectors' armed agents battled over rich fossil sites in Wyoming and Montana, were soon to begin. Museums both great and small were forming all through the East and were grabbing anything that might adorn their cabinets.

Fired with this enthusiasm Cushing turned his nocturnal excursions into week-long ascetic journeys in search of rock specimens and Indian relics, which he accumulated in quantity. A "wigwam" which he had constructed on the grounds of his father's farm turned into a cluttered museum of these finds. Seated inside he conducted "experiments" in archaeology: he analyzed the workmanship of artifacts and reproduced copies of them by native methods, copies so accurate they could be confounded with native arrowheads chipped from obsidian or wooden idols carved with sharpened beavers' teeth.

On one of his long walking trips Cushing met Lewis Henry Morgan, then at work on *Ancient Society*, and showed Morgan some samples of his artistry, which Morgan warmly approved. W.L. Ledyard, who befriended Cushing after he caught the amateur geologist trying to pry loose a trilobite from a rock Ledyard had situated on his lawn, recommended Cushing to C.F. Hartt, geology professor at Cornell. With a keenness that should enter him into the folklore of collecting Cushing brought back a bushel of artifacts from a piece of land which Hartt claimed was barren. The seventeen year old Cushing was quite likely unsuited to the quiet theorizing of university geology: soon he headed for Washington and a position at the Smithsonian Institution.

S.R. Baird, the Assistant Secretary of the Smithsonian, had heard of Cushing through Ledyard and requested a contribution for the *Annual Report* (Cushing 1876). Cushing complied with "Antiquities of Orleans County, N.Y." a raw inventory of his finds with some remarks on archaeology sites and methods of manufacture. In 1876 Cushing was entrusted with the National Museum exhibit at the Philadelphia Centennial, where he flaked stones and fashioned primitive utensils for the multitudes. Three years later he was called into service at the Bureau of American Ethnology by Major John Wesley Powell.

Major Powell was one of the foremost scientific entrepreneurs in a time of many entrepreneurs. Although the Civil War left him with only one arm, Powell braved the Colorado River as leader of a scientific expedition to fill in the vast white space about the river on maps of the southwest. The disasters that beset the explorers made newspaper headlines; Powell was even presented with his own obituary when he returned, though he did not respond as Mark Twain did under similar circumstances. Only some friendly pressure from a Congressman impelled Powell to edit his journal for popular readers: it is a hard, forcible recounting of massacres and rock formations that still reads very well (Powell 1878). The drawings of the Grand Canyon at the end of the book are only less stunning than the Canyon itself.

Powell was named head of the Rocky Mountain Survey and he used his political and bureaucratic connections to agitate for the formation of the Bureau of American Ethnology. He was convinced that the Indian cultures of American were being swamped by white incursions and lost through acculturation. A government Bureau charged with gathering Indian traditions and handiwork was imperative; through its efforts significant portions of Indian life could be placed in the drawers and cases of the Smithsonian. When the Bureau was created Powell was named head and supervised myriads of collecting activities the fruits of which were proudly displayed in the Bureau's *Annual Bulletin*, which began publication for the year 1878.

Powell's efficacy as an administrator curtailed his plans to return west to make full ethnographic observations "on the marvelous savage and barbaric culture" of the Pueblo Indians, the Zuni in particular. Powell's *Exploration of the Colorado River and its Canyons*, contains several pages of notes on the Zuni, their kinship system, tribal government and "Shamanistic government," a rule of priests "of as great importance as tribal government."

> With some tribes the cult societies have greater powers than the clans; with other tribes clan government is the more important; but always there is a conflict of authority, and there is perpetual war between Shamanistic and civil government.

The mythic world of animals with minds and monsters dwelling in the mountains joined this endless civil war to enveigle Powell back. But he could not go; instead he chose a proxy.

Chapter Eleven: Frank Hamilton Cushing | 177

Frank Cushing was attractive to Powell because he was observant, a trait Powell demanded in all the Bureau's field workers. His familiarity with almost every division of Indian culture from clothing to wigwams was encouraging; he would do all the work of a scientific team. A collecting expedition under Colonel James Stevenson was sent to the Pueblos in 1879. Powell arranged for Cushing to accompany this expedition as far as Zuni, and enlightened his protege to the essentials of Zuni culture. When familiarized with the Pueblos Cushing formed a resolve (Powell 1900: 364).

> Cushing decided that he would do everything necessary to make the intimate acquaintance of the people by learning the language, and, if possible, gain admittance to the tribe and become a member of one or more of their religious fraternities.

This is exactly what Powell wanted.

Cushing's own account in his narrative "My Adventures in Zuni" serialized in *Century Magazine* three years later must be disingenuous. He does not accord Powell much credit for setting the object of research or arranging the trip, and writes as if he were tyro in Indian studies boldly forging into a savage camp, notebook in hand. As in the etching made to accompany this text Cushing is solitary and singularly brilliant—but, as before, his eyes give him away.

Cushing first began to sketch, measure and note the features of Zuni life most apparent. A dance caught in the courtyard moves him to a lengthy report. As Colonel Stevenson takes in piles of Indian artifacts by trade Cushing ambles through the Pueblo, surprised at all the signs of liveliness in a race he had long believed was indolent. To his great annoyance the Zuni will not permit him to sketch their masked dances, and are antagonistic to his drawing the faces of people. A few of the young men, coming to his tent out of curiosity, teach him some Zuni expressions and stare at him as he writes. The stratagem of handing out trinkets fails to assuage tempers and win confidence; he carps at Zuni resistance to his attempts.

Then, suddenly, he decides that the only way he can pry information loose from the Indians is by living with them. With monumental presumption he lugs his effects into the house of the Zuni "governor" of the Pueblo (the Americans, like the British, found their own government among the natives) who reacts to this invasion with undisguised displeasure. Cushing is a "Washington man," a label which the Zuni associated with mistrust.

The Zuni are entertained by Cushing's endeavors to cook his own food over a fire he has built on the floor of the governor's house. The ineptitude was probably staged; Cushing fended for himself in the wilds ever since childhood. But the ruse works: triumphantly the governor goes off and returns with some food which he fries for Cushing, though not without sharp words. Eating the food is an initiation of sorts, and gives Cushing shaky access to the people. This does not facilitate his sketching (Cushing 1882-83: 204).

> Suspicions seemed to increase in proportion to the liking they began to feel for me. Realizing that unless I could overcome the suspicion and secure the full confidence of the Indians it would be impossible to gain any knowledge of importance regarding their inner life, I determined to remain among them until the return of their party from Moqui, whither it was soon to go.

Cushing starts to discern the "inner life" of the Zuni apart from the physical structures he tabulates, and considers the value of a protracted stay. A momentous decision is forced upon him when the main expedition trails off leaving him no provisions. The governor, whom he addresses as "grandfather," offers him food and comfort if he will only make up his mind to become a Zuni. "Why should I not be a Zuni? I replied in despair." And he is fed in full Zuni style.

Again this sounds contrived. Cushing faults the callous white men of the expedition for leaving him stranded and reliant on the Zuni; they were, however, unlikely to do anything so irresponsible to an employee of the Bureau of American Ethnology, especially if Powell himself arranged the expedition. Cushing obviously wanted his "adventures" to be sharpened by personal danger, and his accepting the governor's offer to seem an obligatory concession.

The rhythm of concession and assertion pervades Cushing's "Adventures." When Cushing seems to be surrendering to the Zuni he is in fact tempting them to do unto him as he desires for the improvement of his knowledge of their customs. He does not admit the reader to his confidence, but behaves as if his helplessness or resignation is quite real, or defers the cause for his behavior to some external, the expeditions, the Zuni, nature. He is more resourceful than he leads anyone, Zuni or reader, to believe; but he wishes the attendance of the former and the attention of the latter, hence he lies back and lets the Zuni rule him while the reader looks on. His pioneer spirit will not let the savages have their will and rule him completely.

Chapter Eleven: Frank Hamilton Cushing | 179

His sketching, therefore, persists after the reconciliation of the initiatory meal and even after he has learned enough Zuni to understand the protests of his portrait subjects. The governor and other leaders urge him to desist-no avail. They restrain him by force—he breaks loose. While imperturbably sketching the "ill-natured" Knife Dance he is accosted by masked dancers who make a pretense of trying to murder him as an enemy (*he* feels it is no pretense but a real intention). He draws his own knife and waves it about, dispersing his attackers. This courage wins over the old governor (Cushing 1882-83: 207).

> I had completed in him, that day, the winning of the truest of friends; and by so doing had decided the fate of my mission among the Zuni Indians.

Bravery counts for more with the governor than obedience to tribal custom. Cushing's mission among the Zuni is guaranteed success; he has seduced them.

> Soon he is called upon to receive more investiture: the vigilant governor decides that Cushing's next step toward becoming a Zuni is the adoption of Zuni dress. First the governor gives Cushing a headband and moccasins which he has made, and destrpys Cushing's hat and shoes so he can wear nothing else. The other whites at the expedition camp (they had since returned) laugh at the outfit when Cushing shows himself there but the Zuni are overjoyed upon seeing him. Knowing the utility of this state of mind in his hosts Cushing "decided to permit them thenceforth to do with me as they pleased." His tentative experiment of dress change promises future gains.

In the second part of the "Adventures" Cushing, having made the dress concession, swings confidently into an intrusive phase. He barges into a room where a group of sacred clown dancers are secluded apart from the public, ritually preparing themselves. He is expelled immediately. When he finally wrangles a grudging invitation to enter he violates an important rule of speech—he says something in Spanish and has to perform a penance. But he wins a surfeit of information on the hidden rites he is most determined to study. He recedes into himself as if to digest the new experience, and becomes receptive.

One detects an element of probing in this bumptious rush into the Zuni sanctuary; in violating the abjurations of the Zuni he gained a glimpse of secrets and he learned what is done to violators. One even suspects that his speech transgression—once he was admitted to the sacred domain—was also calculated to win the information of penance. Cushing must have been cautioned by his "grandfather" that nothing but Zuni was to be breathed between the walls of the clowns' abode. In the "Adventures" he exudes an "angels fear to tread" boldness; his *conscious* purpose is veiled.

When the Stevenson Expedition leaves to return east Cushing stays in Zuni with the understanding that he is committed to a long sojourn. Cushing had received a letter from Powell directing him to stay in Zuni a few months more and though the governor is willing to keep him the old man is still bewildered by the young ethnologist's sketching and writing. When the Stevenson party leaves, Cushing tells the governor he will follow them shortly; "I guess not" is the governor's reply. The governor gives him a new room, freshly plastered and simply furnished after the Zuni style (Green 1979: 90; Cushing 1882-83: 507).

> 'There,' said he, 'now you have a little house, what more do you want? Here, take these two blankets,—they are all you can have. If you get cold, take off all your clothes and sleep next to the sheepskins, and *think* you are warm, as the Zuni does. You must sleep in the cold and on a hard bed; that will harden your meat. And you must never go to Dust-Eye's house [the mission], or to Black-beard's [the trader's] to eat; for I want to make a Zuni of you. How can I do that if you eat American food?

Cushing is fond enough of Zuni food, but the sleeping arrangements torture him. He slings the hammock across the small room, even while protesting that he sleeps well. The governor slyly removes the civilized object. Cushing has no choice but to have his "meat hardened."

The next step, now that his flesh is of the "soil of Zuni" by his sharing the family supper-bowl, and he wears the headband and moccasins, is to fit him with a complete Zuni costume. Cushing at first objects, but the persuasions of interest soon carry him over. The governor's wife gives him a "coarse woolen blanket shirt"; the old man adds a "pair of short, thin black cotton trowsers," which Cushing wears underneath the shirt. These articles, plus leggings, a heavy serape, a crude copper bracelet and some strings of black stone beads fill out the costume. Cushing's anxiety that he will be left exposed to the elements in certain parts of the fabric is more or less allayed in the sum of its parts, especially when he sees the public reaction (Cushing 1882-83: 509).

> The first time I appeared in the streets in full costume the Zunis were delighted. Little children gathered around me; old women patronizingly bestowed compliments on me as their 'new son, the

child of Wa-sin-to-na.' I found the impression was good, and permitted the old Governor to have his way. In fact, it would have been rather difficult to have done otherwise, for, on returning to my room, I found that every article of civilized clothing had disappeared from it.

The last layer of the white man's shell is gone; Cushing, with decorous hesitation is lowered into the Zuni regalia and cannot escape, in truth does not want to escape. Visualize, then, the true spirit of adventure that informs these proceedings. Cushing allows the Zuni to act upon him as an unknown force whose intentions are only known by their actions. Melville used almost exactly the same mode of description in his *Typee*; only there the friendly natives were preparing their guests for cannibalism (or were they?). There is no question of that fear among the Zuni; however Cushing does not know what he is becoming and the tension, which he sloughs off with jocular allusions, is quite genuine. He may well be stranded in a sense he does not understand among these people.

He is learning all the while. He returns from an absence of a few days to find his room redecorated "more luxuriously than any other room in Zuni." The walls are whitewashed, the floor spread with rugs and the walls papered with colorful prints and a photograph of Colonel Stevenson "which the Indians had designed as my companion" (the photograph, apparently, not the Colonel). Next the clinching formality of adoption, the ear-piercing ceremony, which the Zuni enforced upon Cushing despite his usual balking. In a stroke Cushing becomes a Zuni named Ta-na-sta-li, the adopted son of the governor, and a qualified student of Zuni adoption.

Early in the third section Cushing states a major aim he conceived not long after arriving in Zuni. The "secret Priesthoods" which Powell had mentioned (and perhaps even told him to study) attract him because of the secrecy of their rites and the authority of their members. Cushing is fixed upon the Priesthood of the Bow, inviolate but with access to all other guarded ceremonies, and he commences a drive to be himself initiated. To start he tries to gain access to the initiations, a story which is full of bluster, bluff and subterfuge.

One night during the intermission of a long myth-reciting session, Cushing hears an old priest complain that he has no black paint to renew the tablets of his altar in time for the initiation. Cushing "fell to thinking how I could turn the priest's difficulties to account." Producing a book of colored prints he piques the Indians' curiosity about the coloring technique then demonstrates, using his own watercolors. The black Chinese ink bar he touts grandly, informing the wide-eyed Zuni that it is a rare substance made by the Chi-ni-kwe, "who were a Celestial people and lived on the back side of the world;" it is a priceless ink that he will not give to anyone. His tantalizing the priest works marvellously; at the time of the initiation he receives a request for a little ink, and parlays the Indians' eagerness into an invitation to deliver it himself to the initiation chamber. He deposits it in the morning knowing that this is an excuse for picking it up at night, when the ritual is in progress.

The curses of a bypasser and the scolding of his family do not prevent him from keeping his appointment in the secluded room (Cushing 1882-83: 509).

> Several of the members started up and motioned me out with their flat hands; but I only breathed deeply from my own, until I reached the place of the old priest. Knowing that Mexican was forbidden, I pretended not to understand what was said, when the latter advised me, in his own language, to go home; on the contrary, I wrung his hand, and, as I pulled off my moccasins, incoherently expressed my thanks for the privilege of remaining, and immediately seated myself as if for the night. It was a heavy 'game of bluff'; but utterly bewildered by it, the old priest said nothing for some moments, until, evidently in despair, he lighted the cigarette, blew smoke into the air, uttered a prayer, and then handed the cigarette to me.

Cushing is allowed to stay but he must smoke ceaselessly "to make clouds for their little world"; since he never smoked before this his head reels and he is unable to stand. Soon, however, physical adaptability comes to the aid of the adaptable intellect and he is puffing pleasurably as the ceremony goes forward. The all-night ordeal batters his less than rugged constitution and leaves him bed- or rather hammock-ridden for weeks.

His recovering raises the "subject of Lai-iu-lut-sa" the governor's niece and the mate he has chosen for Cushing. He catechizes Cushing by dictating to him the entire formula for introducing himself to the bride's parents without mentioning what the formula is for until the end. Cushing navigates this narrow strait and escapes marriage, to the governor's intense displeasure. As the old man is leaving the pueblo to do some farming he gets Cushing involved in another courtship by inviting a girl to bring some food to Cushing. This requires even more direct management by the beleaguered ethnologist since his "mother" is offended by the girl and by her bringing the food—for she *does* honor the governor's request. He invites her and her aunt to eat with him one evening then after a formal greeting leaves

Chapter Eleven: Frank Hamilton Cushing | 183

them alone. Since this is an insult, and was engineered as such to create a rift, the girl is nonplussed and soon parts. Cushing makes his peace with the old aunt and with the reader, since he desires the episode to be taken as proof of innocence before "charges and criticisms" i.e. that he had taken a Zuni concubine. There were people in Cushing's day, as there are now, who could not believe that he spent years in Zuni without acquiring a "squaw." Acquire he did, but never something so uncertain.

Cushing's resistance to the various matrimonial plots draws the line against total assimilation. Even when he is selected for the Priesthood of the Bow, the pinnacle of his success, the priests must waive the marriage requirement. Furthermore Cushing will not countenance any Zuni activity which runs counter to his sense of right. Revolver in hand he stops some Bow Priests from executing an old man whom they consider a sorcerer responsible for a protracted drought. He even tries to halt the ritual torture of a turtle. There is an element of bravado in these and similar events; Cushing the lone bearer of civilization is pitted against the barbarous Zuni; he opposes their superstitions even though he has reached high office in their religion. But the closing note of the "Adventures" shows Cushing a child of the Zunis in feeling if not in opinion; he sorrowfully describes the passing and funeral of an old "uncle" rounds out his informal account of Zuni life with a few words on the burial ceremony.

Among anthropologists there is a professional twice-told tale that Cushing became totally assimilated into the Zuni and after his initiation into the Bow Priesthood kept the vow of silence and never spoke to his colleagues of secret matters. Another tale, just the opposite, is being told the first time today, in the wake of Native American indignation over the predatory habits and distortions of anthropologists: Cushing in fact did disclose much of arcana in his writings and was for that reason chastised or even exiled by the Zuni. On the face of it these conflicting opinions present a delightful double bind. Cushing was the first and last ethnologist to become a Bow Priest; since only a Bow Priest can tell what is secret and no such qualified person has, to my knowledge, ever written a critique of Cushing's writings or made his own disclosures there is simply no way of telling whether Cushing was guilty as charged or not. Only the Bow Priests themselves know for sure, and they are not telling. Anthropologists may say what they like.

Cushing's adaptation should not be reduced to his loyalty or disloyalty to his "foster-people." As his subsequent history proves there are intricate elements in his treatment of and by the Zuni which only have meaning within the confines of his own psychology, and should not be judged by thick criteria. Cushing's mission was to collect data. His manipulations reported in the "Adventures" were justafiable as means for gaining the confidence of the Zuni and taking what he could: tricky tactics were admired in that era of American enterprise. He was with the Zuni for scarcely a year before he sent back to Powell the manuscript of "Zuni fetishes" profusely illustrated with figures of the sacred objects and containing versions of some Zuni myths. This appeared in the *Second Annual Report of the Bureau of American Ethnology* (Cushing 1883) and it was lucky for Cushing no Zuni subscribed: fetishes were evacuated of their power by duplication and depiction. But since Cushing did not believe in the power of fetishes it made no difference.

The foremost instance of the many levels of Cushing's relationship with the Zuni once his period of apprenticeship was over is the "aboriginal pilgrimage" he concocted with a *Boston Herald* reporter named Sylvester Baxter. Baxter, possibly lured by newsworthy reports of Cushing, went to Zuni in 1881. Late in that year Cushing led a party of Zuni on a long tour of the East, including Boston and Washington. The esoteric, and highly publicized, reason for the trip was that the Zuni were going to collect some water from the Atlantic Ocean, the "Ocean of Sunrise" for an unnamed ritual use. There was a political underlayer: land speculators, the bugbears of all Indian tribes, were menacing Zuni properties with their writs and deeds. They were even stirring up the Zunis' eternal foes, the Navajo, to herd their sheep over Zuni range. Cushing thought (and he must have had positive confirmation from someone in Washington), that a Zuni embassy in the Capital would act as a lobby in the Indians' favor. Baxter agreed: the likeable frontier color of the Zuni would controvert slanders that painted them as savages. Finally there was the element of showmanship, not to be forgotten after Buffalo Bill's Wild West Show.

The article which Baxter wrote for *Century Magazine*, "An Aboriginal Pilgrim" reports on the Indians' progress in a smiling sympathetic prose that underlines the childlike wonder of the natives faced with American technology. Cushing is their austere leader. They obey his commands and even allow him to wear American clothes and, more reluctantly, to cut his long locks in order to satisfy his own people. Cushing compromises by attaching the hair to a headband which he wears when the occasion calls for him to resume Indian dress for a ritual or for a show.

The Zuni revere machines and are struck by the loftiness of buildings. President Chester A. Arthur, whom they deem the very person Washington, stretches forth a welcoming hand. At the Paint-and-Clay Club of Cambridge, Massachusetts the Zuni sing and perform. Cushing, in Indian garb, sits among them and interprets (Baxter 1882: 530).

> The striking faces and brilliant native costumes of the Indians, almost wholly of articles made by themselves—beautifully woven serape shirts, deer-skin knee breeches, and leggings adorned with rows of close-set silver buttons, moccasins and massive silver belts, necklaces of shell, coral, coral and turquoise—captivated the artists' eyes, and sketch-books and pencils were in use all the evening. The Governor, with his strong profile, was particularly in favor as a subject.

This material array was the most important aspect of the Zuni, who must have been exasperated when they were attacked by an entire nation of sketchers.

The Zuni are shuttled about to a number of similar sessions, where they are always the subjects for the pens and discourse of gentlemen. People who hear them relate folktales at a meeting in Old South Church are pleased to discover in the Zuni faith "intrinsic gentleness ... marked as it is by certain cruel and barbaric practices" and evidences of an awakening scientific sensibility. The Zuni find the young ladies of Wellesley College and a collection of Japanese art objects owned by Professor Edward Morse both "beautiful." While enacting a rite before the ocean, on an island off the Maine coast the Zuni begin the process of inititating Cushing into the order of ka-ka.

While this pilgrimage might seem to have brought Cushing closer to the Zuni, especially with its denouement of initiation into the "most sacred, though least esoteric of the dance organizations" its true effect was the establishment of Cushing on the margin of Zuni society, and within permanent reach of American society. "My Adventures in Zuni" was published in *Century Magazine* directly after Baxter's article and it confirmed the idea of Cushing which Baxter had rejected: an able young ethnologist who is trusted by the natives and shares their interesting, fable-filled life. Furthermore, Cushing married Emily Tennison McGill of Washington, D. C. and brought her and a servant back to Zuni. Cushing had forever turned down intermarriage and, since his wife was unlikely to adapt, had also given up living with the Indians as one of them. His domesticity was a separate sphere. Having won a place among the Indians he treated it as a job, attending to his priestly duties but maintaining an American establishment, with a Negro cook.

After the return to Zuni Cushing spent less time in general at the pueblo. When he was not off on archaeological expeditions or visiting other tribes, the Hopi at Oraibi, he was indulging in more showmanship. In 1883 he conducted a group of Zuni to the Santa Fe Exposition, more to participate than to watch, and the same year he was in Chicago, at the Exposition there, exhibiting his collection of fetishes. Fetishism was a singularly prominent topic in international ethnology and Cushing's expertise was widely heralded; in 1895 the Museum für Volkerunde in Berlin published Cushing's catalogue of his collection in translation, and thus made his collection a unit in the elaborate comparisons and compilations which the German cultural historians were undertaking.

His publications on Zuni multiplied. *Popular Science Monthly* for June 1882 carried a brief article on "The Zuni social, mythic and religious systems" (Cushing 1882); he contributed a chapter on "Zuni weather proverbs" to a general study of the subject; and in the 1882-83 *Bureau of American Ethnology Annual Report* there was a long study of Pueblo pottery which ingeniously correlated the design changes with cultural growth. Cushing was alert to the latest developments in the theory of cultural evolution and was applying them to his favorite manual crafts. The greatest profusion of Zuni lore Cushing put into print during his lifetime, *Zuni Breadstuff* also saw the light in this period. Unfortunately it appeared in an obscure trade journal, *The Millstone* (of which it filled two full issues) and was never available to those scholars most concerned with its contents (reprinted Cushing 1921), some of whom complained that Cushing failed to share his findings on Zuni myth and ritual.

The obscurity of the publication is ironic because *Zuni Breadstuff* is the sequel to "My Adventures in Zuni" and the endpoint of Cushing's personal experience with the tribe; the book is Cushing's last gala trumpet blast before the later quiet. In it the former showmanship is subsiding beneath folklore, which Cushing, his physical presence among the Zuni curbed, turns to as the symbolic staple of his life.

In outline *Zuni Breadstuff* is a series of loosely related chapters on the common theme of food. Most of them are Cushing's adaptations of Zuni myths and in many there are vignettes of Zuni life. Cushing figures into a few, if only to frame the tale with the context of its telling. The long story of the origin of Corn Priests is so long because, he says between parentheses at the end, an Indian companion "maliciously told me this story that he might make me 'wait the morning watching,'" on a cold winter night. The precis of an Indian lawsuit over rights to an orchard shows Cushing simultaneously acting as presiding officer and tartly observing the Indian method of justice, his usual balance; his excursion with some American army friends to the top of a hill ends in an accidental intrusion on the making of baking-stones and another tale. He finishes a section on the wheat foods of the Zuni with a wistful remark on "a most excellent fried cake called *mu'-tsi-k'o-we* or 'contorted cakes'" (Cushing 1920: 108).

> ...these twisted and shriveled little cakes formed my favorite luxury during that extended period throughout which I was required to 'change my flesh, that I might indeed, become of the *blood of Zuni.*'

Several chapters near the end recount the prolonged adventures of a young hunter who runs afoul of supernatural beings and must live the life of a mouse before he is restored to his proper body and his family. It may be my fancy, but I see Cushing himself in this.

No one has satisfactorily explained why Cushing left Zuni in 1886. Rumors of his falling out with the Zuni over publication of arcana were rife; a recall may also have been issued by the Bureau of American Ethnology. Cushing had interefered on behalf of the Zuni to protect land from speculators, and that had repurcussions in Washington. His promoting the Zuni over the previous five years had drawn the attention of wealthy admirers; Cushing soon returned to the Pueblos on an archaeological expedition financed by a Boston woman, Mary Hemenway. He supervised the excavation for nearly two years before illness drove him back East. This mysterious illness plagued him for the rest of his life and imposed restrictions on his writing and activities. Yet he was still attached to the Bureau of American Ethnology and still consulted on the Zuni. When Colonel Garrick Mallery was composing his classic *Picture-Writing of the American Indians* (*Bureau of American Ethnology Tenth Annual Report*, 1887-88) he questioned Cushing on Zuni sand-painting, and received a two-page statement, based on Cushing's observations during his "first sojourn among the Zuni" (Mallory 1972: vol. 1: 210-11).

Like Lewis Henry Morgan after his "Schenandoah" phase Cushing turned to more general studies, mostly on the evolution of material culture. His paper "Manual Concepts" in one of the early issues of *American Anthropologist* (Cushing 1892) related the maturation of handicrafts to the progress of culture in a fashion akin to Ruskin's "shaping hand" theory; in another issue of the same he serialized the arrow forms of American Indians in order of cultural sophistication. His "Outlines of Zuni Creation Myths" (Cushing

1897) disappointingly brief for his colleagues, was in the Bureau's *Thirteenth Annual Report*.

Cushing's physician Dr. Pepper, apprehensive about the effects of the cold and damp on Cushing's health, offered himself to pay some of the expenses of an archaeological expedition to Florida; he solicited another sizeable contribution from Phoebe Hearst, and the Pepper-Hearst Expedition was under way. Cushing spent three years on the Florida Keys, made several fabulous artifact finds and wrote a brief "Preliminary Report." But it was as if his life had reached a stasis. In 1900, at the age of 43, he choked on a fishbone and died.

The rush to cull his papers, under the expectation that they contained extensive notes on the secret Zuni priesthoods, was stopped cold. A bulky manuscript of folktales, some archaeological minutae and travel notes were the sum of his literary legacy. The folktales, edited by Powell as *Zuni Folktales* and published posthumously (1903) bear Cushing's stamp. They are not Zuni folktales really, but spirited beautiful collected reflections on a mythic past already lost to their author.

In one of the folktales a girl who has been sequestered by her father in honor of the gods is visited by the Sun in human form and conceives a child. Fearful of her father's wrath, she exposes the child, but a female deer comes upon him and raises him as her own. The child grows to young manhood among the deer, carries the report back to the council of priests; a grand hunt of the deer is planned to snare the strange being. Alerted to this prospect the deer decide that the youth must be restored to his own people and an elder deer conducts him to the gods of the ka-ka dance... (Cushing 1986: 285).

> And Shulawitsi appeared and waved his flame around the youth, so that he became convinced of his mortal origin and of his dependence on food prepared by fire. Then the gods who speak the speech of men gathered around and breathed upon the youth, and touched to his lips moisture from their own mouths, and touched the portals of his ears with oil from their own ears, and thus was the youth made acquainted with both the speech and the understanding of the speech of mortal man. Then the gods called out, and there were brought before them fine garments of white cotton embroidered in many colors, rare necklaces of sacred shell with many turquoises and coral-like stones and shells strung in their midst, and all that the most beautifully clad of our ancients could have glorified their appearance with.

Chapter Eleven: Frank Hamilton Cushing | 189

References

Baxter, Sylvester
    1882 "An Aboriginal Pilgrimage." *Century Magazine* 24: 526-36.

Cushing, Frank.
    1876 "Antiquities of Orleans County, N. Y." In *Annual Report of the Smithsonian Institution for 1875*. Washington, D. C.: Government Printing Office. 375-77.

    1882 "The Zuni Social, Religious and Mythic Systems." *Popular Science Monthly* 21: 186-92.

    1882-83 "My Adventures in Zuni." *Century Magazine* 25: 191- 207; 500-11.

    1883a "Zuni Fetishes." *Bureau of American Ethnology 2nd Annual Report, 1880-81*. Washington: Government Printing Office.

    1883b "Zuni Weather Proverbs." In *Weather Proverbs*. ed. H.H.C. Dunwoody. Washington, D. C.: Government Printing Office.

    1886 "A Study of Pueblo Pottery as Illustrative of Zuni Cultural Growth." *Bureau of American Ethnology 4th Annual Report, 1882-83*. Washington, D. C.: Government Printing Office. 467-521.

    1892 "Manual Concepts: A Study of the Influence of Hand-Usage on Cultural Growth." *American Anthropologist*. 5: 289-317.

    1895 Katalog einer Sammlung von Idolen, Fetischen und priestlichen Ausrustings gegenstanden Zuni oder Ashiwi Indianer von Neu-Mexico. Veroffentlichungen Museum fur Volkerkunde, Berlin. Band 4, Heft 1. Berlin: D. Reimer.

    1897a "Outlines of Zuni Creation Myths." *Bureau of American Ethnology 13th Annual Report, 1892-93*. Washington, D. C.: Government Printing Office.

    1897b "The Need of Studying the Indian in Order to Teach Him." Board of U. S. Indian Commissioners *28th Annual Report*. Washington, D. C.: Government Printing Office.

    1920 *Zuni Breadstuffs*. Indian Notes and Monographs, VIII. New York: Heye Foundation.

    1986 [1903] *Zuni Folk-Tales*. Tucson: University of Arizona Press.

Green, Jesse, ed.
    1979 *Zuni: Selected Writings of Frank Hamilton Cushing*. Lincoln, Nebraska: University of Nebraska Press.

Holmes, William.
    1900 "In Memorium: Frank Cushing." *American Anthropologist* 2: 356-60.

Mallery, Garrick.
    1964 *Picture Writing of the American Indians*. 2 v. New York: Dover.

Powell, John Wesley.
    1875 *Exploration of the Colorado River of the West....* Washington, D. C.: Government Printing Office.

    1900 "In Memorium: Frank Cushing." *American Anthropologist* 2: 364.

Wilson, Edmund.
    1956 *Red, Black, Blond and Olive: Studies in Four Civilizations: Zuni, Haiti, Soviet Russia, Israel*. New York: Oxford University Press.

XII

Evangelical Changes:
Karl Gützlaff and Hudson Taylor

To the awakened conscience of early nineteenth century Protestant evangelism there was no more grievous thought than the crying heathen multitudes who had not been touched by the Gospel. The Roman Catholic Church had been methodically capturing souls abroad ever since the age of discovery, adding its dangers to those of heathenism. The evangelists had a stunning vision of souls rotting in superstition with the saving Faith so near them. Anyone who believed that there could be no salvation outside the Faith, and that direct, dramatic exposure to the Word could fire even the most sluggish soul to eternal Light was obliged to act immediately, lest Satan's Kingdom shroud the entire world.

China was the most unhappy nation in the empire of the damned. Although an ancient civilization covering great stretches of territory and encompassing an enormous population, China had never been touched either by the Gospel or the refinements of technology. Millions were casually playing themselves into the Pit while the Emperors and Mandarins sported in unchecked dissolution. But labor in this bountiful field was not easy. Missionaries were barred from Chinese territory except for a few trading ports. Even the traders themselves had to be content with only the slightest contact with licensed merchants who handled all the goods brought into China from the outside. The ruling Manchu Dynasty, which had occupied the Dragon Throne for over 150 years had no interest in foreign contact beyond receiving tribute (the fiction under which trade was conducted). Unauthorized foreigners trying to penetrate the mainland were unceremoniously evicted. The missionaries had little hope of going among the common people of the interior whose souls they were most intent upon saving.

China yielded only to a certain touch, and then very slowly. The man who first applied this touch was Karl Gützlaff, a Bavarian medical missionary. Gützlaff had been working among the overseas Chinese of Malaya and Siam—but he felt the call of the mother country and of "China's millions." He took ship for China determined to start a mission; he was eminently qualified for the task (Schlyter 1946:46).

> Since the time he had been at Bintang he had belonged to the Kua family of Fujien, and had already mastered the Chinese language. In addition he took to wearing Chinese clothes, adopted Chinese manners, left off reading European books and sought to become Chinese in all things, to merge himself with the Chinese.

Gützlaff was an "individual missionary," that is unaffiliated with any particular denomination or mission society. By upbringing he was a Moravian, and the Moravian ideology imbued his mission work: he sought to spread the Gospel as far as possible rather than to institute Church organizations among bodies of converts. The aspiration became even more expedient under the straitened circumstances of the mission as Gützlaff focused his efforts on preaching and the distribution of Chinese tracts he had composed or translated.

Gützlaff's Chinese appearance made it slightly easier for him to move along the China coast and make pamphlet-distributing sallies into the interior. His finances were limited, therefore an offer from English opium traders to accompany them as an interpreter was hard to refuse. Gützlaff, and his employers, had various justifications for this sinister marriage of interests; it brought trade and religion to the strangely stubborn Chinese, they explained. Linking opium and religion in practice this way creatively anticipated the famous Marx-Engels metaphor by decades. But Chinese beneficiaries of the expeditions preferred the powdered drug to the verbal drug, and Gützlaff profited accordingly.

It would be a mistake to reduce Gützlaff to snide comments on his condoning the opium trade. Robert Morrison, sent out by the London Mission Society long before Gützlaff, also interpreted for the opium merchants and gentle Quakers from Philadelphia, persecuted for their non-violence, took to the nasty traffic with alarming gusto. Gützlaff was not only adapted to Chinese customs but to the state of China-West relations; he exonerated himself by the belief that China would gain more through Christianity than its loss through addiction. He was considered a "pirate" and a "hypocrite" by many of the traders, but he was indispensible to them because he knew the language and the attitudes of the Chinese to perfection.

During his trips up and down the China coast Gützlaff handed out tracts, preached to the masses where he could and organized agents for his Chinese Union (Gützlaff 1834). Financed partially by English missionary societies this project trained native disciples and sent them off to the interior laden with tracts. Each was supposed to return with a diary and a convert from the province to which he was assigned; but it was easy enough to falsify the diary and find some loafer who would pose as a convert. The disciples spent their travel allowances on opium or other pleasures and came back to Gützlaff with inspiring words on the opening of the interior to the Word of God.

The missionary was only part fooled by his errant followers, and reaped further advantage by having some of them double as spies for the British, learning of troop movements and gun placements. English missionaries who, lured by Gützlaff's apparent success, came out to China were astounded by his shady methods. But in 1839 the Opium War broke out (Gützlaff was interpreter on the English frigate that precipitated the incident) and the missionaries held back while the soldiers cleared the field.

Gützlaff's adaptation was instrumental, for his mission work but later for his idiosyncratic trade-mission-spying activities. When he was at his residence in Macao he wore European clothes and obviously was able to maintain good relations with the traders and with other missionaries. He was not accused of going Chinese as the Jesuits had been centuries before or other evangelicals would be later. Gützlaff's adaptation was as great as its usefulness to himself and to his employers-no more.

The scandal over Gützlaff's Chinese Union broke not long after the Opium War and he had to exert much of his persuasive energy to convince his European societies that he was still reliable. The irregularities which an investigation of his Chinese missionaries uncovered were surprising even to him; he decided that European missionaries must take the place of the Chinese. With the signing of peace treaties and the opening of more ports to trade the chances for European missionaries improved. Gützlaff visited Europe and recruited for the new campaign.

A result of his inspiring visit to London in 1850 was the formation of "The Chinese Association" with the stated purpose of directing English evangelical energies toward China. Mr. Pearse, the Association's Secretary and a prominent member of the Stock Exchange, received late in that year a letter from a young man, James Hudson Taylor, inquiring about the Society's work and asking for written materials. When Pearse replied in an encouraging vein Taylor sent a further communication deploring the state of affairs in Gützlaff's mission: the malversations of the Chinese "converts" were just becoming known. Taylor did not blame Gützlaff, but the Chinese, and he was certain that this setback would not be fatal for all missionary efforts in China (Hudson Taylor to George Pearse, Aug. 7, 1850, quoted in Taylor and Taylor 1912:92-93).

> Notwithstanding that the character of the Chinese seems very favorable for the reception of the Gospel, we have promise that all shall know Him, whom to know is life eternal.

"The harvest is great, but the labors are few," he concluded. Hudson Taylor realized that dedicated proselytes were required to facilitate the ultimate success of the mission. It was typical of him to maintain without question that the harvest of China must someday be gathered, as Christ had promised. He had already dedicated himself to the labor.

Taylor's character was formed by evangelism in its first, fervent period. His family was single-minded in its devotion; in his youth he distributed tracts to sarcastic, irreligious neighbors and joined in family prayers for the redemption of all wayward souls. The dying millions of China were frequently mentioned. After some spiritual meandering, in 1849, at the age of 17, Taylor had an illumination. A voice said, "Then go for me to China," and that sentence became his life's directive.

The inquiries addressed to Pearse were an initial contact with a group interested in the conversion of China. As the correspondence continued it became apparent, amid all the remorse over lost souls, that Taylor would be grateful were the Association to prepare him for missionary work by underwriting some medical training which, it was well known, had immense value in eliciting the attention of Chinese sick in body as well as in spirit. Gützlaff and the American Peter Parker had demonstrated that fully. The Association agreed and Taylor, after some apprentice time in a local surgery, moved to London. He survived the worldliness of the metropolis and a near-lethal infection; in 1854, his training adequate, he made a solitary departure for Shanghai.

Arriving after an arduous journey he was welcomed and housed by Dr. Medhurst, the cotranslator with Gützlaff of the Bible into Chinese. Under Medhurst's able tutelage Taylor perfected himself in the Chinese language. As soon as possible he was pushing inland from Shanghai, there to meet with the abuses so frequent during his long career: irascible officials, cheating tradesmen and living conditions of extreme discomfort. He might tell himself that conditions were like those prevailing in England at the time of his grandfather who was mobbed and beaten many times while out preaching the Gospel. Taylor welcomed martyrdom but he also felt a call to do great work in China—for that he must live.

As his knowledge of both Mandarin Chinese and the local dialects progressed he was induced to adopt the same tactics as Gützlaff and avoid unwanted attention by accommodating himself to native ways (Hudson Taylor 1951:59).

> At the suggestion of the Rev. Dr. Medhurst, the veteran leader of the London Mission, I was led about this period to adopt the native costume in preference to foreign dress, to facilitate travel and residence inland. The Chinese had permitted a foreign firm to build a silk factory some distance inland, with the proviso that the style of the building must be purely Chinese, and that there should be nothing external to suggest that it was foreign. Much benefit was found to result from this change of costume, and I, and most of those associated with me, have continued to use native dress.

The factory analogy is just as unappetizing as the opium one, but it is neater. Taylor was convinced that the Chinese were unreservedly xenophobic and would not let him close enough even to accept a tract as long as he was dressed as a Westerner. The Christian machinery had to operate within a Chinese facade—but then factories were only trade outposts.

Taylor was attentive to detail in his costume, making sure to append a feature which had become characteristically Chinese since being imposed by the Manchu conquerers, the queue, or pigtail (Taylor and Taylor 1912: 316).

> That night he took the step he had been painfully considering—called in a barber and had himself so transformed in appearance that his own mother could hardly have known him. To put on Chinese dress without shaving the head is comparatively simple a matter; but Hudson Taylor went to all lengths leaving only enough of the fair curly hair to grow into the queue of the Chinaman. He had prepared a dye, moreover, with which he darkened this remaining hair, to match the long black braid that at first must do duty. Then in the morning he put on as best he might the loose, unaccustomed garments, and appeared for the first time in the gown and satin shoes of a 'Teacher,' or man of the scholarly class.

The Englishman's adoption of a sign of slavery—the queue symbolized the horse's tail and the horse's (to the nomad Manchu primarily) servitude—would not have set well with others of his nation. Lord Macartney, an

English emissary to the Ch'ien Lung Emperor in 1793 jeopardised the mission rather than render the degrading tribute of a kowtow to the Emperor. But Taylor was no diplomat, and his "English flesh and blood" could take a great deal of punishment for the sake of Christ.

The clothes themselves inflicted this first. However convenient the dress may have been it rode upon Taylor rather ill, as can be gathered from letters he wrote after his "transformation." He complained to a friend in Hull that the turned-up shoes were "especially uncomfortable" and catalogued for his sister Amelia the myriad contentions of Chinese fashion against his English flesh: the head shaving gave him prickly heat and the dye aggravated the soreness; the socks were inelastic; the shoes were flat-soled; and the trousers "unheard-of garments." When he went to a barber for an obligatory "shampooing" he found himself tackled and assaulted nearly beyond endurance. To finish matters he had to obey the Chinese dictum against wearing any cap in the summer, thus exposing his mistreated pate to the rigors of direct sunlight (Hudson Taylor, Aug. 28, 1855, quoted in Taylor and Taylor 1912: 319-20).

Hudson Taylor's conception of the body in comfort differed greatly from the Chinese conception which he must literally take upon himself to present a good front. The botanist and tea company agent Robert Fortune, traveling disguised through China 1848-51, also was afflicted by the shaving ceremony and the stiff dress but Fortune made light of his discomfort. Hudson Taylor had the same tactile response but his experience was altogether different: it was a trial of faith and a labor of evangelism, not just an amusing inconvenience.

A few months after his changeover Taylor wrote to Amelia that he had "such a *sensible* presence of God" as never before. The outward trial bolstered his inner purpose and he headed inland again, confident he could raise Christ among the slothful Chinese. He was associated with another missionary in Chinese clothing William Burns; together they passed through a number of inland cities. Taylor was troubled by accidents and persistent illness and became exceedingly discouraged over the prospects of proselytizing in the interior. He decided to establish a medical mission in the Treaty Port of Ning-po. Cutting himself off from the debt-ridden Chinese Evangelisation Society (as the Chinese Association was called) he built up his own independent organization.

There was already a small English community in Ning-po, and it was inhospitable to Hudson Taylor: wearing Chinese dress was not a respectable practice in the mission fellowship. Taylor was a pariah among his own people and just marginally acceptable among the Chinese. He founded a small hospital and surmounting the fierce opposition of a guardian (Taylor's class background was not exalted enough) he married a young Englishwoman. But in 1860 the T'ai P'ing Rebellion drove him and most of his colleagues out of the country.

Hun Hsiu-ch'uan, the Supreme Ruler of the T'ai P'ing Rebels, failed civil service candidate and visionary, was spurred to form his peculiar ideology by a pamphlet based on Morrison's translation of the Bible. The Medhurst-Gützlaff translation was, however, a great excitement to Hung; Medhurst himself said that Hung's understanding of the Bible or of Christianity was quite limited. Not much could be expected of a man who had announced himself the younger brother of Christ. The Christian element in the rebels' dogma should have indicated to the missionaries that the handing out of tracts and the delivery of sermons, even in Chinese, would not be adequate to make the Chinese total Christians. For the time being they had no opportunity to modify their approach since the T'ai P'ings executed Christians as well as Manchus.

Back in England Taylor lectured on China to raise money for the mission work he contemplated once the T'ai P'ings were quelled. On June 27, 1865 Taylor and the perennial Mr. Pearse deposited ten pounds sterling at the London and Country Bank in an account for the China Inland Mission. This was the name of Taylor's new society, non-denominational and designed after his own principles. He was very successful in gleaning funds and volunteers from an English public horrified by the reports of barbarism in the recent revolt and thus assured of China's need for the Gospel. With the rebels subdued and the Manchus once again in control it only remained to start the new mission. The first party of fifteen missionaries, led by Taylor and his wife, entered Shanghai harbor in 1866.

During the period of exile Taylor, who had become a mission patriarch, considered the matter of adaptation carefully and concluded that assuming Chinese dress and custom was the best strategy for all missions, including those in the Treaty Ports. In a letter intended for the indoctrination of China Inland Missionaries-in-training he explained that though Europeans can go anywhere under passport protection this does not mean they can reach the people (Taylor and Taylor 1912: 89-91).

> Merely to put on their dress and act regardless of their thoughts and feelings is to make a burlesque of the whole matter, and will probably lead the person so adopting it to conclude, before, long, that it is of very little value to him. But I have never heard of any

one, after a *bona fide* attempt to become Chinese to the Chinese
that he might gain the Chinese, who either regretted the course
taken or wished to abandon it.

These are words which reverberate over immense distances with the young
Roberto de Nobili's wish to "become Indian to save the Indians," ultimately
echoing St. Paul's "be all things to all people" enjoinder. But Taylor jams in
a corollary that diverts the call—"become Chinese *to the Chinese*." de Nobili
suffered greatly because he had convinced many of his own compatriots that
he had become an idolatrous Hindu while he was really serving as an
intermediary between Hinduism and Christianity.

Taylor was more circumspect; not a mote of Chinese conviction would
foul his religious consciousness, dress as he might. His work was delivery of
doctrine to the Chinese. Yet the China Inland Mission was not half-hearted;
Taylor knew that Chinese civilization was as complex and deep-founded as
European civilization and would not be totally excluded by conversion. He
made an important distinction, again sounding like Ricci and de Nobili.

> It is not the denationalisation but the Christianisation of these
> people that we seek. We wish to see the Chinese Christians raised
> up—men and women truly Christian in every right sense of the
> word. We wish to see churches of such people presided over by
> pastors of their own country men, worshipping God in the land of
> their fathers, in their own tongue, and the edifices in a thoroughly
> native style of architecture.

Being Chinese and Christian need not be incompatible; coexistence was
possible. Taylor moved in advance of many other Protestant missionaries but
having gone this far he went no further. His Christianity was still the pre-
eminent, exclusive Gospel he had known since youth, it was something to fit
inside Chinese life, like a better part replacing an inferior one in a machine.
He never made an effort, as the Indian Buddhists had long ago on introducing
their faith into China, to take stock of China's traditions and graft the new
faith onto them. Taylor had just grown more subtle in his delivery, in his
expectations. Comparative adaptive theology concerned him very little.

By neglecting to evolve a detailed program for conversion which took
Chinese belief as the point of departure Taylor threw the main work of
doctrinal assimilation upon the individual convert, a good Protestant
atitude perhaps but dangerous under these circumstances. Left to make his
own peace with God an English convert would usually find a God similar to
the One found by other converts but a Chinese convert given the same
opportunity might find a God less congenial to the Lord of his Christian

teachers. Taylor still held the old view of the Chinese as hollow shells overlaid with a civilised skin: the hollow space was ready for Christianity. His version of the skin was thick and more elaborately figured than Gutzlaff's but it was still just a skin: nothing inside but particles of superstition that would quickly effloresce before the new Light.

Taylor expected congregations to be formed painlessly, with little confusion or conflict among converted individuals brought into a wholly novel relation with each other. Christ would change the hearts of those who resisted; the petty quarrels were schemes of the Devil impeding progress of Christ on earth and did not stem from any incompatibility between Christianity and the "great but benighted people of China." The Jesuits erred on the side of complexity, making their message so intricate that only the literati could grasp it. The Inland Mission erred on the side of simplicity, taking it for granted that the Chinese, permitted to retain the forms of their civilization, would tenant them in praise of the Christian God with no explanations required. The Chinese have always required explanations.

At the end of his instructional letter Taylor outlines the philosophy of adaptation.

> Let us in everything not sinful become Chinese, that we may by all means 'save some.' Let us adopt their dress, acquire their language, seek to conform to their habits and approximate to their diet as far as health and constitution will allow. Let us live in their houses, making no unnecessary alteration in external form, and only so far modifying their internal arrangement as health and efficiency for work absolutely require.

Taylor would make every imaginable concession to the Chinese, but he saw something unhealthy and unclean in Chinese living conditions. Some aspects of Chinese behavior were just sinful and should not be tolerated. Taylor's missionaries were hygienically aroused, nutritionally revised and spiritually correct Chinese; they were models for Chinese Christians. The Chinese were thus invited to adapt in a simplified version of their own culture, while those English volunteers who entered the Mission were assuming a sophisticated but still evangelical conception of Chinese identity. Rarely if ever had so large a body of people pledged themselves to take on the ways of another people in obedience to a consistent ideological program: Taylor's China Inland Mission was organized change of cultural identity on the group level.

The original band of missionaries met with setbacks. The English settlements in China were civilised; Chambers of Commerce and cricket teams made the round of life more "English." Taylor had seemed ridiculous in 1860; he and his missionaries were even more ridiculous in 1866. Assessing the likely response they decided to defer putting on Chinese dress in order not to give "unnecessary offence." The clothes, when finally donned, were impossible. Maria, Taylor's wife, carped at the proprieties governing women's behavior; she could not even take her husband's arm when out walking. Furthermore in the cities only Manchu women and prostitutes were not foot-bound. The women of Taylor's company were clearly not Manchu. But Maria Taylor also felt that taking Chinese dress helped the missionaries reach the Chinese (Guiness 1894: vol. 1: 319-20).

Some of the missionaries who expected more glory and less drudgery, felt silly and degraded in their new identities. Lewis Nicol and his wife, transferred to a remote outpost, rapidly reverted to Western clothes and tried to dominate the natives. The local official shipped them back to Taylor in Hang-Chow, where they caused further trouble by allying themselves with a dissident, anti-adaptive faction. This group retailed scandal. Letters were sent back to London picturing Hudson Taylor as an Englishman who had adapted to the extent of taking two Englishwomen as concubines. Taylor quickly obtained affidavits from the two women denying the charge but this was the start of a schism.

A cadre of the mission remained loyal to Taylor and the rolls of volunteers grew. An effort to preach in Yang-chow, previously untouched by missionaries sparked a riot and massacre of Christians. Taylor and his companions escaped without serious harm but the incident raised an anti-missionary mood in the press and in Parliament. Gladstone's government, which would refuse to relieve Gordon in the Sudan several years later, did not take a militant stance against the Chinese. Taylor and his followers were left unprotected. As the recruits multiplied Taylor strung together a missionary network which drew people and funds from many sources, from Cambridge to the London docks, and apportioned them to posts all over China. The China Inland Mission was the hardest hit by the Boxer Rebellion of 1900, losing 58 persons, yet the next year applications to the Mission were at a new high.

Taylor died in 1905, but the Mission moved under its own power for years afterward, bringing hundreds of Christians into China. There is nothing else to say about Taylor's evangelical adaptation; it extended from his own experience, became a movement, but only went so far before it stopped.

References

Benoit, Jean Paul.
   1952 *Puissance du Seigneur: Vie de Hudson Taylor*. Starsbourg: Editions Oberlin.

Broohall, Marshall.
   1930 *Hudson Taylor*. London: China Inland Mission.

Fortune, Robert.
   1853 *A Journey to the Tea Countries of China (1848-51)*. London.

Guiness, Geraldine.
   1894 *The Story of the China Inland Mission*. 2 v. London: Morgan and Scott.

Gützlaff, Karl.
   1834 *Journal of Three Voyages Along the Coast of China in 1831, 1832 and 1833*. London: Westley and Davis.

Hudson Taylor, James.
   1951 *A Retrospect*. London: China Inland Mission.

Macindoe, Betty
   1974 *Hudson Taylor: God's Man for China*. London: Hodder and Stoughton.

Pollock, J.C.
   1962 *Hudson Taylor and Maria*. New York: McGraw-Hill.

Schlyter, Herman.
   1946 *Karl Gützlaff als Missionar in China*. Lund: Hakan Ohlssons Bocktrycken.

Taylor, Dr. and Mrs. Howard.
   1912 *Hudson Taylor in Early Years*. Philadelphia: China Inland Mission.

   1917 *Hudson Taylor and the China Inland Mission*. London: Morgan and Scott.

XIII

Joseph Hardy Neesima

Looking at the document called the Black Ship Scroll one would think that the Japanese had never seen Westerners before. It is a crude, fascinating set of drawings that depict Commodore Perry's ship and crew when they first landed at Uraga in 1853, on their heady mission to pry open the tight-shut island nation. Perry comes off as a "hairy barbarian" with staring eyes and hirsute face; his sailors seem to be wild animals and the one Negro on board is actually drawn with all conventions reserved for demons. But the Japanese had seen Westerners; that is why the island was "closed" and why Perry had to seem a barbarian.

The Portuguese had found their way to Japan in the early sixteenth century and, taking advantage of the political disorder, gained a foothold for trade and religion. After nearly a century of continuous Western presence nearly four percent of Japan was Christian, an impressive record; even more impressive, however, was the almost complete elimination of Christianity when the government became recentralized under the Tokugawa Shogunate. The missionaries and their converts were executed, the Portuguese forbidden to trade. Only the Protestant Dutch, confined to an island in Yedo harbor, were allowed a modicum of contact. A Japanese Christian uprising, sponsored, the authorities thought, by the Portuguese sealed the government's hostility to the barbarians and their religion. One of the chief articles in Japan's closure was the permanent exclusion of Christianity.

The Japanese realized they had other things to fear from the West when Russian ships began probing Japanese harbors early in the nineteenth century. The Russians caused some military incidents in the Kurile Islands and Hokkaido, but one Russian officer, Captain Golovnin, captured along with his surveying party by the Japanese, showed his captors that all Westerners were not barbarians. Later incursions by the British and Americans may have confirmed the old opinion; Perry's well-publicized expedition of 1853-54 (which just outdistanced a Russian party with the same intent) signaled to the Japanese government that it must treat formally with the Western powers, repugnant as that might be.

The mystique of Perry's "opening Japan" should not be taken too seriously. Perry himself was an able diplomat but he was also a very able publicist. The earlier contacts with Western powers had already raised a body of sentiment among the Japanese and, most important, the Japanese were at the time of Perry's visit in the throes of sweeping social change. The samurai class was impoverished and losing respect; their military government was unable to keep order as it had before; the wealthy townsmen were exasperated by the exactions of an expensive government and the peasants, who were rising up in revolt more than ever, were even more exasperated with even heavier exactions. Perry's arrival had the makings of a good excuse.

Science and technology interested the Japanese who had any interest in Western learning much more than Christianity; yet Christianity would not be left out. Townsend Harris, the feckless American envoy who followed Perry, "read the full service in an audible voice" under the sole protection of the "powerful and potent" American name (Harris 1964:17).

> This was beyond doubt the first time that the English version of the Bible was ever read, or the American Protestant Episcopal Service ever repeated in this city.

Harris negotiated his treaty in 1859 specifically to allow the open practice of Christianity. American Protestants, the Presbyterian Dr. Hepburn for example, soon began teaching in the open ports; the Russian Orthodox missionary Nikolai set up an outpost in the northern trade port of Hakodate, where he ministered to the tiny Russian community but also encouraged Japanese in his faith. But there were not many converts.

Japan would only receive Christianity borne in the person of a native who could show himself the favorable changes wrought by Christianity. Joseph Hardy Neesima thought himself that vessel, ordained to bring Japan a Western technology tempered and beatified by the Christian ideals which had fostered its growth.

The transformation of Niijima Jo into Joseph Hardy Neesima is summarized in two letters, both written by Neesima to his American patron Alpheus Hardy, the first in 1865, when Neesima had just arrived in the United States and thrown himself upon Hardy for assistance and the second in 1885, from Japan (Hardy 1892: 5-6).

> (1)   I am very thankful to you. You relief, me but I cannot show to you my thankfulness with my words. But I at all times bless to God for you with this prayer: O God! if thou hast eyes, look upon me. O God! if though hast ears, hear my prayer. Let me be civilized

with Bible. O Lord! thou send they spirit upon my Hardy, and let him relief me from sad condition. O Lord! please! Set thy eyes upon my Hardy and keep him from illness and temptation.

Your obedient servant,
Joseph Hardy Neesima

(2)

Kyoto, Japan
Aug. 29, 1885

To Mr. and Mrs. Alpheus Hardy:
    To whom I owe more than my own parents for their boundless love and untiring interest manifested in my welfare, both temporal and spiritual, I most affectionately dedicate this narrative of my younger days.

Their ever grateful child,

After the second letter there comes a long narrative of Neesima's early life, written in impeccable English.

These two letters are juxtaposed in the main English biography of Neesima, *The Life and Letters of Joseph Hardy Neesima*, published by Alpheus Hardy's son Arthur in 1892, three years after Neesima's death. Hardy compares the letters to demonstrate the progress Neesima had made; they are an advertisement of Christian improvement. The godless Japanese had dropped his crude ways and become a true believer. Hardy felt that Neesima's greatest attainment was imbueing himself with Anglo-Saxon manners enough to become an intermediary between Christian America and heathen Japan (Hardy 1892: 222).

> Anglo-Saxon straightforward methods of procedure, so foreign to a semi-indifferent, indirect Japanese made a middle-man an absolute necessity, and both by nature and by education Mr. Neesima was admirably fitted for this position.

The nineteenth century stereotype of the Japanese was still very much alive when Arthur Hardy wrote this: It was before the Russo-Japanese War. And the Anglo-Saxon self-concept, accurate if Townsend Harris was an example, increasingly emphasized directness and "rugged individualism." As Hardy saw it Neesima had become fully educated not only in American learning but in American national character; he made Anglo-Saxon bluntness of expression palatable to the circuitous Japanese without losing the essential Christian message.

Neesima concurred with this conception of his mission, but he shifted the emphasis. Hardy thought Christianity most important; Neesima, and this is clear from his life and from his letters, was most devoted to Japan. Christianity was the least corrupt means of bringing Japan up to the level of the West. Neesima did not consider himself a Christian messiah sent to topple the pagan regime of Tokugawa. He saw the practical difficulties of converting Japan and knew that the task could not be done in one enthusiastic whirl. Yet he did confess a sense of divine mission which inspired him quietly to his labor of upraising Japan.

It is emblematic of Neesima's spiritual nationalism that he sought to spread Christianity gradually and through education, by founding Christian schools where Japanese students could learn technical subjects along with prayers and catechism. He elicited fair sums of money from American supporters to build and maintain these schools. The Americans felt they were contributing to the missionary effort; they were really helping to train Japanese youth in all aspects of technology in a Christian environment.

Christianity was not just a front for Neesima. He complained bitterly when the Japanese government set up secular schools on the Western model and began to draw students away from the Christian institutions where he had hoped to nurture their best tendencies. Neesima envisioned Japan one day becoming the Kingdom of Christ on Earth with all the blessings of modern technology. But to bring this about he must become a vessel, crude at first but eventually refined by the civilizing touch of America into a model vessel for Christianity's most advantageous doctrine.

As he saw it later his youth was mostly spent in spiritual darkness. He was misled by the pretentions of Japanese religion and even prided himself on gifts as a spirit healer. His hunger for learning saved him from provincial narrowness; his father, a samurai writing-master in the retinue of a nobleman, taught him to read early. On his own he studied Chinese and Dutch, reading what works in these languages he could find. The "Dutch learning," mostly second-hand versions of Dutch works on astronomy, physics and medicine, had been cultivated by a few scholars for several hundred years and was the only conduit for Western ideas into Japan.

This influx of ideas made Neesima restless. Though his father demanded that Neesima prepare to enter the nobleman's service Neesima revolted against his hereditary position and the servitude it entailed. He became truculent toward traditional religious observances too; at age 15 he exhibited a precocious skepticism by stopping his offerings to ancestral idols because they did not eat the food left for them. This was the kind of reasoning revolt Western divines always envisioned in the awakening heathen.

Some Christian books in Chinese, smuggled into his room and read on the sly gave him a jolt. Though he was "partly a skeptic and partly struck with reverential awe," the story of the Creation transformed him, made him want further instruction (Hardy 1892: 31).

> Not being able to see any foreign missionaries then I could not obtain any explanation on many points, and I wished at once to visit a land where the Gospel is freely taught and from whence teachers of God's words were sent out. Having recognized God as my heavenly father, I felt I was no longer inseparably bound to my parents. I discovered for the first time that the doctrines of Confucius on the filial relation were too narrow and fallacious. I said then: 'I am no longer my parent's, but God's.'

The Book of Genesis is most antipathetic to Confucian doctrine; it teaches a definite beginning of things and the dependence of Man upon God where Confucius teaches indifference to beginnings and ends and the dependence of men upon a network of interpersonal relations. At once Neesima's earthly father, whose commands he did not wish to obey, was replaced by an infinitely sublime abstract father. He strained for a chance to travel to a place where he might better serve this higher, better parent.

Obtaining leave to visit Hakodate he found a benefactor in Father Nikolai, who had hired him as a teacher of Japanese. The charitable works of the Russian missionary, the free hospital he had established, encouraged Neesima by proving the practical advantages of the "new light" he was determined to bring into Japan. Conversations with an English-speaking store clerk and other young Japanese determined him to choose America as the place for his Christianization. Abandoning his filial compunctions and his fear of the repressive government, he located a captain willing to take the risk of carrying him to Hong Kong whence he might board ship for America. His companions aided him in eluding the dockside authorities. He paid for the passage by doing menial chores. When a passenger beat him because he did not comprehend an order given in English, Neesima, still a samurai, ran to his quarters for his sword in order to punish the lout. Then he reconsidered, realizing that he must stand trials more severe than this without recourse to material weapons. In Hong Kong he sold the sword to purchase a Bible.

The trip to America saw him in the hands of his first surrogate authority figure, the ship's captain, who patiently taught him English by pointing out objects and enunciating the correct English names. He forbade Neesima to associate with the sailors in the forecastle fearing that he would unwittingly add a few indecorous terms to his growing vocabulary. In Boston the captain introduced Neesima to the ship's wealthy owner, Alpheus Hardy, a former China trade captain himself, who after some meditation adopted Neesima, paid for his education and funded his projects for the rest of his life. In Hardy Neesima found a father who took care of practical details which the greater father, God, overlooked.

When Hardy died in 1887 Neesima, then in Japan, consoled Mrs. Hardy in language almost Biblical (Hardy 1892: 302).

> I feel my real father is gone; yea he has been to me more than my father. I believe that he knew me more than all my Japanese friends here. I have lost the friend of Japan.

The link between Hardy and Japan in this passage is made almost iconic by the presence of an engraved portrait of Hardy on the opposite page, one of the very few illustrations in the book. Hardy stares out from amid cloud-like Dundreary whiskers, as becomes a New England patriarch. The face and the forces it embodied were the dominating energies in the America Neesima now entered.

In the same letter Neesima compares Hardy's death to a recent eclipse of the sun; implicit in several of Neesima's letters is the similarity of Hardy to the sun. He is a very material sun, casting his own brightness but also enabling other lights to illuminate the world. Neesima was one of these lights. At every point in his life he turned to Hardy for counsel and financial assistance. The advice Neesima often sought was usually approval for a pre-ordained course of action—but he still sought Hardy's approval. Hardy stood beneath God, a divinely designated manager of His abundance. In fact, Hardy himself believed this.

Hardy saw his own vocation answered in Neesima's call to the ministry. In his youth Hardy had gone to Phillips Academy in order to "fit" for the ministry. Then, after a bout of ill health, he realized that he would never be able to meet the call. In the midst of his despair he had a vision and experienced a conversion. As he told the Psi Upsilon Society of Amherst College much later in his life (originally published in *North Wisconsin Evangel*, August 1893, Davis 1894: 33-34),

...One evening alone in my room, my distress was so great that I threw myself flat on the floor. The voiceless cry of my soul was, 'O God, I cannot be thy minister.' Then there came to me as I lay a new vision, a new hope, a perception that I could serve God in business with the same devotion as in preaching, and that to make money for God might be my sacred calling. The vision of this service, and its clear nature as a sacred ministry, were so clear and joyous that I rose to my feet and with new hope in my heart exclaimed aloud, 'O God I can be thy *minister*!' I will go back to Boston and I will make money for God and *that* shall be my ministry.

In the context of Max Weber's remarks on the relationship between religion and capitalism this might seem a caricature; but to an audience at Amherst College in 1893, with the example of the great captains of industry in mind, this was a noble recitation. Hardy experienced his personal conversion as a coalescence of faith with commerce which he then might pursue with the knowledge that it was good in the eyes of God. His success in the China trade affirmed the divine direction in his choice, and his final salvation. As a "minister" of commerce he was under a vow to utilize his profits for the Gospel. The instrument given him was, he would agree, tainted, condemned by Christ, hence it was that much better turned to pious deeds.

Hardy was consistently munificent to all Christian charities; Neesima's arrival on one of his ships was providential. Here was a man whom Christian charity could transform into the preacher of the Gospel Hardy could never become. Hardy was God's steward to Neesima, placed by God's will in control of resources which could accomplish great works.

With Hardy assuming the role of his new father Neesima was beset by the need to elide him with his real father, who now seemed lost in superstition. From his earliest letters back to Japan he urged his father to accept Christ and baptism though he did not have words in Japanese for the concepts he was trying to put across. There was a heart-breaking imbalance between the two foci of paternal authority, Japan defiled but still claiming his fundamental allegiance, America vigorous and truly civilized but not home to his spirit. Neesima's program of personal change in America was formed by this conception of Japan's relation to America. He turned himself into a worthy representative of the ideal Christianity most beneficial to Japan, an abstraction that invited imitation not of Neesima but of its principle. Neesima's assimilation to America was not an end in itself, the result of being cast ashore and deciding to "go American" because it was no longer possible or desirable to be Japanese. Neesima prepared to mold himself into whatever pattern made the transfer of Christianity possible.

Of all the lives reviewed in this volume one finds Neesima's the greatest predetermination; he knew exactly who and what he was going to become and he was impatient to proceed with his changes. There was no frivolous deviation, no masquerade or lark in another identity. His dead ahead seriousness mowed down all obstacles to his advance to an American and therefore Christian life.

Logically his path was through the system of education. From preparatory school to college every step was defined and each individual was tested concretely against the standard of the grade. The Anglo-Saxon pedagogy that Neesima encountered when Hardy enrolled him at Andover Academy presupposed that all students were embryo gentlemen and engaged them as much in the conduct of etiquette as in memorization of Latin grammar or English rhetoric. Because Neesima was an alien—and somewhat older than most of the other students—he received much extracurricular coaching in his subjects and his behavior. He first lived with his tutor and then, when he graduated to Amherst College and his classmates were mature enough to support him, he lived in the dormitory. The cameraderie of American college students resembled the group associations that Neesima had experienced with agemates in Japan; his fellow students were even from class backgrounds roughly equivalent to his own. Thus he progressed regularly in surroundings which formally and informally invested him with the qualities of a Christian gentleman. His education was a rationalized translation of cultural identity from Japanese into Christian able to impress everyone around him with the degree of his politeness.

The rationality of the college system apportioned change in small doses, and allowed Neesima to select what he valued most in learning and in social relations. He studied the Bible, Christian literature, mathematics and the sciences; he had a talent for avoiding the college counterpart of the forecastle, which must have made him seem stiff to his classmates, and he was punctilious in the observance of all social forms. In his letters to Hardy and his parents he specified how each minute was made to count toward the final result and in his personal diary he noted down not observations but moments of edification which might arise from any cause, a prayer meeting or a conversation with another student. Neesima was in a process of pure education in which every eventuality was converted into knowledge and modulated by his accepted categories of Christian life.

After he had entrusted himself to the educational process long enough he began to act upon American reality with assurance, as if his regulated change needed more field and he was ready to expand. While still at

Amherst he took up mineral collecting. He requested Hardy to procure for him a copy of Dana's *Mineralogy*, a systematic classification of mineral types much in use among students and collectors. On his walking tours of New England, which had started as trips to church congregations interested in hearing about Japanese heathenism, Neesima visited quarries and mines. He sought out large collections of minerals at colleges and private homes, displaying his own acquisitions and discussing geology with specialists. He began to keep notebooks in which he not only listed the minerals he found but also described (in English) and sketched factories and mills, their machines and their products. His letters filled with technical names and classifications.

The landscape which he traveled became uniform in his experience as a collection of important things each of which fit into a scheme of knowledge which he thought part of his personal education. His emotion and aspiration were governed by the adequacy of collection. The only overt feeling in his letters is when he calls the minerals "beautiful" or his "loving objects," when he has a fit of pique over a quarryman's refusal to free some coveted fossil specimens. This was not a bad experience for Neesima, but a failure to experience. Upon his return to Japan he continued his mineral hunting but with a characteristic twist; he prospected for ores which might prove indicative of important natural resources. The American learning was for Japan's benefit.

In years when many curious tourists from Europe were setting down opinions on American life and manners Neesima never thought of remarking from his outsider's viewpoint on the peculiar traits of Americans. This was not because the Japanese were insensitive to the oddness of Americans; in their popular prints and satiric writings they surpassed most other peoples in capturing the less attractive aspects of their invaders. But Neesima had assimilated to an ideal of Christianity and his comments on the Americans were those of a Christian critic. Some of the congregations he addressed seemed to him less than zealous in their services; on trains he met people conspicuously indifferent to the Bible, and he berated them there as well as in his letters. He was no fanatic foaming with deranged conviction, but a man oppressed, and embarrassed, by the failure of Americans to live up to the goodly enjoinders of the faith which had led them to material bliss. The model which Alpheus Hardy always provided should have been more widely practiced in America.

Neesima himself merged with Hardy's ideal. After Amherst College he was accepted at Andover Theological Seminary and began the studies preparatory to ordination. His original conversion experience and the equation of fathers it engendered broadened into a theology of the same heavenly father existing everywhere. Neesima was not confined by the Bible and by Christian myth—the story of Christ, the execution of the Son of God as a criminal, never attracted him very much—instead his advanced education emphasized the verification of his absolute beliefs through the much more credible propositions of science. Luckily the old course in Natural Theology, which following Paley, Newton and other devout scientists admitted the evidence of natural history into the trial of faith, was still followed in the New England Seminaries. Darwin had not yet stirred up the peace between science and theology with polemics; Neesima's teachers were convinced, and they passed the conviction on to their student, that science would always verify religion. They instilled into him the modern scientific arguments against the superstition which he would have to combat if he ever returned to Japan.

The possibility arose sooner than he expected. In 1868, in the wake of complex political and ideological realignments, the Emperor was formally reinstated as the ruler of Japan, and the Bakufu, the military government of the Shogun, was eliminated. This apparently conservative move was accomplished by a group of progressive leaders who needed to stifle the backward samurai government before effecting changes. One of the pledges made by the leaders of this Meiji Restoration (after the young Emperor's reign title) was the "Five Articles Oath" which promised that the new leaders would search the world for knowledge and improve the education system in Japan to make the absorption of this knowledge more efficient. Neesima, a few other escapees and some official students sent overseas by the Shogun or by provincial lords were the whole of Japan's pre-Meiji foreign education cadre. In 1871 Iwakura Tomomi, a moving force in the Restoration, headed a major Mission to the United States and Europe. Iwakura expected to persuade the United States and Britain to rescind some of the disadvantageous clauses of the initial opening treaties but he also planned to observe government, industry and education abroad. In addition to the 48 members of the mission proper there were 54 students who were to be placed in Western schools, a sign that Neesima's solitary committment to Western learning was being adopted as a policy.

The Mission solicited Neesima's aid as an interpreter and expert on America. They discovered, however, that no amount of palavering would move President Grant's government to liberalize the Harris treaty. They went on to Europe accompanied by Neesima, who had obtained leave from Andover.

Though the Mission was equally unsuccessful in negotiating with Disraeli's government they left a trail of Japanese students everywhere. Neesima's diary (Niijima 1962) is probably the most diagnostic of the Mission's actual accomplishment: every new device or process, from a ship's navigating instruments to a wine press, he noticed and drew. The envoys were deaf to Neesima's exhortations to Christianity but they joined him in looking and taking note. Neesima did have some effect on them. He turned down the Mission's offer to return and accept a government post because Christianity was still banned for Japanese and he would, on reentering the country, be imprisoned both as a Christian and as a disloyal retainer. He explained that he had tranferred all loyalty to the Christian God. This must have had some influence on the government's lifting the ban not long after the Iwakura Mission returned in 1873.

Neesima rapidly finished his studies and was ordained a Congregational minister. Aplpheus Hardy was Chairman of the American Board of that church and secured Neesima the designation as the Board's missionary to Japan. Neesima persuaded the board that a Christian school would be the best base for his efforts, and was awarded a further grant for its establishment. He planned to reconstruct his own training process in an institution which could make Japanese Christians without going to America.

In Japan Neesima at once converted his father and other relatives then challenged the opposition of local rulers—strong despite the decree legalizing Christianity—by holding services wherever he could assemble the congregation. This defiance brought him and his disciples into open conflict with the more conservative lords but he was abetted by the central government, where he had friends from the Iwakura Mission. The modernizers could also use Neesima's movement (never very large, but a movement just the same) to break up reactionary enclaves.

Neesima pressed his advances by renting part of a building for his Christian university directly across from the Imperial Palaces in Kyoto. Under the old regime this sacrilege would never have been tolerated but Neesima relied on his backing to penetrate the sacred space of the capitol. Few students enrolled initially, but in 1876 the Doshisha, as the school was called, received an influx from the provinces that had every prospect of perpetuating Neesima's adaptation on Japanese soil, as he had planned.

The Lord of Kumamoto in Kyushu had in 1871 decided to add a teacher of English to the staff of his domain academy, where the sons of his retainers were educated. On the advice of Guido Verbeck, the Dutch Reformed missionary, he hired Captain Leroy Janes who being a foreigner and a

Christian soon drove the other teachers out of the Academy. Janes adhered to the still-existing law and did not teach Christianity but he did regroup the students into the semblance of an Anglo-American boarding school, and imposed upon them a roster of work and a moral code much tighter than was common in other schools. Janes' personal influence worked upon the students subtly; one morning 35 of them took an oath which joined common fidelity to the Christian God with a rededication to Japan. This Kumamoto Band, persecuted by their own parents and neighbors, became the nucleus of Neesima's Doshisha University in 1876.

Neesima's own adaptation, then, passed over into implementing the adaptation of others to his solution of Christianity and technology. The national interest, interpreted as rapid and clean modernization, was always part of the program. It might be said that the Kumamoto Band in entering the Doshisha was potentially the fundamental exteriorization of Neesima's experience in America: the individual experience of training for a scientific Christianity was embodied in a group of Japanese students. The content of their common ideals and their group rituals may have been derived from Christian and Western models but the yoking of the personal transformation to a group ethos was the crux of "Japanization" of Neesima's idiosyncratic experience. The oath of the Kumamoto Band was a mutual affirmation of conversion which most of them already had separately. Ebina Danjo, one of the Band and later an important Christian teacher, recalled in his autobiography that he rose to Christianity out of a sense of his own duty to God, but became one with the others when their community was recognized. As Janes had catalyzed their conversion and they themselves had formed a union, the Kumamoto Band came to the Doshisha presumably ready to follow the same path as Neesima to Christianity.

The auspices were favorable. Neesima organized the school in a fashion similar to Janes' Academy and the students, united against the contempt of society at large, supported each other in their study and in their proselytizing. It seemed that Neesima might indeed have perpetuated his adaptation in a small but dedicated group of students; Japan would be served by his creating a generation of devout and educated Christians.

But there were difficulties. The evangelical missionary Neesima engaged to teach the Bible underestimated the readiness of his students and gave his lectures in clumsy Japanese rather than the English which they understood. While he was covering the elements of Biblical revelation the graduates of Janes' school were writing meditations and disputing theology among themselves. Neesima, who had the respect of all, tried to keep order but he was faced with an inherent conflict between his Christianity and that of the people who had taught him. He was outmoded in Japan almost as he began.

The Protestantism which Neesima embraced was vocal and demonstrative but Japanese Protestant converts soon favored a less belligerent faith, over assertions which constantly put them at loggerheads with their relatives and dismissed their traditions as pure paganism. Graduates of the Doshisha generally remained Christians but they rarely adopted the hortatory style which their *sensei* had used when he returned to Japan. An inner confession which did not disrupt the calm of interpersonal routine was the preferred Christianity after the first upheavals of conversion.

Furthermore the government and non-Christian scholars rapidly separated Christianity from modernization and built schools which taught technical subjects only. Neesima himself worried that the Bible was too prominent in the curriculum of the Doshisha and that science and mathematics, which would help Japan, were not adequately taught. Yet he also deplored the secular schools and their failure to sweeten knowledge with religion. He argued with the historian and journalist Tokutomi Soho who after having started a proponent of "progress," which included the adoption of Christianity in the company of Western technology and education, gradually dropped Christianity in favor of the new Japan, which could make its way among nations without the crutch of an alien religion (Akimitsu 1963; Sansom 1973: 248-74).

Neesima's was only one small, isolated Christianity among a plethora of sects, groups, and bands that the divisions among the Protestant denominations induced in Japan. And Protestantism itself was second to Catholicism, which Japanese Christians preferred because it was not subject to schisms and heated disputes. Even so all the Christians in Japan during the latter years of the nineteenth century scarcely amounted to one-quarter of one percent of the population. Although Neesima educated some important leaders and writers his program did not amount to much in history, and was far outdistanced by the secular schools which produced the elite of the next generations.

Neesima's adaptation, although pitched at the Japanese nation did not for the comprehensiveness of its aims affect more than a few men whose effect on Japan itself was negligible. The whole of Japan and thus the world widened out before Neesima from where he stood; but in that world he was very small.

Neesima, saintly in his persistence, never ceased to associate Christianity with the highest borrowings Japan could take from the West, and in the Doshisha he cultivated the Christian group life that would make the religion Japanese. His followers venerated him as a *sensei* for he taught and therefore represented something definite which happened to be the result of personal adaptation to another culture. In his maxims, which were later collected into a book (Niijima 1967), he asserted the overwhelming majesty of the Christian God which requires the Christian to leave his parents and follow the path of learning. From his deathbed he wrote again about his beloved school (Hardy 1892: 326):

> The object of the Doshisha is the advancement of Christianity, Literature and Science and the furtherance of all education. These are to be pursued together as mutually helpful. The object of the education given by the Doshisha is not Theology, Literature, or Science in themselves; but that through these men of great and living power may be trained up for the service of true freedom and their country.

He then warned the trustees not to treat the students roughly, admonished them against letting the university become mechanical and impersonal. As the end neared he spoke of love; his last words were "Peace, Joy, Heaven."

References

Akimitsu, Morinaka.
     1963 *Niijima Sensei to Tokutomi Soho*. Tokyo: Doshisha University Press.

Davis, Jerome D.
     1894 *Rev. Joseph Hardy Neesima*. New York: Fleming H. Revell.

Hardy, Arthur Shelburne.
     1892 *The Life and Letters of Joseph Hardy Neesima*. Boston: Houghton-Mifflin.

McKeen, P.F.
     1890 *A Sketch of the Early Life of Joseph Hardy Neesima*. Boston: Lothrop.

Minoru, Watanabe.
     1959 *Niijima Jo*. Tokyo: Kichigawa Kubukan.

[Niijima Jo Shokan Shu]
     1967 *Niijima Jo Shokan Shu*. Tokyo: Iwanami Shoten.

[Niijima Sensei Kinenshu]
     1962 *Niijima Sensei Kinenshu* [Niijima Memorial Volume]. Koyukai: Doshisha University Press.

Tokutori, Ichiro.
     1955 *Niijima Jo Sensei*. Tokyo: Doshisha University Press.

XIV

Sea Breeze: Paul Gauguin

Paul Gauguin's son Emile, in his Preface to Gauguin's *Intimate Journals* (*Avant et Apres*) refers to a "fantastic Gauguin legend, distorted in many retellings." (Gauguin 1958: 9-10).

> Everywhere this story has captured the popular fancy. Once upon a time there was a middle-aged, somewhat commonplace and moderately successful stockbroker. He had a wife and three children to whom he was extremely devoted. Neither his family nor his friends had reason to suspect that he entertained any other ambition than to finish his days as a prosperous business man and a good paterfamilias. Then one night he shed all of his domestic virtues in his sleep. He awoke an inhuman monster. Gone was his love of family. Gone were his bourgeois ambitions and respectability. A burning fever to paint possessed him. So he fled to Paris, with never a thought or a care for his dependent family, and devoted himself to his newly adopted art in sublime defiance of academic tradition. And at last, finding civilization too irksome to be borne, he retired to Tahiti, where he lived and loved and painted and died like a savage.

Emil is correct; the story exists, and is told very much as he describes it. Naturally it is an error and a misjudgement; it cannot be sustained with even the slightest authentic knowledge of Gauguin. Most of the biographies of the painter are written with the refutation of this elementary tale uppermost in the writer's concerns. To the scholar of Gauguin the tale is a falsehood which must be put down or an oversimplification which must be corrected. The response is automatic, and seems impelled by more than the love of truth or some such intellectual cause. We are afraid to admit that the romance affixed by ignorance to Paul Gauguin's life is attractive, especially to those of us who know better and want everyone to know that we do.

The attraction lies in the simplicity of the tale but the simplicity is not that simple. The instantaneous transition from stockbroker to bohemian artist has implications reaching far beyond Paul Gauguin and his paintings. It is entertaining, the kind of sudden, dramatic change of life that is the stuff of popular literature and theater; it is relevant to our social system, which stresses profession and life tasks over family or is at least wrapped up in the conflict between the two; it is psychoanalytic in the popular sense, that is, Gauguin's switch tantalizes us with dark, mysterious forces operating within ordinary people—but never reveals anything. Whether we enjoy watching or worry about participating Gauguin's simplified life holds many things we cannot, no matter how insensate our existence, escape from considering in life. And outside of all this it electrifies us with the superb, scary tremor of Art.

Gauguin's change is the primordial myth of identity change for modern times; it is the shorthand for all the types of change that mean the most, and though we do know better we still repeat it, for like a new, vulgar word (it is new as myths go) there is nothing quite so expressive. That Gauguin chose to go to Tahiti is a further boon: it certifies the idea of the artist as untrammeled savage which has been manifesting itself in various ways ever since the early nineteenth century. Gauguin's identification with the natives is one possibility; the other, madness, typified by his friend van Gogh, has proved more compelling.

Truth, then, is not the issue in Gauguin's change; its suggestiveness is far more important. While many documents exist to render up the truth it is hard not to respond to the suggestive form. No matter how assiduously the real Gauguin is anatomized and laid out to dry the necessary hero rises up and does his deed. When he seems pegged and most removed he comes back with a redeeming explanation that incurs our esteem.

For example Gauguin wrote while in Tahiti a small newspaper called *Les Guêpes*. It was assumed by writers who never saw copies of the newspaper that Gauguin used it to sting French officials and defend the natives whom he had joined. This joined step with the rest of the Gauguin myth because it turned him into a champion of justice, which any great man should be. Then, as usual in Gauguin biography, came the revisionist. Bengt Daniellson, who traced Gauguin's life in Tahiti and the Marquesas exerted much effort to locate copies of the newspaper (Daniellson and O'Reilly 1966). He examined 23 of the 25 numbers edited or written by Gauguin and was amazed to find French-Tahitian relations mentioned only four times in the lot. In one article, a reprint of a public speech in Papeete, Gauguin attacks intermarriage between the Tahitian natives and Chinese immigrants, charging that this will foster a race of defectives. At other times he suggests that the natives be taken in hand and educated by Catholic missionaries, that resident gendarmes be situated among them to discourage their thievery and that since the natives are instinctive drunkards it will do no good to withdraw liquor licenses from tavern owners. Gauguin was the spokesman for the Catholic political party, which financed the newspaper and his diatribes were directed against French officials who were trying to forestall the worst effects of "civilization." on the Tahitians. But Gauguin recovers his grace in *Avant et Après*. There was at the time an election battle between a "dirty priest and a miserable Protestant." The Catholic Chruch controlled most of the land in the Marquesas, where Gauguin wanted to settle (Gauguin 1958:37).

> Never, never in my life, not even when I made my first communion,
> was I so ardent a Catholic, and with good reason.

The admirable rogue just wanted to go to the Marquesas, where there were fewer officials.

I do not care to withstand the cultural and personal force of the Gauguin myth, which Gauguin himself seems to have aspired to assert. I will not give in without some resistence, but that will be only formal; my surrender to the myth will be gracious, pleasurable yet not contrived, in the form of a simple narrative of Gauguin's life that stretches the myth along the full length of his personal history. To my own regret I will not pay much attention to the paintings—that is only true to the myth, which reverences them and passes them by—except in the constant awareness of what events made these beautiful, costly objects possible.

Gauguin's life was from the start the great effect of great causes. The material of his unconventional creativity lay within his germ plasm: his parentage states the source of these genetic characteristics, and this history of his childhood confirms their presence in the forming person. His maternal grandmother, Flora Tristan, was the illegitimate offspring of a Frenchwoman and a Spanish grandee from Peru. Flora lived through an unsettled youth, a tempestuous marriage, a scandal-ridden divorce and attempted murder by her estranged husband to become a feminist and socialist, the self-proclaimed redemptress of the down-trodden (Tristan 1987). She wrote, talked and campaigned herself into an early grave leaving a daughter, Aline, to be raised by relatives.

Spain, exotic enough heritage, was mixed with Peruvian, perhaps even royal Inca ancestry in young Aline who despite this and her mother's termagant fire was quiet and reserved. She relished an occasional joke, a bon mot, like placing a dish of extra-hot peppers before an army officer who had volubly craved the condiments. Aline married Clovis Gauguin, a journalist whose anti-Bonaparte leanings dictated rapid flight away to his wife's relatives in Peru when Louis Napolean mounted his coup d'etat in 1851. Clovis died in the Straits of Magellan and Aline with her two children, Paul and his sister, continued on to Lima where they were warmly welcomed by an old uncle (illigitimacy being no bar to kinship in the Spanish Americas) and given berths in his sprawling patriarchal household. For the next four years Paul lived in this exotic setting which stocked his self-avowedly strong visual memory with images both brilliant and dark, solar and lunar (Gauguin 1958:19).

> In those days in Lima, that delicious country where it never rained, the roofs were terraces. If there was a lunatic in the household he had to be kept at home; these lunatics would be kept on the terrace, fastened by a chain to a ring, and the owner of the house or the tenant was obliged to provide them with a certain amount of very simple food. I remember once my sister, the little negress and I, who were sleeping in a room the open door of which gave on to an inner court, were awakened and saw a madman climbing down the ladder. The moon lighted up the court. Not one of us dared to utter a word. I saw, I can still see, the madman enter our room, glance at us, and then quietly climb up again to his terrace.

The chemistry of exotic heritage with exotic locale already formed a reaction in the child which laid down deposits for the full period of exile. The family's return to France in 1855, when Paul was seven, was more of an exile than the residence in Peru. He longed for far-off places all the rest of his life.

Gauguin could not concentrate on his studies at the local schools and lycees where he was sent; he found no companions among his agemates, whom he despised as he would later despise all "foul bourgeois." He had planned to study for the Naval Academy; instead he joined the merchant marine in 1865 as a pilot's apprentice and for several years sailed back and forth between France and South America, mostly Brazil. He enlisted in the French Navy and took part in minor maneuvers during the Franco-Prussian War. His mother's death in 1870 terminated his nautical vagaries; he had, however, heard of the South Pacific from some of the sailors on the ships he sailed.

His guardian found him employment in the brokerage of Bertin. How to explain Gauguin's success on the Bourse? It would seem that a man of artistic temperament could never reconcile himself to the dullness of stocktrading. The French exchange was, in the years after the defeat in the Franco-Prussian War, the fall of the Paris Commune and the rebirth of the Republic, very venturesome, reaching out with its capital to Panama and Suez to cut canals and Africa and the Pacific to move trade these canals would swiften. Gauguin charted his way through the transactions of this high finance very capably; it was a sea and symbolic seascape to him. There was more dreaming in the presence of nature going on at the Bourse than ever there was in a painting academy. Far from stifling his imagination the stock business probably heightened it.

After a few years of this prosperity Gauguin married a young Danish girl, a minister's daughter who had been sent to Paris in light domestic service before returning improved to Denmark (P. Gauguin 1959). He drew a picture of her shortly after the wedding but it was not his artistic talent that had won her. The prospect of a comfortable home provided by Gauguin's exertions in business had persuaded her and her family to consent. Mette was, for Gauguin's biographers, for Gauguin himself and even for their children, the future painter's anchor in the bourgeois bedrock. For the time being he rode lightly, fathered his three children and pursued his awakening interest in painting only by daubing a few canvases and collecting the works of the Impressionists. He showed all the traits of a well-to-do connoisseur who concentrated on a school of art and followed them with marginal efforts of his own.

Gauguin's acquaintance with the artists themselves increased. An uninspired little landscape was even accepted among the academic works for the Official Salon of 1876. But Gauguin's basic sympathy lay with the revolutionaries, though with their more conservative wing, and he found a mentor in Camille Pissarro. His painting was still restricted to the Sundays and to the rural landscapes which a thousand other bourgeois painters saw. His acumen as a broker was more useful to his avant-garde allies than his canvases. In return for his patronage and in recognition of his enthusiasm the Impressionists included Gauguin's paintings in their own shows, the Fifth and Sixth Impressionist Exhibits of 1880 and 1881, though his entries earned more contempt than praise from critics who took the movement seriously. "Watered-down Pissarro," Huysmans said; Gauguin abhored Huysmans ever after.

1883 was the Year of the Change and it was seeded with omens. Manet, the prophet of Impressionism, died; the group began to split into factions announcing their own theories. There was panic at the Bourse caused by some overinflated stock and then a severe crash that affected Gauguin's own investments. He quit his job and dedicated himself to Art.

There are many versions of Mette Gauguin's reaction to Paul's sudden folly. According to one she berated him for casting off his responsibility as a provider and embarking on the egotistical pursuit of fame as a painter;

according to another she meekly bowed to his wishes; and in yet another version she consoled and supported him even when his hopes to earn a living as a painter were dashed. The family—there were five children—moved to Normandy and tolerated privations as Gauguin cranked out more typical Impressionist landscapes. Then, their savings exhausted, they threw themselves under the ungracious protection of Mette's kin in Copenhagen. Gauguin made motions toward self-support by trying to sell canvas for paintings and for sails. An opportunity presented itself (Gauguin 1958: 43).

> I, who asked for nothing, was earnestly invited and entreated by a certain gentleman, in the name of an art club, to exhibit my works in a hall *ad hoc*. I allowed myself to be persuaded. On the day of the opening I set out—but not till the afternoon—to have a glance at it. What was my astonishment, on arriving, to be told that the exhibition had been officially closed at noon.

> It was useless to seek any information whatever; on all sides were closed mouths. I took one leap to the house of the important gentleman who invited me. This gentleman, the servant told me, had left the country and would not be back for some time.

The Danish Academy had ordered the show shut. Taking his son Clovis, Gauguin returned to Paris.

That winter the city inaugurated in Gauguin's life the second great essential in his life myth-poverty. Without poverty there could be no grin when his paintings became very valuable later. Gauguin froze in a miserable pension at night and stuck bills during the day. Yet that spring, at the Eighth Impressionist Exhibition there were 19 canvases by Gauguin—and enough quarrels among the Exhibitors to end Impressionist Exhibitions forever. Gauguin was no longer sheltered by the Impressionist ethic; he was free to leave Paris and go to Brittany.

Brittany offered him cheap living, open vistas and a handy exotic culture, peasants who spoke a language other than French and who wore unusual costumes. Gauguin had seen stranger people, though, and in 1887 he shipped with a painter friend to Panama, where he hoped for an even easier life and brilliant subjects. It was all for naught: he was reduced to working on the Panama Canal which in his earlier incarnation he might have helped to finance. The French Canal Company failed anyway; Gauguin and Laval moved to Martinique where, barely staying erect for the sickness, Gauguin completed some canvases. The brief sojourn in the tropics lit up his drab scenes with brilliant colors. Though he soon returned to France the gap between heredity and genius had been bridged; he knew he must return to lush, fragrant places.

In the summer of 1888 he was again at Pont-Aven, Brittany, this time in the company of a young enthusiast named Emil Bernard, and a few other less gifted painters. Bernard came up with theories of painting, or he later claimed he did, new ways of distributing colors on the picture plane: cloisonnism, in which the areas of brilliant color were encircled by heavy black lines like the ornament on cloisonné vases; synthesism, which dictated a harmonization of color saturations. Gauguin improved on Bernard's word, and in his paintings, by embodying these ideas in extraordinary execution. Again in Paris he had his first one man show courtesy of Theo van Gogh, Vincent's brother and an agent for Paris art dealers.

Gauguin's involvement with van Gogh has always provoked good theater. Gauguin had known the Dutch painter for a few years when van Gogh invited him by letter to live with him at Arles, in the south of France. Gauguin resisted for a while but then "overborne by Vincent's sincere, friendly enthusiasm" he took the trip. The first few months were fruitful. Gauguin slowly warmed to the locale and went to work; he coached Vincent on the latest color theories. They formed a curious ménage which afflicted by poverty and the peculiarities of van Gogh's cooking (he mixed his soup as he mixed his colors, says Gauguin) was still the first stability Gauguin had known in years. Van Gogh's growing derangement ended all that. For no reason he flung a glass of absinthe at Gauguin's head; the next day, he used a razor blade with which he had earlier threatened Gauguin, to cut off one of his ears, sending it to a prostitute and then burying himself in his bed. Gauguin hastened back to Paris and saner, if less brilliant, companions.

The bourgeoisie was safely behind Gauguin but also, clearly, was the lunatic fringe of art. With Mette safely contained in Copenhagen and only rarely begging him to return and van Gogh committed to the Saint-Remy Asylum Gauguin found company with the "Impressionist-Synthesist Group." But the bourgeoisie at least had found an effective weapon against him; they refused to buy or even look at his paintings. The commercial success which Impressionist painters not much older than he had achieved was denied him. He and his friends put together some abortive shows. After the Academy (always the villain) excluded their paintings from the official exhibit at the Paris Exposition of 1889 Gauguin (always the broker) prevailed upon a cafe owner to allow them to hang their paintings on the walls of his shop. They only earned ridicule by this backdoor assault, and made no sales. Gauguin, the habitually starving artist, went back to doing odd jobs.

At Pont-Aven once more he became the doyen of a small group of painters who debated the latest color theories while following Gauguin about, awaiting his definitive declarations. It is customary (but no longer obligatory) to imagine the existence of a Pont-Aven School made up of several minor but interesting painters under the tutelage of Gauguin himself. Gauguin's increasing competence was set off against the slavish imitations of his followers who copied his style without having his insight.

Here finally the spirit of Gauguin came forth fully armed, personally victorious after his fights with the artistic establishment and with other painters of his own school. Buoyed by his secure talent and his ability to see Nature in a unique savage way Gauguin opposed the dogmas of his time. He acknowledged the other painters who would be accepted into the annals of art—Monet, Degas, Cezanne—but all these masters were only grudging in their appreciation of Gauguin, who was to them an untrained amateur with vague ambitions and loud opinions. Cezanne, the particular object of Gauguin's admiration, a stuffy, unfriendly character, responded to Gauguin's praise with suspicion, rancor and accusations of plagiarism. Only van Gogh saw the worth of Gauguin's painting, but van Gogh was dead by his own hand.

Through all the episodes and encounters of these years Gauguin asserted himself against all the other relevant personalities of his time. Neither the Academy nor the sturdy fold of Impressionism nor the mad universe of van Gogh held him tight for very long. His refusal to take seriously the modish art theories that followed the breakdown of Impressionism caused a dispute between him and Emil Bernard. Ties with the French artists who had drawn him out of the bourgeoisie were also breaking, and the old vision of distances returned.

While at Pont-Aven Gauguin and his companions had matured a plan; they would emigrate in a body to the French possession of Tahiti and establish an art colony there, taking inspiration from the unspoiled surroundings and reaping handsome profits by painting portraits of vain colonials. There were possibilities of official preferment but in extremity one could lead a satisfied existence plucking fruit from the trees and fishing in the surf. And there were the Tahitian women. Gauguin had seen a Tahiti exhibit at the Paris Exposition (a deliberate discouragement on the part of the French government). Gauguin was ravished by their vitality, and envisioned their oceanic island.

Gauguin mythology dictates that at this moment one must evoke the longings for paradise in French art toward the end of the nineteenth century. The poets Baudelaire and Mallarmé breathed it in their verse; the painter Douanier Rousseau spread canvases with jungles he had never seen. Pierre Loti, a novelist of considerable magnetism for Gauguin, conjured up a densely perfumed Tahiti in *La Femme de Loti*, gave Gauguin the island and the women he desired. And Loti had been to Tahiti. Gauguin's scheme for escape was not just a fashionable intention but a personal realization of cultural trends which solidified more concretely in Gauguin than in others. While his friends talked Gauguin readied himself for action.

Met with the possibility of actually going to Tahiti Gauguin's disciples backed down, Bernard to get married, Meyer de Haan because his family would not support him if he departed. Gauguin was willing to go alone but he did not have the money for the passage. A telegram from Theo van Gogh promised him funds in memory of Vincent—but it turned out that Theo had gone mad with grief over Vincent's suicide and the mirage hope evaporated. He tried to sell paintings and pottery. As Symbolists, the most recent innovators in art theory, adopted him as their oracle since he was the eldest and had done some paintings that seemed to illustrated their ideas. In order to help him earn the money for his fare to Tahiti—a trip which was itself a symbol—they arranged an auction. The catalogue and publicity were handled by Charles Morice, a poet and later Gauguin's biographer.

There was a slight amount of interest in Gauguin's paintings in the art market and Gauguin assumed he would sell enough to meet his immediate needs. To boost bidding he made the mistake of entering high initial bids himself and thus purchased many of his own paintings because no one bid higher. Nevertheless he realized 10,000 francs total and was encouraged by the prospect of further sales which this held out. The time to go to Tahiti had come; the resulting pictures would surely have a market. A quick trip to Copenhagen assured him that Mette and the children had no inclination to go with him to Tahiti. In diaries and letters he referred to himself as a savage reborn and yearning for the wilds: Paris and even Brittany had to give way to Tahiti.

He arranged his affairs and even obtained an "official mission," a nebulous document that conferred status on Gauguin, and a promise that the government would purchase a painting for 3,000 francs upon his return, for he did plan to return. During his absence too his friend Morice agreed to market more of Gauguin's paintings and send him a steady stream of cash; the proceeds from a benefit the Symbolists were arranging for the master

Chapter Fourteen: Sea Breeze: Paul Gauguin | 229

would alone yield enough money for years of unharried existence in Tahiti. After some enjoyable years in Tahiti Gauguin would return to France bearing his tropical landscapes. All these fragile suppositions were bound to be crushed in the jaws of reality.

The trip to Tahiti was miserable but the reception given to Gauguin by the resident French officials was heartening; the "official mission" temporarily deceived them into thinking he was a painter of prominence. He was feted royally by the first citizens and received a few inquiries that might have led to commissions had not his behavior and paintings given him away. He did not tally with what the French colony expected in a painter; he slipped from his foothold with the elite.

Although initially quartered with the officials in Papeete, the capital, Gauguin was soon elbowed out of that prestigious residence and as his funds diminished had to be satisfied with shabbier housing. Making an open, and unusual break with the French he moved out into the countryside. Loti had lied about the abundance of fruit and game; Gauguin could not live from the land itself. He spent his money fast; unrelieved by further sums from France he knew poverty again, in festive guise. He took a Tahitian mistress—at least he was not disappointed in the women—and constructed a hut of his own. He was déclassé, no better than a native, in the eyes of the island's French rulers but his antithesis to their bourgeois livelihood gratified his perversity.

Amid the collapse of practically all his ambitions Gauguin was moved to paint by the physical beauty of the island and his work was enriched by the culture of the natives. He discovered to his dismay that they were vaguely Christianized and otherwise polluted by French customs and diseases. No longer themselves able to provide for their own wants, they purchased canned goods at the stores. Gauguin admitted, however, that the packaged food tasted better than the natural produce.

Gauguin was more Tahitian than the Tahitians because he rejected Christianity and turned to the native gods and myths, incorporating them into his paintings with a personal touch. Since this is also a myth and the paintings are not on display it will have to be true that Gauguin just absorbed Tahitian motifs and made them his own. Covetously we stand by and watch the new images fall into paint as Gauguin assimilates to the native world. *Noa Noa*, a book written by Gauguin and much revised by Charles Morice, is the mythic textbook of this assimilation; it does much to rectify the biographers' deviations from the correct symbolic version of Gauguin's two years in Tahiti.

Immediately it is apparent how much the biographers have gulled us. Gauguin fell out with the officials, especially with the Governor—"the Negro Lascasade"—immediately after his reception. The old King Pomare had just died and with him "the last vestiges of ancient traditions." Since Gauguin was considered an artist the Director of Public Works consulted him on the artistic arrangements for the King's funeral. Gauguin just pointed out the Queen, who "made everything she touched a work of art." The insipid officials and clergymen read their boring speeches to a crowd of natives then rode off in their coaches; the Tahitians suddenly bloomed into colors and gaiety.

Shortly afterward Princess Vaitua, the daughter of the deceased King, came to the chamber of the exhausted Gauguin in order to care for him. He wore only the pareo, or native girdle, hardly fit to receive royalty, but the Princess was unaffected. He directed her to a bottle of absinthe which sat in a corner of the room (Gauguin 1964:14),

> Showing neither displeasure nor eagerness she went to the place indicated, and bent down to pick up the bottle. In this movement her slight, transparent dress stretched taut over her loins—loins to bear a world. Oh, surely, she was a princess! her ancestors? Giants proud and brave. Her strong, proud, wild head was firmly planted on her wide shoulders.

Gauguin was living a scene from Loti's novel. The Princess seemed first a hideous cannibal then grew beautiful as the absinthe was drained and she recited a fable from La Fontaine, The Cricket and the Ants. The Princess, however, preferred the cricket's singing to the ants' labor; she remembered Tahiti before the stores and officials had come.

Gauguin found in a city a vahini named Titi, half English, half native. She was so unlike the courtesans he had known in Paris, full of amorous passion and with fire in her blood, but her many contacts with white men had erased her racial differences; she had brought any number of lovers to their graves. When Gauguin left Papeete he did not take her with him.

He was disgusted with the European city, which had no genuine natives left (Gauguin 1964:14).

> I felt that in living intimately with the natives in the wilderness I would by patience gradually gain the confidence of the Maoris and come to know them.

In the hut he saw the images he had come for, a half-naked woman in a fishing canoe, the rays of the moon through the bamboo reeds. Here he learned to know the silence of the Tahitian night. In this sensual richness, however, he was nagged by a physical demand: his provisions were depleted and he was unskilled in the native techniques of collecting food from the trees and the oceans. His neighbors noticed his plight and invited him to dinner. He was too proud and too mortified to accept. With becoming delicacy they placed a meal of vegetables and fruit outside his hut, and were pleased to know they had made him content.

He was watched from the shrubbery, the observed as much as the observer. One young woman dared to enter his hut and look at the photographs of painting she had hung on the wall. She believed Gauguin when he told her the Ingres' Olympia was his wife, but made off when he tried to sketch her—not because she was frightened like the Arabs or the Zuni but because she wanted to trick herself out in her best finery. Gauguin knew that these young women were free for the taking, that island custom favored simple rape, yet he had neither the audacity nor the confidence. The spoiled Titi, whom he invited to live with him, was unsuited to the rural simplicity of her own island, and soon had to go back to the city.

The natives admitted him into their evening councils and paid him regular visits. Seeing that they were displeased with the dilapidated condition of their huts he roused them to form a team for making the repairs. The suggestion was approved unanimously in the meeting; the morning brought indifference to the problem. Gauguin came to the conclusion that he would have to stop playing the civilized improver of the natives. What counted for a virtue in France, industry for instance, had no place among the Tahitians; its opposite, procrastination, was invested by the natives with their own positive value. He became more like them when he understood this.

The people were united with Nature to give him his next lesson. A young man, Jotefa, had attached himself to Gauguin; he watched the artist paint and carve, encouraged him with generous words Gauguin had never heard before. The time came when Gauguin needed some rosewood for a sculpture. Since the best trees grew deep in the forest Jotefa volunteered to lead Gauguin there along paths invisible to all but the most experience native. As they walked, naked except for their pareos, through the luxuriant growth Gauguin gazed upon the youth who went before him and reflected on the similarity of the sexes in Tahiti (Gauguin 1964: 47-48).

In spite of all this lessening in sexual differences, why was it that there suddenly rose in the soul of a member of an old civilization, a horrible thought? Why, in all this drunkeness of lights and perfumes with its enchantment of newness and unknown mystery?

The pure, primitive sensuality beckoned the decadent European to an unthinkable act. Gauguin was fighting himself when the youth turned to cross a stream; at once his full face was that of a man and the feel of the cold water in the brook baptized the awakening conviction that he had vanquished "the corruption of an entire civilization" within himself. Nature embraced him with all her ambient maternal softness. The felling of the rosewood trees was the felling of the evil forest (Gauguin 1964: 51).

Yes, wholly destroyed, finished, dead, is from now on the old civilization within me. I was reborn; or rather another man, purer and stronger, came to life within me,

Gauguin's change of identities was the extirpation of all the sinful old habits in a soul then freed to glide newly savage into the jungle.

Avidly I inhaled the splendid purity of the light. I was, indeed, a new man; from now on I was a true savage, a real Maori.

On his own he voyaged to the center of the island and braved the demons to see the sacred mountain by moonlight.

His peace lacked only the pleasant disruption of the vahina's chatter. Work was affected as were his spirits in general so he left his hut on a wife-hunting trip. In a small village on the untouched eastern shore of the island he was given hospitality by a family whose young daughter, Tehura, agreed to come and live with him. There were no elaborate arrangements or ceremonies, just the approval of the relatives easily given, then, after a few weeks, the trial of Tehura's return to her mother, the affirmation of her coming back finally to settle as Gauguin's vahina. Gauguin lived Tahitian myths and superstitions through Tehura. His slight tremor while exploring a grotto suggested that he might be turning enough into a Tahitian to experience even their fear of sacred places. The motion of eels swarming and the look of a turtle swimming in the sea seemed to communicate an awesome energy. Tehura asked him, when he returned to her, if he had been afraid and he blurted out that Frenchmen have no fear. He knew, however, by one single shift of her eyes as he went to pick her a flower that she did not believe him.

Chapter Fourteen: Sea Breeze: Paul Gauguin | 233

Tehura related to him great long Tahitian myths during their latenight dreamy conversations. Their texts dominate the later portions of *Noa Noa*, myths in a myth (and for the most part it is a myth that they are genuine). One afternoon out fishing with some of the men he learned by an augury of the fish that Tehura was unfaithful to him. When he confronted her with this knowledge her instant look of mystic majesty caught him unawares and transformed this petty issue into a sublime moment. Tehura cowered, and abjectly pleaded with him to punish her but he refrained. He set to rest even the greatest dread of European males, cuckoldom, in the Tahitian calm. But he returned to Europe, on urgent family business, not long afterward.

In Europe and beyond the pale of Noa Noa though still within the further boundaries of his life myth, Gauguin discovered that he had been left a legacy by an uncle. Borrowing some money for train fare he went to Paris to await payment. His friends had been cheating him on the sale of his canvases and had not been remitting his portion to Tahiti. Yet when he arranged his Tahitian paintings in a show there were no buyers, when his inheritance arrived, 15,000 francs, it was rapidly squandered. His strange clothing and collection of tropical pets drew some hangers-on, but he won moderate notoriety rather than great fame and he was always verging on poverty. In an attempt to exploit at least the notoriety he wrote *Ancien Culte Mahorie*, based mostly on his research in French libraries; Morice helped him expand it into *Noa Noa*, which was not published until 1897, when he was back in Tahiti.

His new mistress, a Javanese named Annah, completed the exotic ensemble but at a great price. On the shore in Brittany, which Gauguin found nauseatingly changed by tourism, coarse words spoken to Annah by some sailors precipitated a brawl. Gauguin always fancied himself a good pugilist but the young Bretons were too much for him. One of them broke his ankle by kicking it with his wooden shoe as he lay on the ground. Annah abandoned him there, hastened back to Paris and robbed his studio of all the valuables she could find—which did not include his paintings.

A last trip to Copenhagen had proved to him that no reconciliation with Mette was possible. He worked on a few more "Tahitian" pictures, and he had the status of a treasure among the Nabis, a group of symbolist painters and poets, but the high regard of a few creative people could not break the dead calm. Even the subjects of his paintings brutalized him and left him stranded. There was no place to go but back to Tahiti; this time he was not granted an official mission.

Right before his departure, in March 1895, there was an auction sale of his paintings to help defray expenses. It was an abysmal failure, most painful because it encompassed the full range of his artistic development. The only soft words in the sale were August Strindberg's letter (which was included in the catalogue) refusing to write a preface for the catalogue. The dramatist grasped something about Gauguin while unreservedly accepting the myth.

> I cannot understand your art and I cannot like it. I have no grasp of your art, which is now exclusively Tahitian. But I know that this confession will neither astonish nor wound you, for you always seem to me fortified especially by the hatred of others: your personality delights in the antipathy it arouses, anxious as it is to keep its own integrity.

Gauguin too had become exclusively Tahitian. He disembarked in Papeete to find that the island had grown flaccid with civilization, electric lights illuminating tennis courts in the capital. He withdrew to the most remote part of the island but—and it is as if Strindberg himself conceived the stage setting—he built his hut right across from a Catholic church. In the yard he set up an imaginary pagan Tahiti of carved panels and idols he had designed. His native nature was his own artistic instinct; what he made was Tahitian, wild against the civilized people. He knew even better than the natives what their culture was.

The death of his favorite daughter Aline back in Europe sent him into despair. He painted masterpieces, but his shattered ankle made him a cripple and the encroachment of syphilis contracted last time in Europe undermined his health. His suicide attempt was not a success—perhaps it was not sincere—and worse than suicide he took a clerk's job in a government office. That was not sincere either. After he threw the job over and went back to his hut he was well enough informed about island politics to write and illustrate satirical broadsides. When the Governor and his minions saw a number of *Le Sourire*, filled with its "Tahitian" woodcuts it must have seemed to them that vengeful gods were reawakened and not quite comprehensibly ridiculing them.

The slow trituration of fame into a name had meanwhile advanced the cause of his art in Paris. The publication of *Noa Noa* had raised a mystique; his paintings began to sell. In 1899 an art dealer arranged with Gauguin to pay him a monthly stipend in exchange for 25 pictures a year at 200 francs each. Considering the prices his paintings were starting to bring this was rank exploitation. Gauguin did not know; or did not care. The income enabled him to move to the Marquesas and build a studio house far away from the officials. But he was never far enough away to avoid embroiling himself in affairs with the politicians, the police and the clergy. They reciprocated by making his life hard. As the ravages of his illness worsened he weighed returning to France for treatment. He wrote to an old friend hinting at that possibility but the friend replied with the most drastic sentence of exile any man can receive. It is better, he told Gauguin, to remain a legenedary artist

> who from the depths of Polynesia sends forth his disconcerting and inimitable work—the definitive work of a man who has disappeared from the world. (Daniellson 1966:258)

Gauguin had "passed into the history of art." The living man would be just an embarrassment to the undying legend.

There are several ways to end this protracted Gauguin story but if scholars are right about myth all should amount to the same thing, though I think that each has a different flavor. For mystery: Gauguin died alone in his house, visited after death as he had often been during life by the aged native priest Tioka, who removed a wooden staff Gauguin had carved with deities. For dignity: he was attended near the end by the Protestant pastor Vernier who on his last visit found the dying painter "reassured and calm." For memory: his last painting was of a Breton village deep in snow. For irony: his son by a native woman lived for years in Tahiti doing portraits of tourists, much more successful than his father had been in selling original Gauguins. But last, an unclassifiable end: Gauguin once wrote to the symbolist painter Odilon Redon that he was sure (as Richard Wagner had said)

> that the disciples of great art will be glorified, and that, wrapped in a heavenly cloak of rays, scents and melodious chords, they will return for all eternity into the bosom of the divine source of all harmony. So, my dear Redon, you see that we shall meet again.

References

Chasse, Charles.
    1965 *Gauguin sans legendes*. Paris: Editions du temps.

Daniellsson, Bengt.
    1966 *Gauguin and the South Seas*. London: G. Allen.

Danielsson, Bengt and P. O'Reilly.
    1966 *Gauguin, journaliste à Tahiti*. Paris.

Estienne, Charles.
    1953 *Gauguin*. Geneva: Skira.

Gauguin, Paul.
    1958 *Intimate Journals*. trans. be Van Wyck Brooks. Bloomington: Indiana University Press.

    1964 *Noa Noa: A Journal of the South Seas*. trans. by O. Theis. New York: Noonday.

Gauguin, Pola.
    1937 *My Father, Paul Gauguin*. New York: Knopf.

    1959 *Mette og Paul Gauguin*. Copenhagen.

Morice, Charles.
    1920 *Paul Gauguin*. Paris: H. Floury.

Neverman, Hans.
    1956 *Polynesien und Paul Gauguin*. Bassler Archiv VI.

Tristan, Flora.
    1987 *Peregrenations of a Pariah*. trans. by Jean Hawke. Boston: Beacon.

XV

Körösi-Csoma Sandor

Körösi-Csoma Sandor or, after the then prevalent fashion for Gallicizing Hungarian onomastics, Alexandre Csoma de Koros, left his native village on foot in 1819. It was a touching scene, one that did not fail to move even his most unkind biographers. Csoma drank a farewell glass of tokay with his revered teacher Hegedüs and then tramped off in the direction of the East. A nobleman who lived on the outskirts of Körös village watched the burly figure dressed in a simple outfit of "yellow Nankin" as he walked steadily past.

Csoma may have thought that he was returning to, not leaving, his home. According to an old and probably apocryphal story the impetus for the journey came from a vow Csoma swore with two college mates, to seek out the homeland of the Hungarian people and of the warrior tribe, the Szekelers, from which the Hungarians are thought to have sprung. Popular as well as scholarly opinion placed the Hungarian land of origin in Central Asia. As early as 1235 Hungarian Christians sent a series of missions to Central Asia, and Hungarians showed a strong interest in the region since that time. It has been emphasized that no one in Csoma's time believed that the Hungarians or their language had proceeded intact from Asia (Schmidt 1921: 6). It was a question of how they had been derived from Asian forebears. Csoma, the legend continues, alone among the parties to the vow, pursued the quest, crossing Central Europe, Asia Minor, into India and finally into Tibet. The vow powered his endurance, enabling him to penetrate the Tibetan frontier and at the moment of his death colored his final words.

Theodore Duka, Csoma's countryman and chief biographer (1885), repeatedly denies that Csoma's wanderings were impelled by a search for a mythical homeland. Only Csoma's craving for knowledge drew him onward. "Untrue," rejoins W. W. Hunter, a British officer stationed at an Indian frontier outpost where Csoma often rested between peregrinations. Hunter (Hunter in Körösi-Csoma 1957: 1-24) deridingly holds out evidence to prove that Csoma was obsessed with locating an imaginary country in Central Asia where people still speak a root form of Hungarian. Duka only concedes that Csoma excited laughter among "meaner spirits" at British outposts and in Calcutta, where he spent some time working under the auspices of the Asiatic Society of Bengal. Hunter and other British writers wished to ridicule a man they did not appreciate.

The British did retell silly stories about Csoma and hint roundly at the cause of their mirth. When Csoma first arrived at the border outpost of Sabathu, it was said, Captain C.P. Kennedy, appalled at Csoma's disgracefully simple Indian dress, urged him to appear in something more suitable, and saw him appear in Hungarian national costume, wide trousers fluttering, blouse, bandana and other paraphernalia. At another time Csoma is pictured in deep despair having learned that Tibetan so long the object of his study is in truth a dialect of Sanskrit. Nothing daunted, he determines to learn Sanskrit which, he reasons, must be even closer to Hungarian than Tibetan is. As the author of a *Tibetan-English-Sanskrit Vocabulary*, not published until long after his death (Ross 1910), Csoma knew quite well the affiliations of the languages: both stories indicate a wish to fix upon Csoma a dedicated and absurd nationalism that governed all his activities. Duka repeats these stories as examples of British misunderstanding and indeed if the circumstances of Csoma's life in India are compared with those of his British patrons, the grounds for misunderstanding are evident.

This was the India where Richard Burton earned a bad reputation by learning native languages and visiting native places in native garb. But much of Burton's behavior was an exaggeration of the usual; he visited more brothels and fought swordfights more fiercely and so on. The life style the British officers liked to display to their Indian subjects was much removed from Csoma's "simple" existence. Victor Jacquemot, a French botanist traversing India in search of specimens, stayed in Sabathu with the same Captain Kennedy who remarked on Csoma's aberrations. He and Kennedy went every morning for a "gallop of an hour or two along the magnificent roads he has made" (Woodward 1953: vol. 1: 253). In the evening, after another ride, "we sit down at half past seven to a magnificent dinner and rise at eleven o'clock. I drink Rhine wine or claret. ... I do not remember drinking any water for a week. There is never any excess but great gaiety every evening."

Csoma's indifference to these luxuries imported with great difficulty into the Himalayas made him seem driven by an obsession, most readily conceived as nationalism. Csoma himself did not record his reactions to life in the British hill stations. Hunter (1957), with the hindsight born of years in the India Service, apologizes for Kennedy's rough treatment of Csoma and compliments the Hungarian for not "satirizing" British life there. That task was left to other, British, hands (Forster, Orwell, Ackerly).

Though he may have treated Csoma roughly, Kennedy did preserve and see printed in the *Journal of the Asiatic Society-Bengal* (1834: 128-33), portions of a letter Csoma sent him that amount to the only autobiography the Hungarian ever composed. By the time the letter was published Csoma had settled into a position as sub-librarian of the Asiatic Society library in Calcutta, firmly under the patronage of the British and subject to their description. He had not settled completely. Between 1823, when he first reached India, and 1842, he made four sojourns into Tibet; he died on the road to Lhasa in 1842, in the midst of a journey which, he had declared, would make him the envy of scholars everywhere.

During these years Csoma's translations and precis of Tibetan writings appeared in the pages of the *Journal*, from an analysis of the Buddhist compilation, the *Kahgyur* (Wilson 1832), to a summary of Tibetan medical work (Csoma 1835) and a translation of a Tibetan life of the Buddha (Csoma 1957). The Asiatic Society published a bibliography of his works in their centenary volume (Mitra 1885: 151). The *Tibetan-Sanskrit-English Vocabulary* remained on the shelf at the Asiatic Society library until it was published in 1910. Its editor, Denison Ross (1910: iv), expressed his surprise.

> One would have thought that a man of his capacity for work might have found time during these five years (1837-42) to give the world a work which had cost him such infinite pains to prepare.

Csoma had begun the *Vocabulary* in 1825 and worked on it for nine years before shelving the manuscript. Ross also mentions a bundle of papers Csoma deposited at the Government Office of Records before his death; Duka found and catalogued them, but they were destroyed before he could study them. Except for his letter to Kennedy, Csoma's remains were scholarly treatises.

In that letter Csoma chronicled his journey eastward. His progress was haphazard, investigating languages and the antiquities of the places he visited. He traveled as a European, then as a Persian and an Armenian. Each step of the way he depended upon the benificence of both European and Asian patrons. This pattern he maintained for the rest of his life, whether calling upon the assistance of an individual like Captain Kennedy, or of an organization like the Asiatic Society. His life as presented by his biographers reads as a continual dependency upon others for the daily requirements as he pursued his arcane scholarship.

Chapter Fifteen: Körösi-Csoma Sandor | 241

Csoma tried various costumes during his voyages about the Middle East from 1820 to 1822, but by the time he reached the outpost of Sabathu in 1822 he had arrived at what A. Campbell, who reported his death to the Asiatic Society, calls Csoma's "blue suit" (Campbell 1842: 308). Dr. Malan, who was at Sabathu when Csoma arrived there, described the costume in a letter to Duka some 41 years later (December 8, 1883; Duka 1885: 20).

> ... A jacket like a loose shooting jacket with outside pockets, of the common blue cloth of India; he wore a waistcoat of figured red, black, brown or yellow stuff of Indian manufacture, and trousers of a kind of light brown stuff, cotton stockings and shoes.

This was the dress which Kennedy reportedly required that Csoma change to appear in polite society, and which Csoma was wearing at his death twenty years later.

Campbell's obituary enumerates the effects Csoma had with him then:

> The effects consisted of 4 boxes of books and papers, the suit of blue clothes he always wore and in which he died, a few shirts and one cooking pot. His food was confined to tea, of which he was very fond, and plain boiled rice of which he ate very little. On a mat on the floor with a box of books on the four sides, he sat, ate, slept and studied, never undressed at night, and rarely went out during the day. He never drank wine or spirit, or used tobacco or other stimulants.

Campbell's description announces a Csoma other than the eccentric seeker delineated by the tales. Here he is an austere scholar, enclosed by his work and without any other life, but this description suggests he was static when Campbell himself knew that Csoma was often in motion on foot heading toward Tibet. Hunter coined an epithet which combines all of Csoma's qualities while retaining a hint of a presumed object: "pilgrim scholar."

The exoticism was that of Hungary, Tibet and of Csoma's small domain amid his boxes. Csoma did much by his traveling, collecting texts and translations to make Tibet less exotic: his Tibetan grammar and essay towards a dictionary (1834) was the basis of more substantial later work, and during its time helped to demystify the Tibetan language. His Tibetan Buddhist texts similarly could could serve as a counterpoise to the superstition-laden cult displayed in the writings of Waddell (1895) and others depending upon heresay and the reports of spies without troubling themselves to examine the religious texts. Buddhists saw Csoma as a disseminator of Buddhism through the delivery of the texts, a time-honored and saintly role in the history of the religion's spread. A Japanese Buddhist sect, conscious of their own debt to such scripture-bringers, proclaimed Csoma a Boddhisattva (Peiris 1973: xxii and Plate 31), a being who having attained enlightenment remains in this world to facilitate the enlightenment of others.

Csoma's travel, austerity, incessant study and personal diffidence lent themselves to images ranging from oddity to saint. It is easy to consolidate one view forgetting other evidence, for instance to notice only Csoma's aloofness and ignore his volubility among friends noted by Ross, Hunter, Duka and Eötvös (1843). The man may truly be assimilated into the wearer of national costume or the bronze figurine. The effects of Csoma's life encourage this.

In the Preface to his *Tibetan-English Dictionary* (1967: 4; orig. 1902) Sarat Chandra Das recognizes Csoma as a predecessor in the work of compiling an acceptable vocabulary of Sanskrit-Tibetan-English terms, and he quotes the Preface of Csoma's own *Essay Towards a Dictionary* (1834), Csoma's *Vocabulary* not having yet been published.

> When there shall be more interest taken for Buddhism (which has much in common with true Christianity) and for diffusing Christian knowledge throughout the most eastern parts of Asia, the Tibetan dictionary may be much improved, enlarged and illustrated by the addition of Sanskrit terms.

Csoma is referring to the efforts made by Christian missionaries from de Nobili onward to fashion a Sanskrit Christian vocabulary. The link between Sanskrit and Tibetan which Csoma was developing in his own *Vocabulary* formed the underpinnings of a Tibetan Christianity. Buddhism had already set Tibetan sympathies in that direction.

The effort which Csoma expended upon the never completed *Tibetan-Sanskrit-English Vocabulary* and his failure to press for publication can be viewed in this context. In editing the text for publication Ross (1910: iv) found many of the word equivalents inexact "which in passing the book for the press would not have been allowed to remain." Having the equivalents was not just a lexicographic task for Csoma; it was an element in the Christianization of Central Asia, of interest to his fellow Hungarians since the thirteenth century. Csoma as a Christian missionary can be urged along with Csoma as a Boddhisattva.

But not too strongly. The third element of the triad Tibetan-Sanskrit-English must always be remembered. Ross found few difficulties with Csoma's Tibetan-Sanskrit equivalents in preparing the *Vocabulary* for publication, and it is the *English* translations which exhibit the "surprising lapses." Ross did not doubt the mastery Csoma had gained over English, but he could not help noting that Csoma's early efforts in the language, including his reports to Captain Kennedy, had "undergone some revisions at the hands of an Englishman" and ventures to name possible amanuenses. Csoma's English equivalents were nonetheless retained in the final publication to give insight into Csoma's mind and methods. Csoma's English, Ross observes, cleaves more closely to the Tibetan than to the Sanskrit.

Csoma found his best patrons in the English, and he attained his final state of life as their dependent and counterpoise. They edited and published his works; they also extracted and destroyed his writings. The long letter he sent to Captain Kennedy, the Assistant Political Officer at Sabathu, was severely reduced in publication and reproduced much more extensively by Duka, but still never in whole. It was in fact a report of the conditions Csoma had encountered on his first trip into Tibet and parts of it were in a sense "classified." During that period of hostilities between the British and the Russians in a long band from the Crimea to the Himalayas, Tibet was a geopolitically contested zone, and the British were eager to obtain as much accurate information as possible about its interior. Csoma's intellectual aims were not incompatible with these political and military aims of the British. This intersection of interest was accomplished with great delicacy.

Csoma was to his patrons an accomplished scholar, master of the arcane lore of Tibetan language and religion, and an indefatigable traveler. In relating the circumstances of Csoma's death to the Asiatic Society, A. Campbell, the Superintendent at Darjeeling, told of Csoma's wish to proceed to "the residence of the Sikim Raja and thence to Lassa [Lhasa]" (Campbell 1842: 303).

> ... As the eldest son of the Sikim Raja is by the usage of the family a Lama, and as the present Tubgani Lama is a learned priest, and said to be in possession of an extensive library, I had some hopes that by making the Raja acquainted with Mr. De Koros' unobtrusive character, and known avoidance of political and religious subjects in his intercourse with the peoples of the countries he has visited, I might have contributed to procuring him permission to proceed into Tibet....

Campbell recommended Csoma highly to the Raja's representative, assuring him of Csoma's knowledge and scholarly intent, and of Csoma's not being in government employ. He was hoping for a favorable reply to the petition for the Raja's invitation and protection when Csoma, refusing medication, died of a fever he had contracted on the road. He left all his effects, his books and papers in Campbell's care. Campbell also related that chief among Csoma's final concerns was the possibility of reaching a nation he called the "Yoogars" (Campbell 1842: 308-9).

> This land he believed to be to the east and north of Lassa and the province on Kham, and on the western confines of China; to reach it was the goal of his most ardent wishes, and there he fully expected to find the tribes he had hitherto sought in vain.

In the note which follows Campbell's piece the editor of the *Journal* adds that he long urged Csoma to publish his speculations on the Sanskrit origins of the Hungarian place names, but the "deceased philologist" had consistently demurred. Csoma was not consistently willing to be guided by his patrons, when he was providing them with guidance into the untravelled reaches of inner Asia. This trait they saw as diffidence or modesty: "never did such acquirements centre in one who made such modest use of them."

Csoma's modesty was offset by the flamboyance of his Hungarian successors in Central Asian travel, especially Vambéry (1863), who did not hesitate to publish his own speculations on the origins of the Magyars (1882), or Aurel Stein, who made astonishing archaeological discoveries where Csoma had longed to travel. Before Stein's researches could be undertaken, however, the British had sent an armed expedition to Lhasa (1902). Tibet was "open" to a wide range of interests.

References

Campbell, A.
    1842 "Report of the Death of Mr. Csoma de Körös...," *Journal of the Asiatic Society-Bengal* 124: 305-9.

Duka, Theodore.
    1885 *The Life and Works of Alexander Csoma de Körös.* London: Trubner.

Kara, Georgyi.
1970 *Körösi Csoma Sandor*. Budapest: Academiai Kiade.

Kennedy, C.P.
1834 "Biographical Sketch of M. Alexander Csoma Körösi, the Hungarian Traveller; extracted from a letter..." *Journal of the Royal Asiatic Society* 1: 128-33.

Körösi Csoma Sandor.
1835 "Analysis of a Tibetan Medical Work." *Journal of the Asiatic Society* [of Bengal] 37: 1-19.

1957 *The Life and Teachings of Buddha*. Calcutta: Sil Gupta.

Mitra, Rajendrala.
1885 "History of the Society." *Centenary Review of the Asiatic Society of Bengal*. Calcutta: Thacker, Spinck.

Peiris, William.
1973 *The Western Contribution to Buddhism*. Delhi: Motilal Banarsidass.

Ross, Denison
1910 *Sanskrit-Tibetan-English Vocabulary* by Alexander Csoma de Körös. *Memoirs of the Asiatic Society of Bengal* 4(1): 1-127.

Schmidt, Josef.
1921 "Körösi-Csoma Sandor." *Körösi-Csoma Archivum* 1: 3-12.

Smith, H. H.
1832 "Abstract of the Contents of the Dul-va... " *Journal of the Asiatic Society of Bengal* 1: 1-8; 375-83.

Vambery, Arminius.
1863 *Travels in Central Asia*. London: Murray.

1882 *Der ursprung Magyaren*. Leipzig: F.A. Brockhaus.

1914 *The Life and Adventures of Arminius Vambery*. London: T.F. Unwin.

Woodward, Philip.
1953 *The Men Who Ruled India*. 2 v. London: Cape.

XVI

Alexandra David-Neel in Tibet

Before the flight of the Dalai Lama from Tibet, that land retained a quality of remoteness which the storied empires of earlier travelers had long since relinquished. China, Japan, India all had been entered and reentered; Tibet continued to be an experiment in inaccessibility. Its culture had become a metaphor of its geographical remoteness. Tibetan culture must always be stranger, less fathomable than any other. And thus it might be understood through journeys of the mind displayed in outré images. We can tell that someone has been to Tibet from the stirking obscurity of what he or she reports.

During the thirteenth through fourteenth centuries the Christian Pope sent several ambassadors to the Mongol khans in Central Asia in the hope that these invincible soldiers might be Christian already or might be converted to Christianity to help in the wars against the Muslim Saracens. The last of these, a Minorite friar called Odoric of Pordenone wrote in his journal of reaching a kingdom called "Tebek" in whose principle city there resided a "Pope," the head and prince of all idolaters. Odoric was preoccupied with a ghastly custom of the land: the son of a deceased man cut up his father's corpse and cast the pieces to the vultures, while the skull was made into a drinking cup "wherein he himself with all his family and kindred do drink with great solemnity and mirth in remembrance of his dead and devoured father." Odoric would divulge "many other vile and abominable things" were his readers ready to believe them.

Marco Polo never claimed to have visited Tibet, but he did watch sorcerer lamas materialize an entire banquet and suspend glasses in midair while a guest at the court of the Great Khan. By this time the reputation of Tibet as the warren of magicians and supernatural wonders was well established. Much that was driven from Europe, whether vile or merely marvelous, found a haven there.

Ignorance of Tibet grew out of proportion to the information available. Yet in the seventeenth century Roman Catholic missionaries had established outposts in southern Tibet and in the eighteenth century the Jesuits built a church in Lhasa. The Tibetan voyages of Csoma from 1822 to 1842 and his publications initiated a sober study of Tibetan religion. Though he sat for days with a lama in an ice-bound hermitage Csoma did not learn to levitate or read minds but just to read Tibetan. He never reached Lhasa, but the few explorers who did cover the forbidden territory after him had aims other than the study of religion.

Tibet's strategic position in emerging Asian politics enhanced its mystery for Westerners. The old traveler's tales, the slanted, mistaken ethnography, merged with spiritualism and the nineteenth century vogue for magic to place Tibet alongside Egypt and Yucatan as the home of the intellectualist supernatural. Madame Helena Blavatsky received mystical instruction from the mahatmas lodged high in the Himalayas. She never claimed to have visited Tibet. Tibet came to her. But her writings and those of her followers concentrated a generation of fancies in Tibet's open spaces. The perfect paradise of James Hilton's *Lost Horizon*, where an ancient Jesuit lama is found in a concealed Himalayan city, or the Bela Lugosi movie *Chandu the Magician*, beset by sorcerer lamas unchanged from Marco Polo's accounts, or the writings of the English plumber turned reincarnated lama T. Lobsang Rampa—the old Tibets continue to circulate and recombine with new fads and in new media. Still very few attempted to claim "penetrating" Lhasa.

In 1924 the fifty-five year old Alexandra David-Neel, accompanied by her adopted son the lama Yongden, made her way from Yunnan province in China to the "forbidden city." Except for Sherlock Holmes who amused himself "by visiting Lhasa and spending some days with the head lama," the British soldier Younghusband, and the Swede Sven Hedin, who went in disguise, very few "white people" had entered the city, and no white woman was known to have braved all the obstacles.

According to the description she read before the Société de Géographie, Paris, December 3, 1925, she scaled mountains, ventured among brigands and camped in frozen wastes, without passport, hunted by government officials but evading all pursuit by a clever disguise, luck and a mysterious power. The book of her travels, *Voyage d'une Parisienne à Lhasa* (*My Journey to Lhasa*, 1927) retells the adventure in lucid detail. This feat of endurance by a woman brought accolades from all quarters. David-Neel was awarded medals, the Legion of Honor and was received into the ranks of Tibet specialists. Some of her colleagues expressed reservations over certain "mystical" episodes in the book, but these were niggling doubts next to the grand achievement.

Two years later she advanced her reputation with *Parmi les mystiques et magiciens du Tibet* (*With Mystics and Magicians in Tibet; Magic and Mystery in Tibet*). The rest of her long life—she died in 1969 at 102 years of age—was spent publishing works on Chinese and Tibetan subjects, from the "secret oral teachings" of Tibetan lamas to a translation of the Tibetan epic Gesar of Ling, often in collaboration with the lama Yongden, who himself authored a novel of mystical happenings, *Mipiam*. Tracing all the editions of David-Neel's books from time to time and from language to language is a major bibliographic task. At any moment at least one and perhaps several of her travel books are in print. Until quite recently David-Neel's books were the only sources of general information on Tibet available to the majority of literate people. Despite many more recent competitors, *Magic and Mystery in Tibet* is still probably the most widely read travelogue on any Central Asian territory.

Scholars, remembering her claims of having employed magic powers on various occasions, have been more reserved. David-Neel's books are too story-like, her writing too adventuresome for critical acceptance. Yet her assertions have gone unchallenged and are condoned by citation in the writings of eminent Tibet scholars like David Snellgrove and Guiseppe Tucci. Stephen Beyer in his considerable volume on *The Cult of Tara* (1972: 251) hedges amiably when he described *Magic and Mystery in Tibet* as "perhaps one of the most delightful books on Tibetan magic ever written." The clarity of the books and their sobriety compared to the excesses of Tibet fantasies have rendered them immune from criticisms graver than a little fondness.

Serious misgivings about David-Neel's veracity gained substance with the publication in 1972 of Jeanne Denys' exposé *David-Neel au Tibet: une supercherie devoilée*. Denys purported to demonstrate that David-Neel could not have been where she said she was on the dates she claimed; could not have traveled the routes she mapped out; and never could have met people she mentioned and photographed. David-Neel was not on a voyage of discovery in Tibet, but was a spy in the employ of the French government sent to reconnoiter railroad-building activities in China and assess their possible effects upon French-dominated Southeat Asia. Far from pushing her way into Lhasa, as she so vividly recounts, David-Neel loitered about the Tibet-China border in a way which fooled her few Western contacts into believing she had made the trip. Her reception back in France is better explained as the government's gratitude for services rendered than as honor for real accomplishments. When Denys, a retired physician who had admired David-

Neel, challenged the aged traveler, David-Neel dared her to prove the allegations.

Denys' exposé has not achieved wide currency among readers of David-Neel's books, and it is all but denied in recent biography (Middleton 1989). It is sour, possibly a little vindictive, and it is irrelevant. The reason for David-Neel's persistent and peculiar popularity may be that her journey, like those of other recent travelers to like places (Carlos Castenda; Lynn V. Andrews, for instance), took place outside of a mundane context. It is a realization in the appropriate setting of the most fundamental change a modern person can experience: the discovery of the true power of the self.

Changing identity is the supreme fiction because it makes an entire life into a conditional narrative with the changing self as narrator. The ravages of becoming a fiction, depersonalization and alienation, are soothed by finding in that fiction a truer self better than any other. Both the fiction and its transcendence as a deepening of the individual are best pursued by crossing a strong boundary into alien surroundings which make what is already within rise up and reveal itself. The "savage" he was becoming was for Gauguin his savage nature completing itself. The "mystic" David-Neel became was also a consummation of her own nature. But David-Neel performed the process for anyone to see. Tibet had to be the background, but a Tibet charged with the fiction David-Neel espoused and unlikely to embarrass her with anything inconsistent with her emergent mystical being. Her crossing was not a crossing at all: it was her identification theatrically for her audience with the Tibet everyone expected.

Born Alexandra David, she had a taste for travel from her earliest youth which her family's relative affluence permitted her to satisfy. After her first visit to India and Ceylon (Sri Lanka) at age twenty-three she returned to Paris to study Asian languages and music. Music became her livelihood when her father's financial failure threw her on her own devices. She interpreted soprano roles in a number of theatres and with such skill that Jules Massenet himself wrote her in praise of her Manon. Under the pseudonym of Mademoiselle Myrial she played on the stages of Hanoi and Haiphong and under the same name issued a pamphlet on Chinese philosophy.

She abandoned the opera in 1903 for a career as an orientalist and journalist. The following year she married Philippe Neel, a Tunisan railroad engineer she met in North Africa. Neel subsidized her wanderings about Asia, which she recommenced in 1911, and until his death in 1941 David-Neel wrote him a steady stream of letters containing pithy, vivid descriptions of her adventures in Asia (David-Neel 1975-76). After five years in India, Nepal and Tibet, David-Neel, already proficient in Asian languages and Buddhism, took ship for Japan. In 1918 she sailed to China and spent five years threading her way from Beijing to the province of Yunnan on the Tibet-China border, hoping to enter the land of magic and mystery from the Chinese side.

On October 23, 1923 she wrote to Neel from Tsedjrong, Yunnan telling him that she had met an American botanist who gave her letters of recommendation to officers of the National Geographic Society but was delaying her departure for Tibet because she did not want the American to know her destination. She also asked Neel to put into safekeeping a letter from Father Ouvrard, a missionary with whom she stayed in Tsedjrong, advising Neel that the date and place of origin on the letter would be important for her in the future. The next letter Neel received from her was from Lhasa and dated (approximately) February 28, 1924. The bulk of *My Journey to Lhasa* fits between these two dates.

In the middle of the book David-Neel is crossing the River Po at Showa, well on her way to the sacred city. She has been exclaiming on the beauty of the decorations found along roadsides in Tibet and China (1927: 207).

> Some travellers have found it proper to ridicule that custom. I find it difficult to follow them. A few lines of delicate poetry, a page of philosophical treatise such as one sees engraved on certain rocks in Thibet, the meditative image of a Buddha painted in a natural cave...seem to me greatly preferable to the advertisements of whiskey or ham which 'decorate' the roads of Western countries.
>
> I beg my readers' pardon. I am but a savage.

During this brief span of words David-Neel has made one of those self-introductory speeches given by characters in classical drama or opera. She states the civilized traveler's likely viewpoint, the savage viewpoint of the native, and bravely identifies herself with the latter. The savage is in truth the noble esthete while the civilized person is a clamorous boor. David-Neel is a Tibetan by fundamental sympathy deeper than the impositions of civilization. When she is in Tibet she reacts in accordance with her true nature. But she is not perfect; she needs a bit more training.

On Christmas Day she and Yongden are without food and must subsist on boiled water and tsampa, a type of barley dough. The adventuress complains of her starvation aloud, praying to a mountain god for some butter and fat that they might have a satisfying meal. Yongden reproves her mildly (David-Neel 1927: 170).

> You are somewhat Tibetan in your ways, but perhaps not enough to
> do what a true Tibetan, in your case, would do…

He suggests using shoe leather for a makeshift stew. David-Neel complies, "the soul of a true Tibetan rising" in her.

On the surface, however, she still had the problems of her physical appearance. Her hair and skin were too light to pass for Tibetan. The countryside was alerted to her presence and local officials were on the lookout for vagrants answering her description. She powdered herself with cocoa and charcoal and caused cooking grease to accumulate on her face in the manner of Tibetan women. Her hair was dyed with Chinese ink and done up with yak hair beneath a turban or hat. The hair dressing was rather tenuous and by threatening to expose her provided several tense moments in the narrative. At one juncture David-Neel inadvertently allowed some of the Chinese ink hair dye fall into her food bowl, blackening the mixture of curd and tsampa a woman had given her. She avoided a contretemps by swallowing the entire mess. Much later as she entered the Potala in Lhasa she was ordered to remove the bonnet from her head. Unfortunately she had not applied the ink according to her custom and the hair beneath her bonnet had reverted to its original brownish color in marked contrast with the worn yak-hair braids. Her nonchalance again carried the day. The tangle on her head was taken for the gross headdress of a barbarous border tribe. David-Neel's abiding Tibetan spirit always held her act together.

The same was true of the clothing and other apurtenances of disguise. David-Neel wore Tibetan clothes but never became technically enmeshed in their perfection. Wearing white lay dress or boots that advertised her as a native of Khams province, she allowed herself to be taken for the mother of Yongden, an itinerant lama. When there were male visitors she fell back, squatted on the periphery and accepted the meaner portion of the food. She resigned herself to these indignities for the sake of knowledge (David-Neel 1927: 76).

> Yet I knew that such penance would not be without reward, and
> that under cover of my conspicuous garb of a poor pilgrim I
> should gather a quantity of observations which would never have
> come within the reach of a foreigner, or even, perhaps, of a
> Thibetan of the upper classes. I was to live near the very heart and
> soul of the masses of that unknown land, near those of the women
> folk no outsider had ever approached. To the knowledge I had
> already acquired about the religious people of the country I would

add another and quite intimate one concerning its humblest sons and daughters.

Faced with humiliation she sprang back from the apparent identity of a deferential woman into the confidence of a knowledge more complete than that of many native Tibetans. There was no breaching her character; neither the physical nor the social threats other disguised travelers faced were cause for alarm. David-Neel accepted what came her way and translated it into an asset of her real self. Her apparent poverty was not the same as the real poverty Tibetan people had to endure.

She was not content to remain the passive receptacle of information. Besides David-Neel's Western person the costume covered alien objects: thermometers, miniature compass, watches, not to mention the photographic equipment implied by the shots of Lhasa and other sites reprinted in her books. She had set herself a series of geographic missions to confirm discoveries and confirm data on maps. In the title of her published Société de Géographie address she refers to herself as an "*éclaireur*," a "clarifier." She earned this title by taking strenuous side trips to determine longitudes and latitudes of landmarks, take temperature and altitude readings.

At first this geographical function and the explicit objectivity of the reportage it requires would seem to be at odds with her being the wife and initiate of a *nagspa*, a "sorecerer." Both she and Yongden had occult insights into the future. Yongden caused snowstorms at will and David-Neel generated mystical body heat to warm herself on cold nights. Alongside the genuine magic David-Neel worked upon the credulity of the natives with contrived rites. She frightened a skeptical servant into returning stolen coins with some contrived hocus-pocus. Yogden terrified hostile nomads with sleight-of-hand. David-Neel and her companion kept the secret of true magic to themselves but were willing to use the superstitious ignorance of Tibetans to protect themselves.

Tibetan magic was divided into two categories for David-Neel, the foolish beliefs that regulated the lives of the multitude and the sophisticated techniques known only to a few. Her scientific bias led her to analyze and utilize the superstitions while reaching for a higher discipline that might complement science. The theophists emphasized the difference between vulgar manipulative magic and the higher spiritual discipline that enabled its initiate to perform remarkable feats. The final magic was less important than the discipline it denoted—Madame Blavatsky rarely descended to such showing-off, but was the casual evidence of a perfected self as technology is evidence of scientific knowledge. David-Neel's false and genuine magic implied that she had achieved the disciplined Tibetan spirituality while retaining her Western analytic outlook. By theosophical standards this was perfection indeed.

In *My Journey to Lhasa* she never states that she is an advanced being. One of the pleasures of reading the book is catching the hints as they are almost imperceptibly pitched toward the reader. The only assertion of her privileged spiritual status, while not ambiguous, remains veiled.

As she and Yongden sat warming themselves beside a campfire there approached a shadowy lama who addressed David-Neel by name and demonstrated familiarity with the details of her life. Sharply ordering Yongden to leave, he engaged David-Neel in a long discussion of secret matters before melting away into the night. No details of the discussion are provided; the reader, like Yongden, is not ready to hear the lama's words. David-Neel had glimpsed this man before, passing her upon a trail, in a crowd or in visions. The circumstances of her discussion with him resemble Madam Blavatsky's interviews with the mahatma Koot Humi which likewise were private and never revealed to her followers but implicitly substantiated all her teachings. Just before she made her first trip into Tibet, in June 1913, David-Neel wrote to her husband from Theosophical Society headquarters in Benares where Madam Balvatsky had received several important visits from the mahatmas so many years before, expressing great ambitions to be a writer on oriental philosophy.

David-Neel's responsiveness to the nocturnal conversations of higher intelligences was conditioned by more than her cognizance of her eminent predecessor. In her autobiographical sketch, which appears in slightly different forms at the beginnings of several books, she declares that her "precocious" childhood was filled with reveries of travel, mostly to "wild hills, immense deserted steppes and impassable landscapes of glaciers." This dreaming brought her to pursue oriental studies even as she set about her opera career. In 1912 her first view of Tibet was an epiphany (David-Neel 1927: xi).

> What an unforgettable vision. I had at last come to rest in the
> calm solitudes of which I had dreamed since my infancy. I felt as
> if I had come home after a tiring cheerless pilgrimage.

There truly are places which when first seen recall themselves in memories that never have been. David-Neel's encounter with Tibet has another agenda: the conviction that she is a Tibetan returning home in another body. That she truly belongs in Tibet is one of the most persistent themes in her writing about the place.

Her disguise was not a disguise at all but an honest statement of her true nationality. Through reincarnation the fiction has come round to a truer reality. Even as her disguise flaked away or the pettiness of everyday magic was revealed, David-Neel became yet more Tibetan than most Tibetans. She belonged without question to the land of magic and mystery older in Western imagination than Tibet itself.

My Journey to Lhasa and its autobiographical outriders identified David-Neel as a true Tibetan and attributed to her unspecified knowledge. Her later books either forwarded the attribution (*Among the Brigands of Tibet*, for example) or they specified the knowledge. Thus her second book, *Magic and Mystery in Tibet* (1931), elaborated upon her sallies into the forbidden land in psychic terms. She is remarkably in control of her complex identity, and writes with an authority evident from the manner of her writing. Science, most convincing to her audience, remains her official mode for the presentation of wonders. The Introduction to *Magic and Mystery in Tibet* is by the psychologist d'Arsenval, whose credentials are listed at the end. He offers us the complete David-Neel (David-Neel 1931: ii).

> Madam David-Neel has become, as she herself says, a complete Asiatic, and what is still more important for an explorer of a country hitherto inaccessible to foreign travelers, she is recognized as such by those among whom she has lived.

> This Easterner, this complete Tibetan, has nevertheless remained a Westerner, a disciple of Descartes and Claude Bernard, practising the philosophical skepticism of the former which, according to the latter, should be the constant ally of the scientific observer. Unencumbered by any preconceived theory, and unbiassed by any doctrine or dogma, Madame David-Neel has observed everything in Tibet in a free and impartial spirit.

All the parameters of David-Neel as she sees and writes are summarized here. The only element d'Arsenval omits—and this serves David-Neel's purpose—is the mystic flicker now behind appearances, giving shadow-depth to science.

Quite early in the book, which is not a travelogue but an anecdotal survey of the departments of Tibetan magic, David-Neel lets some of this illumination fall upon her description of events. By orders of an "incarnate lama" she is assigned a lama named Dawasandup as interpreter. This is the same man who translated *The Tibetan Book of the Dead* for W.Y. Evans-Wentz a few years later. In fact he accompanied David-Neel to Gangtok, Sikkim where he would meet the British scholar. Just before leaving Lhasa, David-Neel and the translator-lama attend a benediction by the Dalai Lama. There they observe a grimy ascetic ridicule the ceremony and curious to learn his views, they hike up to the monastery where this curious naljorpa (an ascetic possessing magic powers) is known to be staying. After a confused session in which the naljorpa defames the Dalai Lama and seems to exalt his own magical powers, David-Neel gives Dawasandup some rupees as a gift for this amusing character. The naljorpa refuses; he already has more provisions than he can carry. Dawasandup steps over him to place the money on a table (David-Neel 1931: 39).

> Then I saw him stagger, fall backward and strike his back against the wall as if he had been violently pushed. He uttered a cry and clutched his stomach. The *naljorpa* got up and, sneering, left the room. 'I feel as if I had received a terrible blow,' said Dawasandup. 'The lama is irritated. How shall we appease him?'
>
> 'Let us go,' I answered. 'The lama has probably nothing to do with it. You, perhaps, have heart trouble and had better consult a doctor.'

In accordance with her advertised attitude, David-Neel will not accept the learned lama's supernatural explanation but interposes her own medical explanation for his discomfort. A few pages later she mentions that Dawasandup was fond of strong drink, which she did everything to curb while he was under her influence. But the atmosphere in which she makes this appeal to Claude Bernard—psychological reasons for apparently magical events is fraught with less explicable magic: a sudden hailstorm, verified predictions and otherworldly scenery. David-Neel's observations are positivistic but her presentation shows that this is a litotes, that the whole is an assertion of magic on a higher plane.

Whenever she describes a rite, a person or place identified with Tibet the same general rhetoric of assertion of magic by its denial takes hold. She and Yongden are traveling in North Tibet one day when they happen across a caravan of lamas transporting a magic dagger, or *phurba*. This ritual implement had been the property of their late head lama, a powerful sorcerer, and after his death had gone berserk, killing one monk and wounding others. The monks tried to deposit it in a sacred cave but its destruction of livestock caused herdsmen to demand its removal. They sealed it in a box plastered with charms and were fearful of taking a look inside. Coveting this souvenir, David-Neel offers to disempower the dagger and removes to a field ostensibly to meditate in its presence but really to plot how to secure her prize. As she sits staring at the dagger a ghostly lama materializes bending over it. David-Neel snatches it from before him and runs back to the camp. She was convinced that one of the monks with his own designs on the dagger had stolen away from the camp but Yongden assures her that no one left during the night. The monks tell her that the phantasm was their deceased Grand Lama and that David-Neel, being a greater magician than he because she has blocked his recovery of the instrument, is entitled to keep it. The reader at the end of the episode is more in the position of the monks than of David-Neel. She must marvel at whatever gave David-Neel the power to obtain the artifact.

David-Neel always guards a jocular tone toward the credulity of the Tibetans, including their proclaiming her a great magician, but "I confess that I allow myself to be easily convinced...." As the genuine efficacy of magic becomes apparent, the Tibetans remain typical nineteenth century natives, fondering in superstition while the Westerner, who has penetrated to the core of superstition and found there real power, dominates them from above and from below, from the inside and from the outside.

David-Neel can explain her superiority. The tales of power are interspersed with sections on Buddhist thought and the rationale of magic. These explanations are curiously slanted toward the magical end of Tibetan Buddhism, and do not begin to suggest the oceanic magnitude of the collections of Buddhist scriptures and the commentaries thereon. In explicating the doctrine of causation central to Buddhist philosophy, David-Neel writes as if it applies only to volitional magic and not to the range of causes and effects that form the circle of being. Her account of how causation figures into the training and practice of a sorcerer is strictly correct. Causing a death by magic requires a funnelling of concentration to bring effects to bear. But this leaves aside the moral issue of what it means to bring about or will someone else's death. Tibetan Buddhism has a body of doctrine on that subject. Reading David-Neel's account one might think that there are no liabilities other than medical and psychological. She confuses the operational nature of magic with the spiritual, and does not give Tibetan Buddhism credit for being the complex religion that it is. By the standards of the lamas she hoodwinked much of her magic is incredible and trivial—but that is another Tibet. In David-Neel's Tibet magic exists only as a potential spiritualization of the magic she and her lamas may control.

As a native of scientific Europe and mystical Tibet and even more of the psychic world that underlies both, David-Neel was both an authority on psychic phenomena and their practitioner. She left off disguise and living among Tibetans to return to Europe and her own small monastery, Samten Dzong at Digne, France. In the last chapter of *Magic and Mystery in Tibet*, she writes of psychic research and which in the context of her time meant the exact study, even the laboratory study, of psychic powers. She will "elucidate the mechanism of so-called miracles."

The Tibet of magic and mystery she had inherited from Madame Blavatsky and before was not substantial enough to anything more than a proving ground for her expertise, then reduced to an incomplete categorization of only one area of Tibetan belief, magic. The categories are interesting, and as her later books explain their contents, appealing, but the miracles were extinguished. And the miracles were her claim to being a Tibetan. She was bound for guruhood, a display of mystical knowledge prophetic of later gurus in their reliance upon scientific rhetoric. When Alan Watts cited David-Neel's *Secret Oral Teachings in Tibetan Buddhist Sects* as the affirmation of his own Buddhist doctrine—the circle was complete.

References

Beyer, Stephen.
      1973 *The Cult of Tara*. Berkeley: University of California Press.

David-Neel, Alexandra.
      1927 *My Journey to Tibet*. London: The Bodley Head.

      1931 *Magic and Mystery in Tibet*. London: The Bodley Head.

      1975 *Journal de voyage: lettres à son mari*. 2 v. Paris: Plon.

Denys, Jeanne.
      1972 *David-Neel au Tibet: une supercherie devoilee*. Paris: La Pensee Universelle.

Middleton, Ruth.
      1989 *Alexandra David-Neel: Portrait of an Adventurer*. Boston: Shambala.

XVII

Status:
James Reavis and Philip Musica

The attainability of so-called status symbols in the United States has encouraged the supposition that status is nothing but its symbols. The puchase of a large enough car or a house is the pinnacle of achievement even if it exhausts the resources whose abundance it was calculated to display. There is no basic change in the individual; his friends and relatives stay the same; he is without position or income. And most of all he is not, by his purchase, part of the elite whose material life he copies, partially and from the outside.

The elite in a hierarchical order, even one with great mobility among classes, have a culture and society. Individuals may reach the material prosperity appropriate to the upper class but they may not be accepted into its society and may never understand its culture. Social climbers and arrivistes are defined by their too rapid rise—but it is their lack of cultural integration into the upper class that makes them contemptible outsiders, their bad manners, inadequate education and revolting taste. Like owning a status symbol wealth is no guarantee of acceptance into the upper class.

This is especially true because in the United States class is still very much a matter of ethnic divisions. Though there is now an Irish upper class and a Jewish upper class their culture is unlike those alongside them on the socioeconomic scale; whatever acceptance ethnicity may have in American society there will always remain the opinion that "ethnic style" is not proper to members of the elite. The old aristocratic patterns, Anglo-Saxon in the East and Spanish in the West (though the Anglo-Saxon installed itself there too) hold in themselves a cultural ideal, and a real culture and society to which none but members are admitted.

By the curious inversion that often governs human life, however, the appearance of cultural identity gains acceptance into these old, prestigious elites much more easily than money or fame. Anyone who learns the right manners, evinces the right education and convinces the right people is received. Unfortunately he who has taken the time to study this culture enough to realize this is probably motivated by a wish for more than mere acceptance; he is most likely an impostor seeking to rob his associates, who are willing to place their confidence in one of their own. In fiction this cunning impostor is frequently a Robin Hood who fools the rich to steal back what they have exacted from the poor. By the time an impostor has fixed himself in an upper class culture he is neither that practical nor that altruistic. He has crossed many boundaries and found an identity he values in itself, but which he cannot keep.

James Reavis was the son of a Spanish-Scottish mother and a Welsh father. His mother, by leaps of imagination more than by memory, recalled the days when her family stood grand in the Spanish Empire. The town of St. Joseph, Missouri where he was raised was almost irrelevant to his upbringing because his mother weaned him on Spanish romances, latter day versions of those same books that addled Don Quixote's brain centuries before. The nimbus of the recently eclipsed Spanish Empire always hovered dark over Reavis. He was schooled to expectations which his adult life was bound to disappoint.

Reavis signed up with a Confederate army at the outbreak of the Civil War, then, when the reverses of the Confederate fortunes made this loyalty unrewarding he deserted and joined the victorious Union army. There his habit of forging furloughs or some other wrongdoing was detected and he took flight. His choice of asylum is revealing: Brazil. He made a long, arduous journey, bypassing much more likely countries with more comfortable climates in order to reach the one country in the Western hemisphere that was an Empire. The Portuguese ruler Dom Pedro I, had become Emperor of Brazil in 1825 after he was forced out of Portugal, and his family ruled there until 1889. Reavis was looking for the chivalrous kingdom he had thoroughly imagined. He knew he would not find it in the United States or any of the Spanish republics.

What Reavis did find in Brazil has never been told, but it did not agree with him. The next year he was back in St. Louis, Missouri doing odd jobs. Soon he had accumulated enough capital to set himself up as a land agent. His functions gave him familiarity with the forms and processes of title transfers; he had a knack for finding in old files unambiguous title deeds which gave clear title of disputed lands to his clients. Somewhere along the line he had mastered every aspect of forgery from the preparation of paper to the duplication of historically correct script.

One day a medicine show doctor came to him with what purported to be a Spanish land grant bestowing 2,000 square miles of territory on a nobleman named Peralta, whose descendant had signed the deed over to the quack. The sight of this coalesced Reavis' Spanish fantasies in one great territory; he made an agreement with the doctor and invested himself and his accumulated abilities in this cause. A cursory examination told him that the documents were crude forgeries, but the concept was planted.

Reavis was a singleminded man and he pursued the Peralta claim with narrowly channeled energy. Sensible of the politics surrounding the confirmation of any sizeable land grant Reavis traveled to California and approached magnates with a proposal to back his claim. For a time he lost contact with his partner and with the deeds but by 1880 he had secured the documents and the support of San Francisco capitalists to carry out his work. Their interest lay in the railroad right of way and the mineral deposits which the claimed lands could bring under their control. Fortified by a contribution Reavis began a pilgrimage in creation of a pedigree.

Over the course of the next two years (1880-82) Reavis did research and manufactured documents to sustain an entire family history at back of the Peralta deeds. First he went over the tattered documents which initiated the Peraltas and doctored them for greater verisimilitude, then he visited the National Archives in Mexico City and once trusted by the archivists stole a quantity of manuscripts to serve as raw material for his forgeries. The documents that resulted were a Spanish romance laid down on legal parchment. Two generations of Peraltas came into existence under the strokes of Reavis' pen: Don Miguel de Peralta, who was granted the lands by King Ferdinand VI of Spain in 1748 and his son, also Don Miguel, who sold the land to the quack doctor in the 1860's. Reavis had foisted his fantasy upon history but so far it was only backing for his claim.

With the funds of interested parties to spend on his campaign Reavis went to Tucson, Arizona in 1882 and filed his claim. Although it was a Spanish landgrant it was valid, if approved by the Surveyor General and Congress, under the Treaty of Guadelupe Hidalgo by which the United States had succeeded to much of the Southwest territory. Reavis had upped the extent of the property considerably to over 1,000 acres. He knew he would have to wait years for government action to be completed; the time for profit was nigh.

Reavis let the filing of his papers and the magnitude of the claim be known through the territorial newspapers. Then he recruited a gang of thugs and, balancing his document in one hand, pointed them at landholders.

Chapter Seventeen: James Reavis & Philip Musica | 261

Empowered to collect the hypothetical rents and quitclaims they badgered people, sometimes even brutalized them until the victims threatened an uprising. Reavis had begun to build a "palace" near the place where, he asserted, the Peralta hacienda once stood; he fled to the uncompleted building, gathered up his papers and went back to California. He had learned that the settlers would not accept autocracy without resistence.

This did not discourage Reavis. He used his expulsion as a stepping-stone to an even more extravagant maturation of his scheme. Finding (somewhere) a young woman of mixed Spanish-Indian ancestry he coached her in polite speech and manners. Since Reavis' earlier forgeries suggested a family lineage he nominated his pupil to the Peralta family as daughter of the second Don Miguel and legal heiress of their estates. He fabricated the necessary records and then married his creation.

Renewing his application for possession of the Peralta lands Reavis marshalled forces in California, New York and Washington. He traveled East with his wife, whom he still described only as his ward. Upon being urged by Spanish diplomats to visit the mother country, he addressed himself to noble families called Peralta, informing them that he had discovered their distant relative, the Baroness de Peralta. Reavis had not built a proud family out of paper to exclude himself from its material and heroic heritage: in Spain he became the Baron de Peralta.

The Constitution of the United States of course prohibits the assumptions of patents of nobility by citizens; even the Spanish laws of inheritance would make his assumption of the title on the grounds of his wife's disputed patrimony rather arrogant. Reavis was aware that brazen action often breaks a principle. He and his wife toured Spain as a baronial couple. They insisted on the forms of address proper to their rank; kept only noble company; and performed with unmistakable gentility all the customs of their rank.

Reavis was finally a noble Spaniard. It is a shame that there is no information on his preparations to assume this status other than the mechanics of forgeries and lodging the claim, for this period in Spain was the fulfillment of the wishes which real life never brought. Reavis spoke Spanish fluently since his youth; but how did he acquire the characteristic accent and intonation of the Spanish upper classes when he knew only Mexicans and Spanish-Americans? He and his wife, indulged because they were American, must have assimilated to the refinements of social intercourse rapidly and with seeming ease. Reavis also made free with his extorted wealth—noble generosity also being a part of his conceived character—and purchased what he was not given. He participated so confidently in the life of the aristocrats that he may even have been party to discussions of a Spanish invasion of the United States.

The dross of nobility did not hide his less savory professional practices. A clerk in the Archivos de Indias spotted the Baron as he was filching a document. There were complications. Reavis left Spain and his reception in London, where he next lay seige to society, implies that his credentials had lost their luster. On his return to the United States Reavis exploited his claim by fostering a series of development companies to milk shareholders in advance of confirmation. But confirmation never came: the forgery was minutely detected and Reavis was brought to trial in civil and then in criminal court. He spent only two years in prison, but many years after that imprisoned by schemes to develop the land he had once claimed. The romance of the land and of the man who controlled it still held him tight though he was nothing more than a guidebook curiosity.

The means by which Reavis had achieved his new identity demanded that he serve them exclusively ever after. Even when he became the nobleman he imagined and lived among the grandees he could not relinquish the laborer's reaching for his tools or the promoter's ballyhoo. He was, ironically, too American to be a Spanish noble. The enterprise was more important than the profit.

Reavis' Spanish excursion was a denial of American principles in achievement of American ideals which, had it been more successful, would have been diabolical. His self-transformation was tinctured with exoticism, with a need to be of a nationality more suited to his fanciful absolutism, and at any rate of a nationality more stringent than midwestern America exhibited in the post Civil War period. Reavis' superficial opposite was Philip Musica, who did everything he could to become solidly American— but also with status.

The life of Philip Musica can be followed in one of two directions, from its culmination in an entry in the 1938-39 *Who's Who in America* or from its beginning, on Broome Street, Manhattan (or Naples, Italy) where he was born in 1884, the child of Italian immigrants. Taken together these two points might not seem all that divergent: what more satisfying to Americans than the tale of a poor boy from the tenements becoming president of a major corporation? However any tale of this sort must have its own demise built-in, as in the revelation that Andrew Carnegie was a remorseless murderer of workmen or Horatio Alger himself was a pervert.

For Philip Musica the demise was contained in the panorama of his success, for the *Who's Who* entry was in the name of Coster. Once Coster was known to be Musica neither could exist for much longer.

Philip Musica was a solemn, intelligent child nurtured by a driving mother and a compliant father. The mother's drive, which had brought the family from Naples to America pushed Antonio Musica from barbering into the import business. At the turn of the century there was little likelihood of Italian-Americans having the credit to capitalize large-scale enterprizes. The store started very small, therefore, with pasta and dried fruit. When Philip left high school to act as his father's partner the firm became more ambitious. Bulk cheeses, including mozzarella and gorgonzola, large wheels and tubes, were the main commodity handled by Musica and Son. They supplied the cheese at good prices to restaurants and neighborhood grocers. For the ostensible volume of their trade the Musica family was faring well; Philip himself began leading a stylish life about town. In a period when most Italian immigrants were locked into the dreary pathos of the slums with Black Hand extortions and unemployment, and were subjected to atrocities like the massacre of twelve murder "suspects" in New Orleans (1898), the Musicas were able to move out of their old neighborhood and into Bay Ridge, Brooklyn. However else modern American society may have reacted to foreigners money improved them.

A stigma soon became attached to Musica's money. Investigators into waterfront corruption found that federal customs inspectors were in collusion with Musica to underreport the quantities of cheese arriving and hence undercollect duties. The good living of the family and the carousing of Philip Musica were founded on the margin between cheese actually sold (much of it on the black market) and cheese reported to the government. Philip, the real culprit, was brought to trial and sentenced to one year in prison.

The twenty-one year old Musica was a hard-core mythomaniac. He had invented in his days about town a story of a more respectable childhood and a college education to bolster his vanity and this he retailed to the prison officials. His imprisonment did not last long enough to infringe on his life seriously; after five months he was released under a presidential reprieve. The Italian ambassador asked this favor from President Taft and his request was, in the condition of international politics, not to be ignored.

The journalistic and crime-book interpreters of Musica's career have overlooked a significant connection which was central from the beginning:

Musica's criminal activity and his life were both filled with the same growing delusion. Musica was already tied up in a round of make-believe which he had to perpetrate on all sides-and he had a genius for perpetrating it. The bon vivant was consistent with the man who bribed customs inspectors; through his public life and his business there curved the same arc of fantasy. This might have proceeded harmlessly after he was chastised the first time except that Musica's criminality, like Reavis', was insuperable. He was one of those individuals who chose the dishonest way of doing things even though, with his abilities and opportunities, he might have profited more by doing the same thing honestly.

Getting by the law, bilking people, especially, it seems, large institutions, the government, compelled Musica and never let him leave off in time and never disposed him to protect himself with saving legalities, as some of his less imaginative fellow extortionists always have done. Musica's object was not crime or profiting from crime but a life style which announced his dominance and his acceptance by the dominant class, accompanied by a power to move things.

The United States Hair Company, Musica's next effort to construct his fantasy in mercantile terms, was a refinement of the cheese dodge that eliminated the loose strand of custom inspectors. Musica set himself up as a buyer of human hair to be used for wigs and other tonsorial adornments. He purchased crates of this valuable substance—between eighty and one hundred dollars a pound—from India, China or Europe and consigned them on the international market. Musica invoiced from a foreign port hair purchased with letters of credit drawn on his firm at a foreign bank, these letters of credit being redeemed by drafts from another bank into which he had deposited the proceeds of the sale of the hair in another country. A web of filaments passed through Musica's New York office joining banks all over the world in an intercourse of commercial paper.

Musica returned to his boulevard haunts again a well-heeled man and he told more stories about his college days. He was believed on all sides: stock from his firm was accepted for trading on the Curb Exchange. The elevation of United States Hair to the Exchange trade, vital to Musica's appetite for prestige, further capitalized his life, but it also wrecked his company and thus his life.

The meddling of other people with their unpredictable appetites in Musica's overstretched web tangled it irreparably. Double-dealing on the exchange caused a panic which devalued the company's stock. Musica borrowed extensively against crates of human hair in transshipment at the

New York docks and an interested bank, concerned over its investments, inspected a crate and found nothing but hair sweepings from barbershop floors and a bulking amount of tissue paper. United States Hair collapsed entirely but by then Musica and his family were on the road with the ill-gotten credit and some diamonds he had coaxed out of New York dealers against the same insubstantial crates of human hair.

Musica had spun his empire from nothing. Cronies overseas outfitted the phony crates in their respective ports, exaggerated the weight on bills of lading which Musica, through more bribery and forgery, had accepted at ports of entry. U.S. Hair consisted of a fleet of these lonely boxes being shipped here and there around the world with charges made here and payments there. Musica's profit derived from the inflation of stocks and the siphoning off of bank credit which was the groundwork of all his dealings.

The banks hired detectives to pursue the Musicas and recover their loan money. The family, except for Assunta, Musica's mother, who was in Naples, was apprehended in New Orleans boarding a ship for Panama. While being hustled to the New Orleans jail pending extradition to New York Musica tried to commit suicide with a revolver the police had overlooked (!) in searching him. The gun was taken away by force. It is interesting that Musica pointed it at himself rather than at the police, not making his getaway like a stereotype gangster. This self-destructiveness continued when Musica, interrogated by the New York authorities, took the rap and shielded his family. He went to the Tombs without sentence being passed.

The total institution of a prison is designed to bind the inmates into a regular life; penance, though encouraged, is their own business. It might be expected that Musica's downfall would end either in a contrite prisoner or a withdrawn prisoner but that underestimates the coherence of his delusional system. Musica discovered that within the confines of prison he could enjoy privileges by swamping the District Attorney's office with inside information on criminal cases. In exchange he was allowed a fancy hairdo and freedom of the walks.

After three years of this life he was given a suspended sentence and went to work for the State Attorney as an investigator. Sheltered by the justice apparatus outside as he had been inside the prison Musica indiscriminately found and invented evidence to convict people or at least impugn them. He sensed out the contours of his superiors' suspicions and then generated or at least located facts to confirm what they liked to believe. In prison he had already sent one man to the electric chair (for nothing more than complicity); outside he steered onto Death Row a gangster who may have been guilty of everything but this murder. Musica had to be in command of the destinies of others by including them in his own surrounding fiction. He always worked in extremities.

Certainly his next intended victim, William Randolph Hearst, was an extremity. Musica tried to expose Hearst as the puppet of German propagandists, it being 1918 and the most anxious period of the War. Musica muscled testimony out of witnesses, concocted meetings between Hearst and German agents at Hearst's country estate. This was more than some of Musica's colleagues of the State Attorney's staff could stomach. At Senate hearings of Hearst's alleged pro-German activities it came out that the New York State Attorney was employing an ex-con named Johnson (Musica's alias) to investigate Hearst. The Hearst newspapers echoed the allegations against Johnson everywhere and though Musica's superior defended him Musica swiftly quit his job. What remains surprising is that a former jailbird could in a brief time reach the position of threatening a powerful publisher.

Musica's delusion was adaptable to many different settings and times. He had the ingenuity to establish his own legitimacy in solid goods then borrow on that legitimacy with false collateral as far as it would take him. In his detective work he proved to himself that anything can be made real if the person asserting it is respectable in the eyes of his audience. The figure of respectability was immensely powerful: he desired to assume it for himself and remove it from other people; he desired to trade from within its protective cloak.

Musica changed his name to Costa and went into bootlegging. This was done respectably and legitimately under the guise of the normal operation of the Adelphi Chemical Company, in which Musica was partners with the fictitious Horace P. Girard. The name Girard, aglow with Philadelphia class, was the badge of Musica's ambition. Apprehensive of some of his disreputable distrubutors Musica betrayed his own operations, lost his alcohol license and reopened shop in the pure air of Westchester, as Girard and Company. The overlay was the same as Adelphi, hair lotion and shampoo, and the underground was still bootleg liquor. Possibly the poet might detect something that scans in the transition from barbershop to fraudulent hair dealing to fraudulent hair-lotion manufacture.

Girard and Company was everything that Musica, now calling himself Frank D. Coster, had learned in his peregrinations through finance and law. As in the cheese business he sold a commodity at a greater profit than anyone by obtaining greater amounts under a legal pretense (for making drugs); as in the hair business he engaged in nimble actuarial prestidigitation; as in the State Attorney's office he duped government agents right and left and used them for his own purposes. He topped these old skills with more specialized knowledge. By hiring a reputable accounting firm, Price, Waterhouse and Company, to audit the Girard books, which he kept in rigid order, he tested himself against the accountants and passed muster without fail, learning what adjustments he must make if he were to step up operations and remain beneath the veil of their approbation. He placed a German chemist on the payroll and thus had next to him a source of wisdom on the preparations under which drinking alcohol could be masked for safe recovery later. The chemist's Ph.D. (University of Heidelburg), some of his technical knowledge and no one knows how many expressions and mannerisms were annexed by Coster for the new amalgam that was emerging.

The private evolution of Musica into Coster will always remain a mystery, but the superficialities are all in a line. In Coster Musica slipped away from his past errors and into the dominance of his ideal identity. When he married he told his wife, who had known him as Musica, that his mother first was wed to an Italian named Musica and then to a German named Coster—he preferred Coster. His mother's maiden name became Girard and his wife (née Jenkins), unbeknownst to her awarded the maiden name of Schiefflin, which called up the name of a prominent New York drug firm. Musica sought the pharmaceutically respectable German nationality for him and his wife.

Musica was planning a passage from Italian-American society and culture into the American upper class, in which well educated, wealthy men with German or English names were welcome. Musica's success, more than his financial coups, was to perceive what was required to rise into that social empyrean and bring it about in himself and his family. His venue of birth changed to Washington, D.C.; he sported a Ph.D. and an M.D. from the University of Heidelburg and a history of medical practice in New York. This, plus the managerial ability the rise of Girard and Company implied, proposed him to the stratum of society he longed to enter.

New York was not a safe place for Coster to hobnob with the great; he had met too many people as Musica. He therefore moved his factory and office to the vicinity of Bridgeport, Connecticut. He was lured to Barnum's city by the antithesis of showmanship: he found the police department capable of winking at the furtive side of his chemical manufacturing when assuaged with cash. Coster settled in his name and character and was taken up by the local elite as the founder of a promsing new enterprise. Bankers and politicians befriended him; he was proposed to clubs. His trade was doing well: reportedly he had himself designated supplier of many New England speakeasy networks while miraculously preserving his above-board identity as a drug dealer.

The demand for his product and the natural corruptability of small-town officials helped him keep his status and his cover. He scrupled to use intermediaries in most of the clandestine bargaining but his genius for organization—the ability to take an overview where none of the petty hoodlums of the area had before him—was his edge. He expanded in both directions both crooked and legal, with the help of a heavy bank loan which he repaid promptly (but not too promptly). He thus established a credit rating, a good name with the bankers and built bigger facilities for his drugs and for his booze. The detective story character who is a respectable businessman on the surface and a cutthroat on the sly is no reflection of Coster; he integrated his two kinds of trade with his social life and participation in the local community, all of them adding up to respectability.

Something in the order of things gambled on Coster and sent his way, in one big piece, a whole facade which he could not have assembled in two hundred years of Girard and Company. This was the McKesson-Robbins corporate name.

The old firm—its proprietary drugs fondly harbored on the shelves of family pharmacies from coast to coast, its famous ointments, unguents, febrifuges and alcohol rubs having lasted through the scandal of the patent medicine era—was slipping; competition from new firms with glamorous new products was ruining its markets. The heirs of the Robbins family and some large outside shareholders decided to put the company up for sale. Coster, always on the lookout for such opportunities, excitedly caucused his banker and stockholder friends. His credit and their confidence amounted to a series of transactions and a stock issue: McKesson-Robbins of Connecticut, F. Donald Coster, President, accepted for trading on the New York Stock Exchange, was born.

All that remained of McKesson-Robbins was a name and some ramshackle factory-warehouse buildings. Coster absorbed them all into his Fairfield, Connecticut plant; behind the name he assembled an organization to fit its stature. A McKesson-Robbins of Canada came into being, a holding company was incorporated in Maryland; but Coster's brainstorm was the idea of bringing regional wholesale drug firms under the McKesson-Robbins umbrella. The main firm undertook to manufacture and supply the local wholesalers with standard formulas in bulk which they could then label and distribute as their popular remedies. Furthermore any local wholesaler could provide himself with a quantity of bottled preparations from another wholesaler if he found a market. The wholesalers took blocks of stock in McKesson-Robbins in exchange for their old stock. Coster had architected a centralization of the pharmacy business which did not eliminate the reliable local brands but did restrict the effects of market fluctuations and supply drops on gross sales.

It was a masterpiece of preclusive vertical expansion which magnified everyone's profits but avoided robber baron methods by leaving autonomy to the wholesalers. Yet each small enterprise was fortified by the McKesson-Robbins bastion, which was not shaken by the small tremors that could have wrecked smaller firms. The Great Crash of 1929 did not destroy the edifice; Coster even directed that the company extend emergency credit to many subsidiaries to keep them from collapsing. More to Coster's satisfaction, though, was his survival of Repeal in 1932 with no ill effects to his aggregate income or to his prestige. He had made the transition smoothly from New York bootlegger to Fairfield businessman, yacht-owner and philanthropist.

This munificent conquest of the wholesalers in hand Coster retired to his favorite game of solitaire, leaving the management of the rest to more mundane minds. He had purchased in his wife's name a comfortable house and lived a retiring life between there and his office, taking pleasure in his yacht and membership in a few clubs. He could have been nicely cushioned for life if he stayed where he was; but the capacity to work this arrangement presupposed in Coster a confabulation that weakened the most solid structure. In truth the visible solidity of McKesson-Robbins was the surface effect of that same dream castle, its most bizarre components buried.

The strangest room in Coster's palace was the Crude Drug Division, shunned by the trustees and the lesser officials because Coster alone seemed to understand its workings. Large quantities of substances with enchanter's names—oil of bitter almonds, ipecac, dragon's blood passed through the division, which bought them in one place and sold them in another, always, the books showed, at a profit to McKesson-Robbins. These purchases and sales never took place; Coster was juggling clouds. He had invented subsidiaries all around the world and a banking house to enter debits and issue letters of credit on his imaginary sales. The money paid to the banking house and to sundry other services was pocketed by Coster—skimmed from the surface of McKesson-Robbin's assets. He drained larger sums—over three million dollars—by dropping money withdrawn to purchase crude drugs into bank accounts under a number of fictitious names. The crude drug business was a bung hole in the McKesson-Robbins capital; it seemed to contribute but gave a controlled opening for parasitic embezzlement. No one ever determined for sure what Coster did with all that money.

Stationed in offices on either side of his own Coster had a pair of collaborators, the Dietrich brothers, George and Robert, who were officially an assistant treasurer and a purchasing agent respectively. The Dietrichs lived not far from Coster in Fairfield but there were few other than business contacts between them. George and Robert Dietrich were George and Robert Musica Germanized. Arthur Musica, the remaining brother, was masquerading as George Vernard, the Brooklyn agent of the contrived shipping firm W.W. Smith and Company, which handled all the drug traffic Coster was deploying.

Coster had housed his entire family in the McKesson-Robbins citadel; they were running in assumed lives all of the support operations that kept his crude drug dodges from being noticed. The Dietrich's helped Coster keep the books in order at the main plant in Fairfield and Vernard was responsible for keeping the flow of mail between the main office and the false bank and shipping firms up to a level which made it appear the illusory business was really being transacted. Vernard had set up in Canada some dummy offices each staffed by a secretary who only readdressed letters—phony orders, bills and receipts—which Vernard sent there to the accounting department in Fairfield and elsewhere as the need arose. In short the multi-million dollar crude drug empire, like the smaller United States Hair Company, was nothing but a flow of mail between outposts in Canada and Fairfield. Since the Dietrich's entered everything on the books the simple apparatus—and the seepage of funds—was checked at both ends.

Coster's mother and two of his sisters resided in a picturesque house on Long Island and Coster solicitously answered their every need. As a finishing touch he paid a midwife to fake a birth certificate in New York, giving his correct birth date and all the assumed parentage he had built up plus the crisp pregnant detail of a new birthplace—Washington, D.C., seat of power, center of America. In his many rooms and looking from the battlements Coster conceived himself unapproachable; he might move and channel his dreamy floods of aromatic, non-existent oils forever. But his old associates remembered him: he was blackmailed and, it is said, he still visited the cafes of the East Side and was greeted as Musica.

Coster could not have succeeded as fully as he did, however, if he was inept or impercipient. For over fourteen years he lived as an executive with many connections in the business world and in the local community, a member of the Episcopal Church and an unenthusiastic party giver. Coster's personality was allowable in a man of his position; his behavior was within the bounds of propriety. This was not due to imposture though it had begun with a will to imposture; it was assimilation to a society and culture different from the one in which he was raised. Assimilation under false pretenses—but still complete. Without being facetious I would even venture to say it was Americanization accomplished with incredible rapidity, and some degree of completeness. The only link among the Musica family members was past history—to which their original culture was reduced—and collusion in Philip's ongoing extortion. It is not to be assumed that the Fairfield house and the corporate presidency were an excuse for embezzlement or satisfying the prestige needs of immigrants, and nothing else. Musica had wanted to enter that society and having succeeded he lived as one of its members, some of whom are embezzlers. How else could he have become assimilated to American society so utterly in fulfillment of an American ideal?

The assimilation did not last for long; although it was complete to Coster others, appraised of his former identity, would demand he be reduced back to its confines.

The first split was from inside. The board of trustees, anxious to reduce McKesson-Robbins' indebtedness to the banks in 1935 ordered each of the departments to make a contribution to the payment. The crude drug contribution was set at one million dollars, which would require the liquidation of drug holdings. To this point Coster had been shielded from inquiry into the concrete state of his inventory by the practice of accounting firms—the Price, Waterhouse partnership he still employed—never to make inspection of the items themselves. When the company's Treasurer, Julian F. Thomson, saw that far from liquidating the one million dollars in crude drug stock another million had been acquired he agitated for a physical check; Coster, backed into a corner, squirmed so violently that Thomson was alerted. The drugs, millions of dollars worth, did not exist!

On December 5, 1938 Coster, alarmed by the extent his operations were exposed, threw the company into an equity receivership, possibly hoping to refract responsibility or escape before more was realized. He did neither. Eight days later, as federal agents aware of his former identity approached his house Coster shot and killed himself and Musica. The suicide note blamed everyone, particularly Wall Street brokers. His brothers went to jail; McKesson-Robbins almost went under—but many people never believed the reports about him were true.

References

Cookridge, E.H.
    1967 *The Baron of Arizona.* New York: Day.

Shaplen, Robert.
    1955 "The Metamorphosis of Philip Musica." *The New Yorker* 22 October: 49-65; 29 October: 39-67.